PRAISE FOR *DESIRE MAKES ME BRAVE*

"Readers will be enlightened, entertained, and moved by April Hirschman's bold hybrid memoir—a delightful blend of psychology, Eros, and poetry."
—Sari Botton, author of *And You May Find Yourself...Confessions of a Late-Blooming Gen-X Weirdo*

"*Desire Makes Me Brave* is a heartfelt, engaging, endearing, modern-day, erotic adventure that is unique. April Hirschman's story is of a young woman's sexual evolution through bisexual dating, casual sex, falling in love, doing three ways, getting her needs met through Tinder, doing it all in every way, in various countries. April shares her naked truth, detailing her thoughts, feelings, and realizations, which makes me fall completely in love with her. You will too!"
—Annie Sprinkle, PhD, author of *Post Porn Modernist, Explorer's Guide to Planet Orgasm,* and *Assuming the Ecosexual Position: The Earth as Lover*

"*Desire Makes Me Brave* gives bisexuality a voice in a way that is playful, captivating, and downright sexy. April Hirschman's raw sharing of her journey being "attracted to sameness and difference" inspires other bisexual or bi-curious folks to shamelessly embrace their true desires outside of the standard binary for sexual exploration and orientation."
—Amy Baldwin, coauthor of *Shameless Sex: Choose Your Own Pleasure Path to Unlock the Sex Life You've Been Waiting For*

"Smart, sexy, and hilarious! This is the book the world has needed for years!"
—Kyle Schickner, Fencesitter Films

"Clever and charming, vulnerable and wise, *Desire Makes Me Brave* is as much about sexuality and desire as about how we humans craft the stories of our lives."
—Kate Evans, winner of the 2015 Bisexual Book Award for *Call It Wonder*

"A fun and sexy romp on the bisexual—trysexual?—side! Hirschman writes engagingly about free love, free expression, and, well, freedom. In her tales of hookups and relationships with people of various gender identities, often in exotic locales, you'll find your eyeballs glued to the pages. Sure, the book's titillating but it's also packed with loads of heart and humor."
—Jake Whitney, freelance journalist

Desire Makes Me Brave

A Bisexual Journey from California to the World

April Hirschman

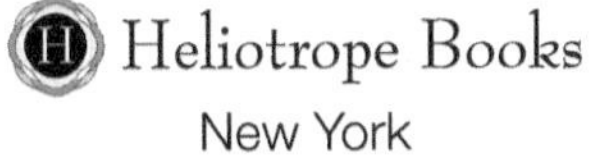

New York

Heliotrope Books, LLC
heliotropebooks@gmail.com

ISBN 978-1-956474-43-5
ISBN for eBook 978-1-956474-42-8

Typeset by Heliotrope Books with AJ & J Design

I could dedicate this book to the ones that got away.
But no one did. They're all around here somewhere.

So I'll dedicate it to the men I lost, out of the blue,
in the midst of the first part of the pandemic:
My father, Marc Henry Hirschman
and my nephew, Devin Yakoushkin—
they both died with memoirs in them.

CONTENTS

Mandala of Me

drawn by April Hirschman

PROLOGUE

"The words 'narrative arc' make me reach for my revolver. If I had known about that shit I would've never started writing."
—Abigail Thomas

"Stay with it!"
—Marc Hirschman

I love a visual aid, and maybe you do too. So I am sharing the Mandala of Me on the opposite page, in hopes it can help orient you to the wild ride on which I am about to take you. To explore so many arts, countries, and experiences as possible is my joy, my conundrum and my legacy. Art is a big part of me, the improvisation of it, the trust in where colors, and pencils, and words, and dance movements will take me. Creativity has given me the strength to keep staying on this beat. To keep it flowing. And no this isn't a big artist's statement of a book. Don't worry, there's lots of sex! But then I guess sex is art too, right?

I started writing this book over two decades ago. And it's had many different titles. Speaking of names, many people I know prefer to let go of the term "bisexual" and let it sink to the bottom of the sea with other imperfect or dated terms. But I believe the history of this word, and our insistent reclaiming of it from its pathologizing beginnings, still matters.

"Bisexual" does not imply a division of lines or binaries. It can mean "attracted to sameness and difference." Like the Mandala, bisexuality is about how the parts of us are discrete and overlapping. Our bisexuality flag has three colors after all, not two.

Without that history—upheld by people who fought to recognize bisexuality—it would still be the love that has no name and no place. Yet still, we are searching for our place. Ever been to a bisexual bar? No, you haven't. No one has.

Our visibility in LGBTQIA+ spaces is still conditional (did you get the special glasses so you can see us?). In seeking to inhabit the elusive bisexual space, I have had to actively create and insist upon it. Extending the honor from other bisexual artists who fought for inclusion, my sister Allegra and I curated what was the only exclusively Bi Film Night at Frameline Film Festival, the biggest queer film festival in the world, for over a decade before the new management unceremoniously ended the program. The struggle continues. But so does the party. In fact, my sisters and I host an annual Bi B Q celebration in San Francisco during pride. You should totally come! It's for allies too.

I hope my words on these pages make you an ally. I hope they give form to how I navigated the big queer and even bigger straight worlds as a bisexual woman, but also how I crafted my own fantabulous bi galaxy, supported by the constellation of my incredible, weirdo family whose identities were not too different from my own. My hippie commune upbringing was not without its pitfalls, but it taught me that life was one celebration flowing into another celebration and that, when in doubt, it's always the right time to figure out what we will be eating.

I had considered beginning the narrative by just dropping you into a hot bedroom scene. My publisher advised me to decorate the door before you entered. Very well. She said: "What was the motive for you to write this book? It's a life the reader may not approve of or relate to. What's your statement?"

Was there a statement in the paragraphs above? Being bisexual means never having to decide. So, now that I decorated the door for you, I hope you can step into the world of this bisexual Odyssey, sit down, eat a little something, and stay awhile.

1: THREESOME

At supper in the hotel restaurant with my girlfriend Quince and ex-boyfriend Kunal, I drank too much Chandon. My first ménage à trois was about to start and I needed liquid courage, but there's such a thing as too much courage.

We got here because Quince, a gold star (a woman who has never slept with a man), wanted to step into my bisexual shoes for a night, thought the threesome would give her such slippers. I wanted to please her, to explore, to be someone that had threesomes. Why not? I was in my early thirties and thus neither young nor old. According to the oracle of Ally Sheedy in *The Breakfast Club,* my heart was already dead.

Kunal and I plotted threesomes when we were a couple, but they never materialized. We were the people who weren't careful about what we wished for.

The hotel room was gray and taupe and made to look like rooms aren't messy. That people aren't messy, leaving our traces everywhere. After some kissing at the foot of the bed we all conjured a plan where Kunal and I would tie up Quince. We propped her now naked body up on a dresser. With ties and socks we tied her ankles and her wrists, fixing them behind her back. We kissed the contours of her creamy skin. The soft current beauty of Quince merging with the past world of Kunal (jazz, cigarettes, beard stubble) was a bit much for me to handle.

Things got blurry very fast. I went into the bathroom and looked in the mirror. I was so drunk my image wasn't still. My lipstick was smeared, hair wild. I could hear things heating up in the other room, Kunal's sweet talking dance of trying to avoid putting on a condom. His slight Indian accent made it all the more charming. But this was the first time Quince had ever had sex with a man. It was too bright in the bathroom and too dark when I stumbled out, looking at them on the bed, Kunal's long light brown body on top, her legs around his hips, him thrusting into my woman. It's not like Kunal's cock was the first to enter her. It's just the previous ones were connected to women, myself and others. It's not like he was getting somewhere I hadn't been. But still.

It was like watching a scene on TV that I couldn't enter. Threesomes are hard. They need a choreographer and a director. What's my motivation again? I didn't know how to enter the scene of these two gorgeous people having missionary sex. I disappeared back to the bathroom. I thought about my struggle. I wanted enduring love with a woman. But I sometimes wanted novelty and excitement with men. And I wanted to experience ALL KINDS OF HOT SEX. So yes, the search for enduring love is going to be one of my themes. But it won't get tied up in a neat bow at the end. Though I will get tied up in ... never mind, that's a spoiler.

I went back into the bedroom and climbed in bed with Kunal. We kissed and hungrily ran our hands along all the favorite places on each other's bodies, suspended in some timeless drunken space. But then something was missing. In a moment of panic, I realized Quince was gone.

One editor, and not just any editor but Dr. Lauren Shufran, who holds a PhD in early modern British literature, said, "I understand the compulsion to open with the threesome; but I think you have stronger options for the opening." Look at me, a Compulsive Threesome Opener! Thank you, Dr. Shufran, but decisions must be made. I can't keep tinkering with this beast for another quarter century.

2: MY LESBIAN HUSBAND VS. THE KINGDOM OF NEPAL

During the 17-hour flight I watched movies, tried to get away with masturbating in my seat, and wrote in my journal. So picture me in a sort of belly dance outfit with green/brown hair. It started out blonde but everyone said crazed Nepalese men would scream-chase me down the street as they had never seen a blonde. This is the stupid shit ignorant Americans tell you. I should have rocked that blonde like the Nordic girls did.

But I guess you deserve to get up to date. I was in a 5-year relationship with my first girlfriend, Harper. She was a solid Midwestern husband of a woman, 11 years my senior. I was 26 years old and I thought I was over the hill (I know, I know).

So if you are so desperate for this memoir to have a theme, Gentle Reader, here it is: shedding my erotic virginity. The dumb dads of patriarchy say we "lose our virginity" in a one-time penetrative event. Spoken like an oaf who believes the world revolves around the penis. I had hetero intercourse for the first time with my high school boyfriend Troy, but intuited early on that it was actually going to take a good many years to become erotically knowledgeable.

Over the course of my early 20s, I gave my heart and soul to Harper. I was crazy for her. But at 26 I was ready to shed some veils. I longed to talk dirty, share fantasies, push the edge, try out a little BDSM. The list went on.

Let's review sex with Harper: We are in our sunny bedroom in the small Northern California hick town where we live. I am silent because the deadly combo of porn plus feminism has me believing that noisy sex is just theatrics invented for horny dudes. I'm naked, having deemed lingerie a sexist uniform. Harper goes down between my legs and negotiates with my pubic hair curled out wild and electric, an emblem of an earthy woman. And she makes me come this way. That's what good sex looks like between Harper and me.

But for some reason the bulk of our sex most often looks more like this: It's after 10 p.m. on a Tuesday night. Harper climbs on top of me and humps against my thigh. My part in this scene is to touch myself with my own hand. And in this way we come together. Do you get it, reader? Or do I have to spell it out? I was jilling myself off for years. I liked that she was on top of me. And frankly I would LOVE to be able to hump against something to come. You people who can do it are my heroes.

So I'd rub the left side of my clit. That's my romance and foreplay section. Then when I was ready to come I would rub the right side. I would imagine this torrid sex/rape scene from a movie where a man throws a woman against a wall, rips off her white dress and pumps his cock into her while she pushes his hands off her perky tits until resistance turns into submission (a classic) and they moan together. I felt shame about it then and I feel shame about it now. So if you are hoping my narrative arc will involve me overcoming this shame, then spoiler: It won't. Yes I know intellectually that I have a right to think of WHATEVER sick little scenarios get me off. But the feminist in me cringes to this day.

Harper makes some breathy moans. I am working the rapey fantasy and move my hand over to the right side of my clit that is the down-and-dirty area where I rub vigorously and come. Of course I come, I am a twentysomething chock full of hormones and youthful optimism and it's my hand. I masturbate and she humps me. That was our go-to sex routine.

I fretted that I just wasn't very sexual. I was still new to womanly love. I had only slept with two men and Harper at this point. So I didn't know the difference between not having chemistry and not being a sexual person. Harper and I had a deep connection but it wasn't urgent, hot, lustful. Sometimes I felt shame about our same-sexness like I was doing something taboo in bed with a sister. Later I would feel the same about men, taboo, like they were my brothers. The double helix of desire would keep intertwining and shifting but never landing.

My coming out as bisexual was so easy compared to most. My hippie parents had no objection. My older sister Celeste paved the queer road for our family by going away to college saying: *I am now only going to date women*. Can you tell she is rather dramatic? She starred in ALL the plays in high school.

I didn't lose jobs or friends. I wasn't raised in any religion that systematically shamed me. My expression of my preferences would lead to more subtle internal struggles around what to share about myself and what not to share, when it was safe or unsafe, where I could see myself reflected in media or art. Many of my relationships would start with an interrogation about what gender I preferred and who I had been in a long-term relationship with. I am attracted to *people*. I was attracted to both sameness and difference.

Nepal here I come! I missed out on the college years of dorm bed hopping because I went to an all-age junior college and lived with my mom. Early in our relationship Harper told me if I ever cheated on her with a guy she would breakup with me. And thus she established the dimensions of the cage. I wanted her love and like most young women I thought I had to morph myself into what my partner wanted in order to get it. I didn't know she was supposed to love and accept all of me, including my bisexuality. I had no intention of cheating on Harper because I was madly in love with her. On a conscious level the trip was all about travel, culture, learning and adventure. There was something else compelling me that I would only learn later.

"It looks like you're moving out," Harper had said that morning after I had everything packed into my suitcases. I understood her concerns. We had barely been apart since we started dating and this was a four-month sojourn. Harper was the perfect combination of earth mother and provider, old-fashioned and steady. So different from my chaotic hippie childhood and my parents who practiced non-ethical non-monogamy.

"I'm not moving out. It's just a long trip and I want room to buy tapestries and presents for everyone. We will be in touch over Skype."

The plan to travel percolated after a case of mononucleosis that had me bedridden for months. I needed to get out there and live again after feeling like a corpse. I chose Nepal because my belly dance student and dear friend Julie had gone there through a cultural study-abroad program. She came back speaking Nepalese, doing Nepalese folk dances, and infused with the spirit of the colorful land. I would be studying Nepalese culture and writing an anthropological paper. That's it for the backstory.

Off the plane through the darkened city and I was deposited in a punishingly bright hotel lobby. The floor was cold white tile against cement walls with some carved wooden beams. The school director, Mohandara, met me and we waited for the mom of my Nepali family to pick me up. Sameera arrived in a full fuchsia sari with gold designs on the hem, tired kohl-lined eyes, smooth brown skin, and wavy ebony hair. Her face was almost mask-like in its perfection.

Back at her house I met her husband and two kids. They don't figure into this smutty version of my story.

On my second day with the family Sameera, clad in emerald, took me to run errands. We came to a major thoroughfare in Lazimpat. It loomed as wide as a highway. Three-wheel Autorickshaws zipped by looking like comical black bonnets made miniature by the military trucks passing them. Cars rushed forward neck and neck with brave bicyclists, transport trucks and wild Newaris fearless on their motorcycles. I was frozen. There were no crosswalks. It was like entering the double Dutch jump ropes of my childhood, only deadlier.

Sameera grabbed my wrist and we crossed. She pointed out

some shops and in a flash she was gone into her hotel job and I was out on the street. I noticed couples walking by. The women looked like goddesses in their saris and kurtas, ebony hair in buns, intricate bindis on their third eyes and the men next to them mere mortals in faded slacks and 1970s style button-up shirts. I wandered around dizzy from jet lag, bought nothing and went home.

That night, Sameera made the first of many epic feasts I would experience: mushroom curry, two kinds of fried bread, fluffy saffron rice, cauliflower curry. The secret to her dhal was adding some uncooked ginger right at the end: *for the fragrance*. The family was quiet and very kind to me.

In keeping with tradition the family wanted me locked in behind their metal gate at 7 at night. I had never had a curfew and this made me bonkers.

The school was a humble building in a part of town with overgrown fields and shabby homes. I was disappointed to find there was only one other student in the program with me. I hoped for a group of people that would provide friendship, camaraderie, and perhaps flirtation. But the other student, Sana, and I never quite got along. Photos on the school's wall of past students in big cheerful groups were evidence of a heyday long past.

Mohandara gave us our class schedule including mythology, language, and history. He ended his first lecture by saying, "You are welcome to predict what the fate of Nepal will be. It's anyone's guess." He said this with the detached wisdom of a sage. Spoiler alert: the next ten or more years in Nepal was a trash fire. But I was dazzled by adolescent monks in orange cloth, spicy incense, temples, sadhus in white with long painted third eyes. Then I would see 18-year-old backpackers off to hike the Himalayas, and I'd feel shabby and old. I wished I was just a nomad instead of a student. I felt stuck inside the locked gates of the compound. I wanted to see all of Nepal, not just its city where we inhaled the smoke of burning trash and had to stay home some days when Maoist bandits threatened riots.

I would walk the streets with my headphones listening to Dylan's *Like a Rolling Stone* and feeling untethered. No one back home new exactly where I was and no one in Nepal knew who I was.

After a month my Canadian friend Mardi offered me a room in her apartment, nicknamed The Love Palace. I quickly agreed. The Love Palace was a two-story apartment in a residential area with a big hammock on the roof where the four other roommates and I would lounge and chat. They came fromSweden, Australia, and Canada and they were all reading *The God of Small Things, Siddhartha,* or *The Bhagavat Gita.*

Back home my life with Harper was chaste. I rarely drank caffeinated tea, coffee, or alcohol, never smoked cigarettes, ate mostly vegetarian, sucked no cock. But in Nepal, a tiger began to pace behind its cage.

My life took on an easy rhythm. In the day I would go to language, dance, religion, and culture classes. In my dance classes I molded my body into the shapes of peacocks, warriors, nymphs, and Hindu goddesses. It was delicious to become immersed in such a rich, colorful world.

There was one decent dance club. Westerners had to pay. Locals got in free. No Nepalese women ever entered. This was a country that didn't recognize the term *girlfriend.* You were either your father's daughter or somebody's wife. I saw about ten Nepalese guys dancing, some European guys in hiking gear, and a few tourist women. Mardi and I hit the dance floor. As usual I peppered in a few belly dance moves. Nepalese men swarmed us. We created a dance move where you spin with one bent elbow out to clear at least two feet around yourself.

I got tipsy from the beer. An English hunk approached me, tall and thick. We made the usual chit chat. He was leaving for a trek in a couple of days. He was giving me *I want you* eyes and I was a sucker for that. He invited me to his place. Kathmandu was a small town and for practical reasons I didn't want to get a slutty white girl reputation, so I gave him a proposition: "You leave now. If I come downstairs in five minutes, we go back to your place. If I don't, then goodnight."

Back in his hostel his pokey beard was a startling contrast to the softness of kissing Harper. Everything about him was bigger, heavier. He made me feel petite. He climbed on top of me and pulled my skirt and panties down.

I thought how Harper was almost comically jealous and possessive. If any one of the male species rang, Harper would say with disgust "some guy called you," even if it was my cousin or a high school friend. Harper would accuse me of "clinging to my bisexuality" as if my set of desires were a crutch and hers the true set, as if my relationship with her could magically turn me into a lesbian. She constantly suspected me of cheating. But for the first four years of our relationship, I had no intention of cheating. I was loyal. I experienced the punishment but not the pleasure of the crime.

The English hunk was licking between my legs while sticking a finger inside. This was my first time with this combination and my whole body perked up to bright attention. If I was told as a budding teenager that a lot of sex consists of someone's finger inside while they lick your clit or you touch it, I would have been alarmed. It's so different from the depictions in movies.

I was shocked at how well he was able to read my secret needs. His finger was so much smarter than a penis. It had been about five years since I'd had one of those. Harper and I made one try with a strap-on and I didn't like it. His tongue was edging against my clit while his knowing finger pulsed inside. And he was super-hot. But I was distracted by thoughts of Harper's steady, loyal love. Out of guilt I stopped it right there.

As I walked home, a bunch of Nepalese guys cackled and gossiped. So much for my clever departure from the club saving my reputation.

Back in my single bed, with the lights of cars flashing across my ceiling, I felt a terrible loneliness and longing for Harper, for home. I began to think of the English Hunk as I circled the left edge of my clit. Time to finish what he started.

After weeks of studying in Kathmandu I was ready for adventure into more of Nepal. As I walked down the street, shop owners tried to get my attention by yelling, "Hey sister, come have a look." There was a lot of addressing strangers as "brother" and "sister." I was learning that the Nepalese treat every stranger with great kindness because they may be a goddess or god in disguise.

I entered a tour company called Ultimate Descent to book a trip near the Tibetan border. The office had colorful signs with oversized photos of exuberant, helmeted people rafting down wild, rushing water. Prakash, a Nepalese man who looked a little younger than me, explained the merits of the different trips in broken English. He had thick, shiny black hair, full pink lips and almond eyes set in a flat moon-like face. His long, sleek body was taller than most Nepalese men. He wasn't just beautiful; he was the most beautiful man I had ever seen.

I was all set for the Borderland trip leaving on the weekend.

"Will you be there?" I asked, coyly.

"I'll be on another trip," he said smiling.

If I dated Prakash then life could be simple for me, like it was for the straight blonde 18-year-old Nordic girls who always had a Nepalese boyfriend wrapped around them. I wasn't like them. I had a girlfriend at home. But here I could temporarily reinvent myself as a carefree straight girl. I got Prakash's card and planned to contact him upon my return.

When I arrived at the parking lot outside Ultimate Descent, a gorgeous gaggle of international backpackers were ready to go. There was an option to ride on the top of the bus and risk my life exposed to the treacherous labyrinthine mountain. I took it. We climbed the verdant mountain, our hair flying all over as the spiraling road took us into the wide unknown.

No one knew where I was. I felt on the edge of the world where anything was possible. The only road signs, oddly, were about urging condom use. We were on the mountains snaky edge, the bus clearing hairpin corners by gravity or magic. Bob Marley sang about his feet being the only vehicle to carry him.

Everywhere I've traveled since, from posh Paris cafés to tiny Indonesian villages, I always eventually hear Bob Marley. He is my totem, part shaman, part welcoming committee, a sign I have officially arrived.

Finally we pulled into Borderlands, a gorgeous backpacker resort sprawled out near the thrashing Bota Kosi River. Most people came there to go zigzagging along the whitewater rapids. It is the steepest river rafted in Nepal, a level 4-5 at high flow. I was one of the few people who didn't want to raft and risk death. I just wanted to flirt, meet travelers, and relax in nature.

Borderlands had two cone-shaped tropical roofs arching over raised seating areas of smooth rocks holding low tables. You step up into your own little stage and sit on cushions. Outside were cascading terraced lawns with tender green grass resembling rice fields.

On the bus we were all sweaty, mussed hair, glasses, pants. For dinner I changed into a tight mesh see-through shirt and a long black skirt. I put in my contacts, painted my face, brushed my hair. As I walked into the candlelit open air dining area with everyone sitting or lounging on low tables I felt many eyes on me like the quiet stare of monkeys, squirrels, and snakes in the trees of a jungle. I walked slowly, taking in the attention a young woman can elicit so effortlessly.

The evening dripped into night as we lounged around eating salads and Tibetan steamed dumplings and drinking beer. I flirted with an English gent named Tim who had a girlfriend (but then so did I) and a slightly older American guy with a round face. As the night proceeded I added on a Nepalese guy. I licked up this attention from a variety of people after being under the gaze of just one person for so long. Finally, I grew tired and retreated to my tent.

Tim appeared at my tent flap all tall, bony, and excited. I liked his accent and his general charming Englishness. Men had become the exotic other to me. I was fascinated by the obviousness of their desire. I was willing to try anything to a point. We kissed. His lips were soft. His heartbeat quickened. He was wearing those terrible canvas traveler pants that can be reduced to shorts with a rip on the Velcro just under the knee. He smelled like beer. He procured a condom and deftly fit it onto his medium-sized manhood.

He moved his arms on either side of my shoulders as if to do a push up.

Here's a little more background on Harper because I owe her that much. I met her at a feminist lesbian naked pool party. She gave me her card and got my number. The next day I found Harper's business card in my pocket. I wanted her to call me but then what would I do? Sure I went to high school in the early nineties so I made out with all the female friends that would have me. But they were femme femme femmie femmes. Harper looked like a handsome *man*.

She rang me later that week and asked me out. Was it a date? Later I would learn the term: *ambiguous queer hangout*. She said we could go to a play in Sebastopol, a concert in Bodega, or a night picnic on the beach. The few men I dated had never offered so many enticing options. I chose the picnic on the beach.

We smoked some pot and drank wine. She brought an elaborate spread of delicious foods: homemade hummus, olives, pita, and triple cream brie. The moon illuminated our feast as if it was our own sanctioned light. Despite all my previous dalliances with ladies I felt pretty green about whatever was happening. This was not a tequila-induced exploration. I was definitely on a date with this butch daddy woman and I didn't know what to make of it.

We chatted pleasantly all the drive back to my home. The darkness of the windows indicated that my younger sister Allegra and mom were already asleep. I looked down at Harper's brown thighs in her gray cotton shorts. Could those be the thighs of my partner? A girlfriend? A woman? Her thighs looked so soft, her hands so small. And her eyes were so full of hope. Our physical actions in this little car could lead to a world of possibility I wasn't ready to enter. Even with my progressive parents and in the landscape of permissive California, I still thought of myself as heterosexual.

I wasn't ready in that moment to kiss her. I wasn't sure if I was even physically attracted to her. But I was drawn to her. I sat quietly for a few moments. A car drove by flashing its lights across our faces. She let her lips softly brush mine as a goodnight kiss. She said she would call me tomorrow.

Back behind the tent flap at Borderlands, Tim painted a stupid grin on his face and thrust himself into me three forceful times like he was hitting a sports target discernable only to himself. In out. In out. In out. Three pumps, reader! Head turned to the side giving me the profile of his awful grin. Troy, my first love, turned his head to the side when he was inside of me. Looking at his profile while he was above me with his cock inside, I thought: *Is this how it's done? We're not even going to look at each other?*

You only have one time to make a first impression. The impression that Tim made with my pussy was very bad. She wasn't having any of it. I quickly expelled him from my pussy and my tent. I've always been proud of the swiftness of my inviting him to leave. As I would come to learn, losing erotic virginity wasn't only about what I permitted but where I made boundaries. This is an important part of eros, no?

We made the long journey down the mountain. I loved the adventure of it all but I wondered why I was ransacking my fidelity to Harper with these disappointing trysts. All my life I was taught to want attention from men. And I did want it. I love their blunt stares, their open desire, their aggressive moves. I didn't always know what to do with that desire though. I didn't know what sexual experiences I wanted with them or how to ask for them. I was in it for that flirtation, being the object of lust. I enjoyed the validation but then felt empty after. Of course I didn't get what I wanted because I didn't *know* what I wanted. In Sex Ed I was taught abstinence, shown anatomical diagrams, warned of pregnancy. I was instructed that it was my job to militantly guard the barracks of my vagina. I was taught in subtle and sometimes blunt ways that my purpose was to please men. The contradiction of constantly guarding and then being taught to acquiesce left me confused. No one asked me what brought me pleasure or taught me how to get it. Becoming a sex coach helped, but that happened over time.

Back in Kathmandu at the Love Palace everyone was drinking tall Nepalese beers and listening to Massive Attack. People go to Nepal for meditation, enlightenment, epic mountaineering, cultural immersion. They don't go looking for torrid sex in hostels or tents. But that's what I was doing.

A week later I met up with Prakash and he took me to his place. I met his short, round mother whose fatigued eyes sunk back into her head in the hopes of retreating from further pain. Many Nepalese women are worked to the bone. She quickly returned to cleaning the kitchen.

Nepalese men weren't supposed to bring some foreign girl home. But as usual, boys can break rules and their adoring mothers allow it.

On Harper's sofa candles flickered at the sides of our vision. This was early courting days when you bother to light candles. We had gone on a couple more dates. She played Toni Child's "Where's the Ocean." Childs' voice sounded like the body of the earth cracked open. We kissed. I said I wanted to slow things down a minute. We talked about what it meant for me to date her. To have sex with her.

"Being with women is so natural," she said with a soothing smile. This philosophy of hers opened up a new landscape for me. I decided to shift past being unsure and give Harper a chance. I ran my hands along her coppery skin that glowed like it was oiled. I touched her gravity-defying breasts with my tentative hands. She found her way between my thighs. I had only received oral sex a couple of times. It felt so vulnerable to be encountered in this way.

But did I want to do the same to Harper? We had only focused on my pleasure that night. I wasn't sure how to connect Harper's face with the part of her that didn't look like you'd expect it to look when she walked around presenting masculine in the world. Do I need to spell this out for you? She looked like she had a dick in her jeans. Years later, after a lot of pussy licking, a friend would say: "Sometimes you have to develop a taste for it."

Despite all my feminist books, women's rights protests, and classes, when I first beheld Harper's vulva, I felt cautious. I hadn't yet developed a taste for it. Sorry Harper! You are THE BEST. Don't worry. There is no chance she will read this.

Prakash and I disrobed each other with slow hunger. Off came my dress, off came his T-shirt. We touched the new territories as they revealed themselves. Kissing him was almost like kissing a woman. He was so feminine in his refined, elegant beauty. His brown cock was a pleasing shape like something thoughtfully carved out of a fine wood. He put on a condom and worked himself slowly inside of me. He fit perfectly. He smelled of dhal and sweet incense. I made a bold move and touched myself. I knew this was the only way I could come with penetration. And with that decision, a layer of my erotic virginity shed. See the theme?

I enjoyed his pleasure and the breathy sounds he made. His moon face was full and satisfied. He came before I could catch up with him but I felt satisfied too. I maneuvered myself into the crook of his neck. In future sexual encounters I would touch myself so we could both come.

Ready for a Rom Com Falling in L*O*V*E Montage? Okay, here we go.

We went for walks and dinners. He had no money so I bought us things. Don't get used to that. I am nobody's sugar mommy. Prakash and I didn't have much to say to each other. But we laughed and I loved to look at him. His features perfect, his movements like a dancer trained from birth. We walked by the begging sadhus at the palace complex of Darbar Square, stole kisses on back roads, and had sex on my mattress on the floor of the Love Palace, our brown and cream skins winding around each other, our breaths merging.

Cue montage music winding and ... full stop.

We were walking along a busy street, people in colorful clothes passing on all sides. He mentioned he wanted me to meet his best friend Aakar. Prakash brought it up with shy giggles, probing and unsure ... almost as if he was hoping for us to have a threesome? Language was limited so I wasn't clear on his intentions.

Prakash and I entered the Love Palace, walking past my roomies slamming tequila shots with beer backs. One of them, Tomas, looked at me disapprovingly. He had tried to date me when we first met but I wasn't attracted to him. His face was endearingly scarred from cuts caused by a ceiling sex mirror falling on him. Like I said, these guys are extras in my movie.

Prakash and I chatted in my room. One of Harper's love letters was out and I shoved it in a drawer. She wrote me long email and paper love letters about how much she missed me. She wrote that her "yoni" missed me. It's a Sanskrit term for the vagina that now sounded too cute to be hot.

I put my hands on Prakash's neck and he put his on my hips. A classic pose for a kiss, his lips so soft against me. Then Aakar walked in. He was short with startling upturned green eyes, light brown skin, and long dark brown hair. His English was only slightly better than Prakash's. We traded their broken English for my more broken Nepalese. They flattered me, saying my accent was good. As if it was somehow ordained, the three of us got into my bed, with me in the middle.

Aakar brought his hand down the muscles of my stomach. Goose bumps covered my arms. He traced a finger under the line of my panties. I barely knew him, which was part of the allure. His hand began massaging and discovering me. I was poised in a perfect embrace with Prakash's arms around me, lips against mine. My hands explored both of their arms and stomachs, brushing against the bulges in their pants.

Aakar's fingers were bringing me very quickly to the brink. I experienced such a delicious sensation of pleasure in my whole being, everything a warm humming beehive. All my needs met at once, the disregarded middle child now the center of attention. I entered a liminal space, kissing one and then the other. Prakash smelled like the incense his mother burned. Aakar smelled like heady British cologne. There was something yielding about them that made me feel safe but also excited. Aakar's long hair was out of its ponytail and I ran my hands through it. I wasn't thinking of consequences. I was cocooned inside the dreamy part of a threesome. The good part. But it never lasts, at least not for me.

Tomas barged in under the pretense of returning my tequila bottle, but his real intent was disruption. The boys were startled out of the easy constellation we wordlessly found ourselves in. Prakash got up and mumbled something about us going on without him. He left the room. I enjoyed some delicious moments on top of Aakar, the sizzle of us doing something forbidden lighting up my clit. But Prakash's absence hung heavy in the air. Soon Aakar got up and dressed.

Prakash was the one who brought over his buddy, which didn't stop him from yelling loud enough for all of Kathmandu to hear: "What kind of a woman has relations with two men at once!?" Then he slammed the door hard. It was jarring to go from the sensual flow of *The Diaries of Anais Nin* to the harsh stamp of *The Scarlett Letter.* If you are still assigning that terrible book then go die. You have no right to teach, and no, I don't care if you are giving it a feminist assessment. Prakash was slut-shaming me but we didn't have that term in 2000. We also didn't have *mansplain* or *manspread*. We thought those were all just normal behaviors we had to endure.

Prakash came back a couple times a week (surprise surprise), knocking violently on the big wooden door, begging for me to take him back, but I never opened it to him.

My time was up. I packed my precious wares: half shirt "choli" tops made for my sisters, patterned bedspreads for my parents, statues, packets of decorative bindis. But I didn't know what to get for Harper. She didn't like the ornate feminine things of Nepal. In fact, like many butch women, she had years of resentment built up towards her family for giving her dresses and perfumes when she wanted jeans and tools. Nothing is more terrifying than giving your butch the wrong present on any occasion. She will kill you with her eyes.

Mardi and I left the Love Palace together for a trip to Thailand. By this time it was December and absolutely freezing in Nepal. We never got a hot shower and were lucky if we got a warm one. We were ready for some warmth and beach. Afterward Mardi would return to Nepal and I would fly home with Harper who was meeting us in Ko Phangan in a week.

On the day of departure, I got up early and snuggled in bed with each of my roommates to say goodbye, knowing I would never see their smiles again. Tomas held me tight saying, "It was great to be with you April." Okay that was sweet. Maybe I should have given him a bigger part.

I looked at myself in the mirror by the door. I'd lost weight eating so much dhal and rice and almost no fish, my favorite protein. My face was winter pale. I remembered my mom sending me off from my driveway in Forestville (the aforementioned hick town). She put her hands on my arms and cast a spell of safety around me saying, "Let me look into those traveler's eyes." Moms.

I wore impractical platform shoes as I set out with my three green suitcases on the busted road. Mardi was tall, sporty, and broad-shouldered. She gave me one look and promptly took charge of my two largest bags. Here's the part where I call back the big traffic street from the beginning of this chapter and instead of imagining it like a Double Dutch death march, I simply walk across it without getting hit by a single autorickshaw. Just making sure we are tracking progress and the character arc and I are growing and changing!

As our taxi flashed by Kathmandu, its kindly people, its wild rickshaws, I tried to memorize it because I didn't know if I would ever return and even if I, did I wouldn't find the same Nepal or the same me. Cue some epic transitional music overlaying this scene and I'd love to randomly have a British accent doing the voiceover:

I was glad I wasn't just a young backpacker passing through. I had lived in Nepal and gotten to know its streets, neighborhoods, language. I departed with a semester abroad certificate, an ability to give a Thai Massage, several Nepalese classical and folk dances, a loss of innocence, a measure of freedom and infidelity, and a masala chai addiction. Paramount was my expanded concept of all the ways there are to live.

Mardi and I drank beers towards the end of our flight. I stored my many suitcases in the airport and emerged with only a backpack of essentials. The bus dropped us off in Bangkok. Being tipsy made me feel young and fun but I was also disoriented and suddenly in a loud, wild, foreign city. Everyone was brown, short, and speaking a language I couldn't fathom. Everywhere the music sounded like songs Hello Kitty would sing if she sang in Thai, sugary sweet. We arrived at a fleabag hotel owned by a defeated Indian family.

I lay flat and wide-awake next to Mardi trying to get through the humid night sans air conditioner. I held the Lakshmi necklace that I planned never to remove in my hand. She is the goddess of abundance and almost two decades later I would choose her as my deity in my yoga teacher training.

I had my identity as a student and a philandering sexual explorer in Nepal. But who would I be in Bangkok? Was I Harper's girlfriend?

After Mardi and I had our fill of shopping, squid on the stick, and dodging carts selling DEEP FRIED FUCKING CRICKETS, we headed to the southeastern island of Koh Phangan, known for its full moon parties, bad rave dancing, lack of consent conversations, and travelers with full body tattoos, which were still novel at that time.

We stumbled out of a taxi to behold a traveler's paradise: a long carpet of coral-colored sand, glistening surfer waves, beach huts and hammocks everywhere. Mardi and I quickly got used to a lifestyle of bikinis, long seafood lunches, and dipping into the warm Gulf of Thailand. After witnessing me eating Plaw Gung (shrimp salad) three meals in a row, for three days in a row, Mardi finally asked, "Are you going to eat shrimp salad every meal here?" After four months of eating mostly rice and dahl in landlocked Nepal, the answer was yes, Mardi, yes in fact I am.

We were staying in 100-baht huts on the beach where the colors of sand and pale blue sky and ocean made everything soft and peaceful. I flirted with a short, muscular black college student named Darren. I sat with him and other travelers on the beach for an eternity. Someone sang Bob Marley songs on a guitar. Darren said men's orgasms were more powerful than women's. He said he saw all the colors, felt all the feelings, spoke in tongues. We debated this point.

That night I ended up in his 50-bhat hut (no bathroom). His muscles were ripped along his chest and arms. We kissed and made out, he played with the belly button piercing Mardi had peer-pressured me to get in Bangkok. I carefully removed his hand saying: "I just got that and it's very sore."

Who was this woman in this hut with a man she barely knew, this wanton woman with bangles on her wrists and a belly button piercing? In just two days Harper would be here.

Darren and I didn't have sex that night and thus we couldn't compare our orgasms. We just snuggled and I quietly stumbled out of his hut in the morning. Okay so THEME: Did I lose any erotic virginity in this case? He wanted to have sex with me. And I didn't feel obligated to have sex with him just because he wanted to. You are probably wondering if I ever had boundary problems, as I have now left a pussy loving English Hunk behind, kicked Three Pumps out of my tent, didn't forgive Prakash for Scarlett Lettering me. I didn't even tell you about the Tibetan dude who had a wife and kid that I slept with in a sleazy hostel. I made a literary choice there. I have secrets, reader, many secrets. None of which I told to Darren. I didn't tell him about Harper, that's for sure. Are we good, can I keep going? Is the protagonist reflecting enough? Growing? What does she want? How about your book club gets back to me on that. Meanwhile I feel some self-reflection coming on:

Thailand wasn't real life. There were huts on the beach, sunsets, hordes of gorgeous men, and no consequences. It was too close to Harper's arrival. So why was I still flirting with men? I wasn't ready to go back to my former self. Men represented sparks of freedom, their blunt lust made me feel powerful and desired. They were each a different dish I was tasting. But none of them was distinct. None of them was worth leaving Harper for. I had no intention of confessing my transgressions. I decided I could leave it behind like all the temples, restaurants, mountains I had left behind in Nepal. But every once in a while, I would get a sinking feeling.

She arrived on the beach sweaty and flustered, her old-fashioned suitcase out of place among the backpacks we all used. I was excited to see Harper and I was not. She felt more like a cousin than a lover; already my actions had changed our constellation.

I took Harper into my hut. She was frazzled. This was natural, given her long journey from America. At this moment our 11-year age difference really showed. I didn't want to rip her clothes off. I was so acclimated to men now that being with a woman seemed like something taboo I did back home in California. This was intensified by the fact that I hadn't seen a SINGLE QUEER PERSON I could identify in Asia during the past four months.

I had discarded my identity and now that its representation arrived in the form of Harper, I felt unsure about it. Though I liked that I had explored, I was also unhinged. I seemed to be pulling away from Harper, with whom I shared a life and a home. But if I were to leave her, what would I be leaving her for? I didn't fully trust The World of Men.

Side Bar

Me: Dad, why don't you join a men's group?

Dad: I don't like men.

Woot!

I love that and I love you, Pops.

I didn't trust that I could bond with men deeply. I was young enough to go with the flow but a fear loomed in the background: Was there even someone out there for me? And if it wasn't one person, how would I cope with jealously, insecurity, the unknown? My childhood had been chaotic and non-traditional. I longed for someone to show me a tradition that fit.

When Mardi and I were alone later that night, she said she adored Harper. She didn't judge me but was curious why I had cheated on her. What I didn't explain to Mardi was that four years on the pendulum of a lesbian relationship made me want to swing to the other side. I was still young. Like many girls I thought I would have sex with lots of guys and have a boyfriend when I grew up. I thought I was missing out on something. I couldn't fully reconcile my womanly relationship with the expectations growing up in a straight-normalizing world had created. I told Mardi that I was bisexual and wanted to explore more.

Harper treated me to oceanside meals and we played like dolphins in the water. We said goodbye to Mardi, which was hard as I knew I was unlikely to ever see her again. I know what you are thinking here. One of my editors thought it too. I'm a total shit and Harper is so kind and saintly. But I'm compelling, right?

Harper and I traveled together to other islands and even found a gay part of town and saw a fun drag show. But sometimes I would catch her looking at me with a quizzical gaze I had never seen before. I quickly looked away. I was now carrying extra baggage of secrets and I kept them out of sight. You know how at the airport they announce, "Unattended baggage will be confiscated and destroyed." Wouldn't it be great if that happened to emotional baggage too? We'd be leaving it in hoards at the airport!

I'm stalling because I don't want Nepal to be over. I don't want to leave sun-drenched Thailand and go back to my small town.

When we finally got back, the first thing I noticed was that Harper had placed my Wandering Jew plant in a big planter with her fichus. I had kept that plant alive since high school. The only plant I had committed to. I moved with it four times in the same little plastic pot that it was perfectly happy in. These plants were so different. They needed different amounts of sun and water.

3: RECIPE FOR A BISEXUAL

Two events in 1985 marked my initiation into the gay half of my bisexual self. Kelly Preston bared her breasts in *Secret Admirer*, and Joyce Hyser dressed up as a man in *Just One of the Guys*, which my older sister Celeste and I watched about 20 times. By the time Cindy Crawford sat astride KD Lang on the cover of *Vanity Fair* eight years later, the deal was done.

The '80s was the decade of gender ambiguity. Madonna donned a suit. Boy George adorned his face and clothes to the point of becoming a bird; Cindy Lauper was his mirror image. Michael Jackson wore more glitter than a showgirl. Annie Lennox looked like a man, at least from behind. Grace Jones's powerful jaw and hairline became weapon-like, a carefully painted arrowhead, threatening and beautiful. The "baby" that Melissa Etheridge was always singing to could have been anyone. Prince was all dolled up and crooning *I'm not a woman, I'm not a man, I'm something that you'll never understand.*

I sat glued to MTV, licking it all up like a Mars Popsicle.

There were other childhood clues about my bisexuality. I liked the part where my girlfriends and I got dressed together before parties as much as when we arrived to flirt with boys. We were always stripping down to our bras and panties, zipping up each other's dresses, brushing each other's hair. All the while I was watching their curves and smelling their scents. Getting ready for the party was intimate. The party was not intimate.

Recipe for a bisexual child
One curious girl
Two wild, permissive hippie parents
Infinite hand-rolled joints and watery bongs
A pinch of that seventies vibe
Mix together in a big soup pot from the flea market. Simmer.

My parents pulled it off three times. My two sisters and I are all bi, referred to by friends as The Bisexual Dynasty (we're kind of a big deal). In fact, my podcast producer just the other day, said, "April you are semi-queer famous." Yes, I also have a podcast, please refer to the glossary!

When I was a sophomore in high school, Mom called me up from San Francisco, where she was living with her boyfriend, to tell me about a sort-of foursome they'd tried. "Me and the other lady dressed up and were sexy dancing for the guys and then"

"Mom!"

Reader, can you believe this shit?

"Honey I just mean that whoever you love is fine," she said in her rum-soaked voice. "It's all love. It can be a man or a woman."

When my older sister Celeste said, "Dad, I'm bisexual," he answered, "Really? Me too!" then proceeded to steal her thunder and ramble on about his brief encounters of the same-sex kind.

Try rebelling against hippie parents. Go ahead, just try.

Growing up on a commune is fascinating. So are my parents. But that's a story for a different memoir. I will say the Guru told us we were all Goddesses and gods, dancing in a new age, and we were immortal. So you can extrapolate a lot from that.

Here's what one editor said: "Your relationship with your parents is challenging, and there is more to dig into with that without this becoming a story of parental saga."

More great advice I couldn't include. Please review this book on Amazon right now to encourage me to finish the other 200 memoirs I am working on. Stay with it!

Harper and I went back to our domestic routine. She made me delicious feasts. I went back to teaching nine belly dance classes a week.

We had converted the garage into a dance studio where on hot days I would just open the big tapestry-covered door to breeze and sun. I loved getting in sync with my students, all of us showing our midriffs, bejeweled scarves on our round hips, making snaky moves and shimmies, looking for all the world like temple priestesses of Amazon isles. Belly dance can be a real gateway to lezzing out.

Real quick, let me introduce Wells. She had long hair (and then short hair, her hair was always changing), she was vegan, she was an activist, and she was hilarious. She was/is a great dancer. She has a longass dancer's torso and a smile so sweet. She should be in this memoir more. If I knew how to slowly develop character, she and my sisters might have their own arc. This is Wells to a T: At a protest, two cops grabbed her on either shoulder. She did a full flip using them as some sort of circus fulcrum. Can you imagine? Anyhow she came over a lot and was friends with Harper and later became my platonic wife. More about that in future chapters.

I read biographies of dancers Martha Graham and Ruth St. Denis. Both their stories alluded to sublimating sex for dance, to working out one's desires through movement, dance being, as Shaw put it, "a vertical expression of a horizontal desire." St. Denis shielded herself from the complications of sex by marrying Ted Shawn, who was bisexual but perhaps on the gayer side. Graham was a petite woman and had a very large older boyfriend for a while. He would be called upon to slap her into focus when she became "hysterical" before a show.

My recent adventures in Nepal notwithstanding, you could still fill a library with all I didn't know about sex. All my fantasies were aggressive or even violent encounters between men and women. I was never the women in my fantasies then. I never wanted to be subjected to their ordeals and humiliations. Women who were pushed up against walls, hands held down, taken from behind, forced. I had nowhere to put the dissonance these images triggered in me, the feminist discomfort and the notion that it was taking me away from the moment with Harper. Only later would I learn that so many women needed images like these to orgasm. Only later would I read Ester Perel's *Mating in Captivity* and understand her concise statement: "What we protest in the day we act out in the night."

I told Harper I wanted to get tested for HIV because I was concerned I had contacted something from getting my belly button pierced in Bangkok. Ha! What a nutbag I was. I could have just gotten tested without telling her such a blatant lie. I had used protection with the boys but I wanted to be sure none of those disease wands contaminated my perfect queer pussy.

Small aside here because I don't have time to write a whole gyno scene.

But when you go to the gyno and say you've been in a monogamous lesbian relationship for five years, they do the exam saying, "Oh sweetie, this is just a formality. You've actually improved your pussy in this relationship." Everything in the room is warm and fuzzy and smells like lavender. But if you come saying you are a slutty bisexual who's recently slept with anything that moves in Southeast Asia, they take you to a dark corridor scented by worn-out leather, the doctor looks at you all dire and gloomy and leaves the room as you await their Verdict of Doom.

I got tested. I didn't have anything but a horrible case of guilt. Which sucked because I wasn't even raised in the guilt factory of Catholicism.

Harper and I were in our backyard where the chard produced endless leaves growing upward towards the sky. Being in our domestic sphere and pretending nothing had changed was a lie. I was terrified of Harper's response. Here in our haven it seemed crazy that I had cheated on her. But I needed to get to the other side of this.

"I had some affairs in Nepal."

Harper's eyes narrowed and her body stiffened. She stood her ground. I thought if she moved an inch, it might send a fissure crackling through the earth, severing the yard, separating us forever. Here it was finally. What she had imagined of me finally happened. I cheated on her, and with men—evil men and their evil penises.

"You took two months to tell me this?"

"I was scared, baby. I still can't believe I did it."

"Do you want to break up?"

"No, no I don't. I love you."

She walked away from me. I got in my car and drove past my old ugly school with its terrible 1970s lion mural. In my teenage years I couldn't wait to get out of Forestville and home to the tiny redwood-crowned town of Occidental each day. I never thought I would end up living near my school. "Touch of Grey" by the Grateful Dead was playing on the radio. I had shattered the basic tenants of our relationship. Harper had said, "If you ever have sex with a man I will break up with you."

But Harper didn't break up with me. She didn't even kick me out or make me sleep on the couch. That night when I nuzzled into her she didn't push me away. I thought to myself, *I'm okay. The earth didn't crack open and devour me. I didn't destroy everything.*

4: JUNGLE BEAST

It was a year since my Nepal trip. I flew to meet my sisters in Yelapa, Mexico. That's right, I had barely patched it up with Harper and was off to slut it up in Spanish.

Before I left, Harper and I had started therapy and I was working up my nerve to ask for an open relationship. Mexico became the next setting where I could play out another life, another self, unconfined by the parameters of monogamy Harper created in our relationship. I had called her bluff. My cheating hadn't driven her away. So my rebellion continued.

Allegra flew in from Bard College on the East Coast and I from Sonoma County. She was witty, joyful and a good four inches taller than me. She was a master of one-liners. When she went away to college in an aura of purple clothes and gold glitter, gay boys flocked around her like drones to their queen.

Celeste bounded towards us at the airport, a woman transformed by tropical Mexico, richly tanned, muscular, her enormous eyes wide with excitement. She had been living in Yelapa for three months with her boyfriend Logan. There was something feral about her. She was bursting with excitement to show us her world. She plopped us on a motorboat they call a *panga* and off we zoomed.

As we raced over the water, Celeste, the sex goddess of the family, let us know that many men and some women in Yelapa had crushes on her. Her enormous mane of hair flew about her face. She and Logan had enjoyed a few threesomes with hot tourist women, but the men were left with their desires unmet.

"So some guys might hit on you," she concluded, given our physical resemblance.

"You told them we have partners, right?" said Allegra with the wild winds turning her short hair into a Mohawk.

Celeste had a tendency to bring orgy vibes and instant harems into any situation. Over the years Celeste had hit on many of Allegra's friends and a few of mine. Celeste's prowess was a wide, powerful spotlight that could land anywhere. Allegra was simply assessing the current risk.

"Yes, I said you had a boyfriend and April had a girlfriend."

I know what you are thinking. You are enamored with my beautiful and enchanting sisters. Story of my life. You meet and befriend me and want to date them! I am not jealous, really. I am their biggest fan. But as the middle child I do have to whine occasionally. We have never fought over any women or men. I have had crushes on one or two of their boyfriends and they took it very well, even saying I could have them when they were done, like a favorite prom dress. As far as I know they never had a crush on any of my babes.

The boat blasted forward until it turned around a patch of rocks and the full panorama of Yelapa spread before us: a long, white sandy beach lined with hut-like restaurants and behind that a jungle, mountains and hilly foliage that hid a peekaboo view of a beauteous waterfall.

This was the storied town where our mom and her lover ran away together, leaving the rest of my family behind. I was nine. Mom had cleaned Mexican houses to pay for their stolen honeymoon. But I didn't feel her presence here now.

Strong Mexican men steadied our hands as we slipped off our shoes and landed barefoot up to our ankles in water. They unloaded our bags onto the beach giving our arrival the carefree vibe of a gypsy caravan. Allegra had brought only a tiny backpack, mostly stuffed with belly dance costumes. I had planned for us to do a belly dance performance during our short holiday and she agreed because resistance was futile.

Like me, Yelapa was in transition. It had survived all these years without electricity. But wooden utility poles were being erected during our visit. The nights lit only with flickering candles were fading, replaced by the dull modernity found everywhere. But it still maintained its status as car free. The main modes of transportation were *en piedro* and a la donkey.

We waded across a swamp and plopped into our round palapa. It had a thatched roof and separate outdoor bathroom and shower landscaped with tropical flowers. That night we headed to the locally famous Saturday Night Disco, an open-air restaurant with wooden tables surrounding a dance floor. Young Mexican couples kissed in the shadows as we walked by. Celeste, Logan, Allegra, and I all sat down. "We Want the Funk" played for the 15 dancers shaking it. It was an odd smattering of white-haired hippies, hot young Mexican studs, Gortex-clad travelers and a couple of local girls. But mostly it was a gringo disco. Celeste gave us the rundown of the scene.

"Juan, the shy one over there, is totally crushing on me. He is handsome but kind of boring and mopey. Don't even talk to the hunks hovering by the bar, they are just after one-night stands and petty theft."

A tall Mexican guy with crazy, curly hair and a huge, uneven smile interrupted her. He had green eyes set in a kind face but there was definitely something wild about him. He grunted something that sounded like "sister." And here was Jungle Beast.

He grabbed my hand and muscled me onto the dance floor. He threw me around in a caveman salsa. I was lurched and twirled, and then flung back into his arms. The music stopped, a new song started and the roller coaster began again. He spun me, dipped me, we almost leveled two ravers with my kicking legs as I hurtled around him. I'm a born dancer, but dancing with Jungle Beast was unlike anything I'd experienced. I didn't even know that you could salsa dance to REM. The song ended and he grabbed my wrists again. I mumbled something about getting a drink and limped back to our table. It was deserted. Allegra was at the bar ordering a drink. Celeste was freaking on a curvy woman with brilliant blonde hair. As I walked passed her she moved the blonde's hair aside like she was in an Abba video and said, "Logan and I can take this lady home with us if we want," then let the hair flop back like a curtain. I was catching my breath as Allegra approached with two cervazas con limón.

"Courtesy of Juan," she said handing me a beer. She turned her head, directing my gaze to a lanky clean-cut guy with bushy eyebrows and a hopeful smile.

"I can't believe you let him buy us drinks. Now one of us is going to have to make out with him."

"Listen, I'm in college and can't afford anything. If the gentleman wants to buy, we accept." Juan made a "cheers" gesture with his beer.

"Why is he smiling at me, he's yours," I said.

"The way I figure it is you have long hair and I have a dyke cut, they probably think I'm the lesbo sister," said Allegra.

I wandered onto the beach. I love having a crew behind me at a bar and then going off on my own to see what happens. I encountered an earnest, very pale Canadian traveler about ten years younger than me. We sat on a rock looking at the moon floating above the ocean. We chatted, we flirted, and then he said:

"How do I possess someone like you?"

Can you believe this? And under the moonlight. I had no idea how to respond.

"How do I possess you?" he said again. He moved his face close to mine. I kissed his dry lips. We made out a bit, but I was giving it fifty percent. When we got up, we realized he had sat in dog poop. I disentangled myself from him and headed back to the bar. Near the entrance I ran into Celeste.

"Did you just make out with that guy?"

"Yes, your little sister is a big slut," I said.

"Being a slut is great," said Celeste. "Take the Slut Pledge. Raise your hand and repeat after me: I'm a slut."

"I'm a slut," I said, hand up like I was solemnly swearing in court. I felt the word alchemizing from shaming slur to self-proclamation. It felt empowering, and also like I was giving something up, perhaps the "reward" for being the "good girl" Shakira sang about in "Underneath Your Clothes."

Reader, I invite you to take the SLUT PLEDGE right now. Raise your right hand, say *I'm a slut* and click your heels. There you go.

After saying goodbye to Celeste, Allegra and I walked along the beach back to our palapa. The moon clung to the watery horizon and small waves crashed peacefully against the shore. Jungle Beast and Juan appeared just as we reached the swamp. This particular pond was full of spawning pollywogs who wriggled around like sexy sperm waiting for the right egg.

"Hello ladies," said Juan with a thick accent.

Jungle Beast just grunted, lifted me up, hoisted me over his shoulder and carried me across the water. As the blood rushed to my head, I looked back to see how Allegra and her beau were fairing. He was making moves to pick her up but she was several inches taller than him. Finally, she picked him up damsel-in-distress-style and carried him. I was enchanted by this tropical life where suitors came out of moonlight and fawned at you. It was a world with its own time and no rules and I drank in the freedom and spontaneity.

We appeared at the wooden gate of our palapa. Allegra said a rushed goodnight and disappeared behind the gate. Juan, looking forlorn, scuttled off. Jungle Beast moved closer to me, his teeth a mosaic of orange, yellow, and brown. Many would be repulsed by this but I was having my beauty and the beast moment. Allegra re-appeared and yanked me backwards through the gate.

"What are you doing with Gingivitis?"

"Just saying goodnight," I replied getting under the netted canopy that had holes the size of cats.

"Does he speak?"

"I'm not sure."

"Exactly," and she turned off her light and rolled over. But neither of us could sleep, the travel euphoria zipping through my nervous system and jetlag tussling her about.

The next night the moon was full and I felt restless. Celeste and Logan were processing their relationship. Allegra was still hungover from all the drinks men had bought her at the disco. With a light still in the sky I walked along the creek trail to get an early dinner taco.

The restaurant was the front porch of a local family's house, nestled between banana and palm trees. An oppressive series of neon lights dampened the outdoor setting. The menu was simply fish tacos, of which I ordered six, and sweet, starchy horchata. Jungle Beast appeared. He came close and kissed me roughly on the cheek.

"Come on baby, there's a party in the jungle, let's go."

As I recovered from the shock of hearing his actual voice, we stumbled along a rocky path that snaked parallel to the rushing creak that lead eventually to waterfalls. The light was dimming as we went further into the overgrown trees.

I halted to stage a revolt just as we passed a particularly steep patch of rocks. We couldn't turn back and my sisters would worry. On the far bank of the river, a makeshift kitchen had materialized, created from long driftwood and a white canvas canopy. A big fire was casting warm glows on the faces of ten travelers. The moonlight hung on the creek water. Candles stuck in the sand gave the scene a timeless, tribal look.

I recognized our hosts immediately: they were a dreadlocked hippie couple I had seen dancing at the disco. This oasis, this shanty town by the river, was the reward for my impulsive trek through the jungle. The tension in my body relaxed. I wanted to be a part of this tribe. We were given big mugs of *atole,* a warm corn drink. A beautiful blond woman who looked like the sun in human form sang songs about longing, the lyrics dripping out like honey off a spoon. I knew of her from Sonoma County. She had been in a band called Wild Mango. There were a couple of Canadians, a few Americans and one Mexican besides the Jungle Beast. After a while he said:

"April, let's go see one of their tree houses," pointing to rooms and beds strung like webs in the high trees.

"Maybe a little later."

Instead, JB led me over to a sandy stretch of beach by the water. We started kissing and he turned me on my side as if to spoon me. He started biting my back in a little row, so just when the thrill and pain of one bite would leave he would be onto the next. I felt goose bumps lift up my spine. Our host brought us another round of *atole* and we sat up to sip it. We rejoined the others.

"Come on baby," said the Beast.

He took my hand and we went towards the tree houses. I was nervous as I got my footing on the tiny steps leading up the tree. The base of the floor was not wood but woven rope so it rocked like a stately hammock. The furnishings consisted of a bed with blankets and pure white sheets.

I looked out eye level to the moon.

"What took you so long to take me here?" I asked.

He wrestled me down to the bed. What he lacked in looks he made up for in healthy aggression. Eventually he was between my legs with his long arms reaching up and his hands squeezing my nipples hard. I looked up and saw the crowning heads of the trees and the black and white shadows of night.

"I'm going to make you come three times on my tongue," he whispered. He took his time. My legs began to shake and I came with a moan. I was pleasantly surprised I was able to let loose with an almost stranger.

"Don't you want to kiss Pepito?" he said motioning downward. This was the beginning of me not doing anything I didn't want to do sexually, especially with men. I would relapse, but this encounter began an upward trend. By the time I had met Harper at 22, I had already done a bunch of things with boys I didn't want to do. None of these stories are sexy and there is no way to make them funny. But if you're a woman, you know the main storyline: *You made my dick hard now do something about it.*

"No, thanks," I said, and Jungle Beast and I fell into a blissful sleep. I had come a long way from the passive girl I once was. I can't do a flashback on that one, just trust me.

By the next morning I was totally immersed in my new jungle community. After a fire-cooked breakfast of oatmeal and quesadillas we headed to a series of waterfalls and pools. I showed a voluptuous woman some belly dance moves as a tall Canadian biologist and Jungle Beast looked on happily.

I got into a discussion about emotions versus chemicals with the biologist. JB stared me down with jealous intensity. I backed up. He moved closer. I backed up again, he approached. I started to jog away slowly. He jogged towards me. I took off running. He sprinted after me. I ran splashing with pagan glee over rocks and zigzagging across the water. He was right behind me and I tripped and fell into the river. He fell on top of me and we kissed passionately, choking on water and spewing it out of our noses. I rolled over so I was on top of him. His crazy hair was moving in the water around his face. I kissed him again and jumped off and took off running. He chased me. I spun around and chased him. This was some wildass sexy freedom I hadn't experienced in my small hometown. Our hippie friends were watching now with interest and clearly hedging bets. I turned around a tree and ran smack into Logan, Celeste's boyfriend.

"Hey! Are you joining our jungle party?"

"No, your sisters are worried sick. What are you doing?"

A tune rang in my head like when you lose an arcade game.

"Come on, you need to come back with me."

The next day, my sisters and I set ourselves up on the lounge chairs by the beach and handsome men from the restaurant brought us cervezas and coconut juices. We read. I journaled. We bought rich, shaved coconut pie from a lady who came around carrying it on her head. When the sun got low, we went back to our hut to change into our belly dance costumes as we were performing at The Lagunitas Hotel. They had made special tagine dinners to accompany our dance. We were bejeweled and bangled in our belly dance tops, midriffs bare, coined belts around our hips. We had to hike up our skirts to walk through the pollywog swamp. Allegra had tambourines stacked on her head.

"Dignity, always dignity," said Celeste, our mantra from *Singin in the Rain*. Lagunitas restaurant had a thatched roof and a sandy floor. Every table was full of expectant guests drinking margaritas and cervezas.

We found the makeshift stage, basically where the sand ended and cement began. We found a hidden spot and did our beginning ritual holding hands and grounding. The music started and we burst forward, arms raised high, as a rabid dog charged us, barking wildly. *Dignity, always dignity*. Finally someone subdued the dog and we finished our dances and were tipped in pesos.

The next morning my sisters, Logan and I packed up our belongings and zoomed on a panga to Puerto Vallarta. Jungle Beast insisted on accompanying us. He stood on the front of the boat, crazy hair blowing, looking back at me with wild eyes.

In Puerto Vallarta he bought me a big bouquet of tropical flowers and whispered, "Tell me what scent you're wearing."

"A woman must have her secrets." I whispered back. I was wearing amber rose.

My sisters and I had one last night in Puerto Vallarta before flying home. We stood on the hotel roof surrounded by white buildings, climbing bougainvillea, palm trees, and twinkling lights, flushed with happiness, the Three Graces clinking our glasses in good cheer. It was the rare decade where our ages lined up so that we were all in our 20s. Celeste and I seemed to have solid partners, but the expirations were looming. Allegra had a college boyfriend and her high school sweetheart both madly in love with her. I knew moments like this were rare. We were out in the world together, in Mexico, just the three of us. Still young enough to feel that gleeful optimism that everything was possible, the whole world a red carpet unfurling before us, bringing us in easy contact with the crowning of our every whim and desire.

As we boarded the plane I thought about returning to Harper and our sedate life. We chugged along on the runway, leaving Mexico and more of my innocence behind. Harper would be coming to the airport, so I handed Celeste the flowers JB had given me. When we landed, Harper was waiting for me with red roses.

I had missed her and we had some nice weeks together. In bed I initiated a new move: instead of facing her full on when I licked her, I angled my body to the side, giving her a full view of my ass. It was hot that I was doing new things, but it was also obvious I'd learned it from cheating. She must have noticed but she didn't say.

I grappled with possession of my body. I felt very clear it was mine to do with what I pleased. To be undressed with whomever I desired. But that was in direct conflict to Harper's and much of the world's idea about the confines of relationship. Monogamy is the agreement. You undress for one person. It was innocent of me to think I could just choose freedom when it suited me. Much later I would long for possession and not novelty. But that too would change:

Harper had an irascible side that she mostly tucked away but was slowly daylighting. The comment that I was "clinging to my bisexuality" epitomized her judgment of my sexuality. There's a linguistic problem with relationships for bisexuals. If I date a man, I am in a straight relationship. If I date a woman, I am in a lesbian relationship. In other words I am erased and reformed, defined by my lover. It would be two more decades before I learned the term "mixed orientation relationship." It's wordy but I'll take wordiness over invisibility.

Harper was slow to motivate, rarely traveled, and took forever to leave the house. She opened a spa in a nearby town. It was a tremendous effort to get it running. I helped out in the beginning by shopping for décor, being a bath attendant, and running the front desk. Owning a spa consumed most of her time and caused great stress. Gone were the carefree days of our courtship. I tried a maintenance breakup. That occurs when you semi-breakup in the hopes that when you reunite, they will have changed. In other words it's a load of crap prolonging the inevitable.

I packed a bag and went to live in my old bedroom at my

mom's place called The Blue Witch House. I liked having few possessions, living in Sebastopol, which was bigger than Forestville, and being accountable to no one. Harper would come over every day with flowers and notes in the hopes of wooing me back. Of course she eventually did. I didn't really want to lose Harper. I loved her fiercely.

Harper and I went to see my therapist. Oh, I love the scene in the saga when they go to the therapist! Yippee.

Her office was all beige and pastels. After hugging us both into her warm body she sat down. She had the kind of compassionate brown eyes that beamed unconditional love directly into your heart. If we all looked at each other that way, there would be no need for therapy. The office had an enormous spongy sofa which is the second thing I look for a in a therapist. The first is a knack for putting all the pieces of my life together and then handing it back to me with a new understanding.

Harper and I sat on the couch. She was erratic, jumpy. Almost like a parent losing their grip on a teenage daughter. I was sure I had subconsciously chosen her because she was a grounded person who would provide the boundaries my parents never did. And now I was rebelling against the very quality that had healed and sustained me.

Our visits started to remind me of my only attempt as a child to ice skate. I slowly pawed around the edge of the rink, gripping the sides but never skating out into the center to cut my metal teeth on the white ice.

"April, you're furrowing your brow. Is there something else you would like to say?"

I looked at the painting on the wall, azure water rushing through two steady boulders in a wild river.

"I am attracted to men as well as women. I would like to open up our relationship so I can see men as well."

Harper tensed, retreating into herself, a thousand flinches infused into one all-powerful flinch.

"How do you feel about that, Harper?"

"I don't see how that can work. I can't do that."

"It seems like that might be too much to ask, April," said the therapist.

Sometimes the whole notion of bisexuality seems to be asking too much of the world. Also, that therapist was wrong. Poly-shamed me, she did. What can you do? She was a great therapist but nobody's perfect.

I was constantly in a sour mood, restless, bored. My traveler's yearning was ramping up. I so wanted to be the girlfriend that I once was for Harper. The one that was fully satisfied by her presence, her warmth. But I couldn't seem to put myself back in the box.

One day, working at Harper's spa, I cleaned pubic hair and other detritus out of a tub. I got up and danced, putting on my best *Sweet Charity* imitation: "There's got to be something better than this. And when I find me some kind of life I can live I'm gonna get out get out get out and live it."

I was seesawing back and forth between my life with Harper and my wanderlust. I loved snuggling onto Harper's warm body at night. We had laughter-filled cookouts with friends. Harper would grill for us all as I made salads and drinks. When everyone left, she'd take me in her arms and say, "It will take a lifetime to love you."

She left little love notes in my clothing drawers covered with hearts and effusive sentiments. But I was ever longing for an April who was living a parallel life in San Francisco, Paris, or Istanbul dressed in sexy heels and colorful blouses. I wanted to travel the world as a belly dancer. After reading *The Summer of Love* I wanted to open a curios shop on Haight Street or be a tour guide in some Asian paradise where the air was always warm, damp, and imbued with the aroma of passion fruit.

The sound of the TV news bleating woke me from sleep. Harper never listened to the news at high volume in the early morning. I went into the living room to scold her for waking me. She turned her head towards me.

"Something's happened," she said.

I looked at the gruesome footage of the Twin Towers burning. I wanted out.

I found a company called Interexchange that sent you to foreign countries to be a Language Assistant. You stayed with a family and spoke English with their children in exchange for room and board.

My belly dance troupe with Allegra and four other dancers was dispersing. So was our band, of which Harper was a member. I ended the dance classes I taught in my garage studio. I sold or stored all my possessions and planned to move to Europe and never look back. I said long passionate goodbyes to everyone. I told Allegra about it in my living room, curious for her response. "You tiny, little determined thing," she said.

I broke up with Harper. Though in my recollection it wasn't so perspicuous. She sadly surveyed all my packing and discarding. She made me a mix tape to take to Spain featuring Ketel Kenig, Michelle Shocked, Madonna. I didn't know how to break up with her. I certainly didn't know how to live in Sonoma County without her. So I moved to Spain.

When Celeste and I returned from Mexico, Harper bought me some sort of proto cell phone. Logan bought Celeste a pager. They both sensed they needed to put tracking devices on us so we would return like homing pigeons. But we weren't pigeons. We were wild, exotic birds raised on a hippie commune and like our mom, we flew away.

5: THE PAIN IN SPAIN

On the plane to Madrid I invented a new self. Her name was Sumaya Douvan. She was first and foremost a belly dancer. I had packed several costumes and my sword. I called ahead since airports had become paranoia centers unwelcoming to Middle Eastern style dancers traveling with sabers. They said as long as it went as checked luggage, they would allow it.

An air hostess handed me a promising lasagna and I got out my journal and wrote a poem while I waited for it to cool. The final stanza read:

If we continue to worship life,
to pray to it, to smile to it,
to make jokes in her honor,
we together will not tire of life.

This poem would be the last bloom of optimism for months. I was violently ill the minute we hit the atmosphere of Spain. When I looked out the window night had fallen and the plane landed with a thud, a big mechanical bird reduced to a clunky car.

Valentina, the mom of my host family, greeted me up at the airport. As in Nepal, a strong matriarch was taking me under her wing. I could barely speak I was so nauseous. We went to her bright lovely home set up with clean surfaces and cozy nooks. I introduced myself to them as Sumaya, my new name, and proceeded to be startled every time I heard it addressed to me. After meeting Valentina's two clean-cut, serious kids, we drove to a nearby apartment. It was small and dark and featured a grandmother that hadn't been mentioned in our correspondences. This would be my dumpy little abode.

Five days a week I spent afternoons helping the children improve their already impressive English skills. In exchange for that I got room and board at their grandmother's apartment.

I saw a notice on Craigslist for language exchanges where I could improve my Spanish. I agreed to meet Arturo at a café near the Plaza Mayor. He was short with thinning hair, a big nose, and large green eyes. He wore a bulky leather jacket that was too long for him. He gave me a kiss on either cheek.

We ordered coffees and sat down. Arturo's phone kept ringing. He finally turned it off saying: "This stupid girl won't take the hint, she won't leave me alone." We spoke to each other first in English. His accent was thick. He was flirty and self-deprecating, stuttering some of his words. When we spoke Spanish I wondered if I sounded like a precocious five year-old. He invited me to a party that weekend. I was non-committal about attending.

I was going to go straight home but I heard U2 coming form an Irish Pub. I ordered a beer at the bar but didn't intend to drink it. All around me clusters of jovial young Europeans laughed and drank together. How had they found each other? A very tall young man sat down next to me. He introduced himself as Jona from Kenya. He had big, unresting eyes. We chatted about what brought us here. I was embarrassed by my story so I asked him about his. He was studying environmental science. There was an innocence about him that made him feel safe. I hoped he could be a friend. We exchanged numbers.

Back at my place the grandmother, my unexpected flatmate, was sitting in the living room. I made myself a cup of tea.

"Why do you drink tea at night?" she asked in Spanish. "It will make you go pee all night." Truer words were never spoken. But I enjoyed my musty, floral chamomile. "Okay," I answered in Spanish. She probably had a whole panoply of folk wisdom I could glean as my Spanish improved.

I put on makeup and my best Spanish boots for the party at Arturo's friends house that Saturday night. The apartment was two stories high with a long balcony overlooking the first floor. It was dark and cold inside. Everyone was standing, which is how the Spanish tend to party. Arturo walked up to me, his already large eyes widening with delight. He introduced me to the host, a pretty lady with the signature eggshell colored skin and long black hair that so many Spanish women have. She clutched his arm and said: "This is a good guy. You should totally date him. He is a good guy." Note: HE WAS NOT A GOOD GUY. But we'll get to that. I kept up with everyone's Spanish as best I could as I nibbled on olives.

Arturo invited me back to his place. His room was cold, messy, strewn with items of transience. I wasn't drawn to Arturo at first. He had a pointy nose and a shapeless stocky body. He smelled like he bathed in only cologne and brushed his teeth with cigarettes.

The first night he tried to get in there was an elaborate seduction. I said I would stay the night but we wouldn't have sex. I know I know. We were still pretending to just be hanging out, or I was. He breathed into my neck, clutched me close to him, kissed me all along my body. He squeezed me in all the right places, making me wet despite my instincts. Men become the best dancers when they think they won't get to dip you. I should have drawn that out for months.

Days passed and I was still thinking of Arturo. I needed a distraction, something to fixate on in this new foreign, cold landscape. Arturo invited me over and I accepted. We kissed and rolled around but he was distracted. Knowing we would have sex took the artfulness from it. He wasn't trying hard this time. I was on top of him, he was inside of me barely moving.

"No movimento" I said.

"No moviemento" I repeated.

For some reason, at this, he sprang up from under me, flipped me onto all fours and entered me hard and fast from behind with his little member. I felt erotically charged and aroused. A thin layer of my erotic virginity was shed. I used it as fantasy imagery for years after.

When I hadn't heard from him in a couple of days I called him.

I said in my growing Spanish. "Estoy confundido Arturo. Que quieres de mi amigo, intercambio, sexo, nada?"

"We can't talk about it on the phone," he said. He was amused by my desperation and emotional outburst. His voice was imbued with an almost mocking laughter that had the odd effect of turning me on more.

"What do you want from me? You didn't call me in days ..."

"Slowly, April, I am from Bolivia," he said managing to be adorable.

We had a date on Friday night. When the time arrived, the hours advanced until I called him. The phone just rang and rang. He was with some other girl and I was the one who couldn't get the hint. And what of the friend who had endorsed him at the party? What of sisterhood? What, exactly, had she meant when she said he was a good guy? I have gotten much better at casual sex in the ensuing years, but in my late 20s, alone and heartbroken in Spain and living in a musty apartment with someone else's abuela, I mistook the chemical reaction my few dates with Arturo had catalyzed for something more meaningful. I was already in an overly sensitive state. His disappearance took on more gravity than it should have.

I couldn't get warm in Spain, I couldn't get a real job, and I couldn't bear the claustrophobic Plaza Mayor. The big buildings on all four sides felt like walls. It was so orderly I felt trapped as on a chess set. For all the celebrations that took place here there were also bullfights and public executions.

I passed alluring hot bakeries, cold slick walkways, women with big hair and small waists, and ancient buildings with statue-bodies clinging to the upper towers in an endless cement dance.

I met the wrong lovers, made and lost the wrong friends. There's no unified Madrid. It's a different city to every traveler. To me, it was a closed society. People made friends in childhood, grew up with them, married each other and were cautious with foreigners. There wasn't a big tourist or expat community to join.

Sometimes I went into the Irish Pub just to hear English spoken.

I called my mom and Harper in tears trying to figure out what to do with all my sadness. I could see no future. I had lost my belly dance troupe, my girlfriend, my pagan community. This geographic cure was only making me sicker. The trip to Spain was catastrophic on such a scale that I had to soothe myself with a nursery rhyme: *The pain in Spain stays mainly in my brain.*

I wrote morose things in my journal. I spent many hours looking out the window, feeling invisible. One day I was belly dancing and I saw a boy stop and look at me through the window. I was so startled. I thought *I am not invisible, I can be seen.* I grew a resolve to take language classes and find places to perform belly dance. My culture shock wore off a little like the final hours of a hangover.

The winter was record-breaking cold. It hadn't snowed in ten years but they rolled out the white powder for me. Everywhere I went I went alone. The days were rainy. One day in the metro I found myself with my fingers entwined holding hands. With myself.

I enjoyed spending time with the children because I had a purpose. No, I am not going to bore you with character studies on the kids. You're welcome. Suffice it to say they adored me in their stoic way.

In my ample free time I tracked down Moroccan restaurants. In the night I would perform two sets with a costume change. Always I danced with my sword. People can't resist a sword dancer. I could see interest, even hunger in the audience's eyes while they sipped spirits and ate olives. The softness of my curves juxtaposed with the sharp edge of the sword. One night I decided not to use it. The owner asked where the sword was. I said I thought I had been using it too much.

"Not at all. Please get it. I have billed you as the woman with the sword."

They do everything late in Spain. I finished my set at one in the morning so he drove me home. He had a distracted air as if he was meant for a different, grander time, presiding over some city-state from a bejeweled palace. We listened to Pink Floyd's *Comfortably Numb* as we sped through the gray city. When he dropped me off he said, "Goodnight Sumaya."

Jona, a man I had met randomly at a bar, invited me out with some of his friends. He was beanstalk tall, had a round open face, and deep brown skin.

I invited some friends from the Spanish language class I started that week. I loved the tiny wine glasses they used in Spain, which meant I could sip and not get drunk. We had one of those blurring international broken English conversations about where we'd traveled. Jona tried to hold my hand. "I only want to be friends," I whispered gently. He smelled too sweet. I wasn't aroused by him.

The family took me to the New Year's celebration in the Plaza Mayor. The kids were dressed like mini adults, the boy in a little suit and tie and the girl in a gown. Everyone was excited about the euro being introduced into Spain. At midnight fake bills dropped from the sky to the words of the Flying Lizard's remake of *Money.* The lyrics are a bit of a dark chant towards capitalism even if they are delivered ironically. I wondered how many people understood the meaning behind the catchy hook.

Valentina handed me an apple dipped in honey for a sweet year. The tart crisp of the apple reminded me of the famed Gravenstein apples of my home. Of walking among the orb laden trees and watching the yearly Apple Blossom parade cantor down main street Sebastopol.

I made weepy phone calls to Harper. I knew I didn't have a right to burden her with my sadness. I had broken up with her and moved to Spain. But I was young and needy enough to seek solace from a familiar place. And though I knew we couldn't be together I missed her terribly. I missed all things that might anchor me. She had supplied such gravity and now I was orbiting alone.

"Talk to your sisters," she said.

"Come home," Celeste said.

"But I'll be a failure," I pleaded.

"I enrolled in therapy school years ago," Celeste reminded me. "I knew it wasn't right for me. Quitting cost me thousands of dollars. But it was what I had to do. Just come home."

Jona and I went out for drinks. He invited me back to his small room with its single bed against the wall. I lunged at him, moved not by passion but by a gaping loneliness. I kissed him and instantly regretted it. The lights were bright, there was no music playing. There wasn't enough foreplay and I was too weak to advocate for it. Once he entered me I felt only pain. My pussy would never really become a good-time girl. The sex in movies where a big cock goes right in with no warmup is sexy to watch but so unrealistic. I need lots of lube, clitoral stimulation, starting slow at the right angle. Sirens blared outside his window. I wanted to be out there, out of this stifling room.

He was very quiet, as if going through the motions of something businesslike. He turned me over so I was pressed belly down into the bed as he took me from behind. I got caught up in the old story: *You started this so you have to keep going*. Finally a small, self-preserving voice spoke.

"We need to stop; it hurts."

He said, "I'm almost done, just let me finish."

Get a load of this guy! The injustice and humiliation of it.

I let him finish and then was furious with myself. I was so out of sorts. Out of my body. Out of my element. Using a new name. Having a woman's body takes such constant vigilance. It was too late to get myself home, so I slept with his long arms around me, barely able to breathe through all his cologne.

I was finally entertaining the thought of leaving. The owner of one of the Moroccan restaurants wanted me to dance more regularly; my expat friends wanted to hang out. I was improving my Spanish. The children acted excited to see me (okay, their stoic version of excitement). Karen Blixen had warned me about this: "I have before in other countries seen them give themselves to you when you are leaving them."

I searched the papers for Original Language American films that hadn't been dubbed beyond recognition into Spanish. *Vanilla Sky* was all over the Spanish papers: Penelope Cruz and Tom Cruise. I sat in the cold theater hugging myself, trying to keep up with the film's jarring leaps through time, confusion, uncertainty. At the climax Tom Cruise is on the edge of a high building as Sigor Ros music played. At great risk he leaps, descends, surrenders. The next day I bought a one-way ticket home.

6: BOY NEXT ROOM

YOU'RE STILL WITH ME? HUZZAH!

I emerged from the chilly winter of Spain into a blissful Sonoma County spring. I almost kissed the tarmac at SFO. Green suitcase in hand, I walked into the Blue Witch House, pale blue on the outside, its big picture windows framing the dining and living rooms. In the hallway I looked left at my old room, the door of which I always kept open. My mom's roommate now lived there. I knew him peripherally as a friend of the family. The door was firmly shut.

So I walked into Allegra's former room, half the size, featuring a bookshelf full of Allegra's books and a strange collection of Advil bottles. The small space felt comforting. I was ready to be simple and thankful. I made a small altar in the corner and put a candle and a Quan Yin goddess on it.

I was so happy to see familiar sites, warm knowable faces, all the lovely vibrations of home. I was in a good mood for six solid months. I re-enrolled at Santa Rosa Community College. I had attended the same college when I lived with my mom after high school. My life took one big, sweeping circle. But on the bright side how many people can brag they finished college in just 11 years!

As fate would have it, Celeste and her boyfriend Logan had also moved back in with mom. They were living in the converted garage. Despite the difficulty in Mexico they were still together. Allegra was still back east at Bard College.

I decided to be a traveler in my own town. I drove with a carload of friends out to Bodega Bay shooting a video I would never edit. We saw the fields of calla lillies I'd always heard about, spread out all white and green like a fairytale come to life.

Next up: Red's Recovery Room, now closed, near Cotati. RIP Reds! It was a funky barn in the middle of nowhere that I drove past all my life going to and from San Francisco. We waltzed through the door and sat down. A sign over the bar said: "Sonoma County, home of fine wines, did you bring any?"

Logan and his friend got me plastered on tequila shots. Logan and I passed out together in my old room. He said it was confusing to snuggle with someone who looked just like his girl but wasn't.

Men hit on me all the time when I had a girlfriend, but now that I was single they didn't seem to notice me. Whatever register of my Kinsey scale, I consistently wanted attention from men, not leering catcalls, just the flicker of desire in their eyes. This was a script I was given in my unconscious youth: You be pretty and they will pursue. But it wasn't happening.

"Men don't know you're bisexual," said Allegra. "It's a small town. They saw you with a girlfriend for years. They think of you as the unavailable pretty lesbian." And yes, I do want a shirt with that printed on it. Black with pink letters please.

Mom was renting out my room to a 25-year-old named Levi. He had round green eyes, tea-with-cream skin, and a tall, willowy build. I was staying right next door. Let me give you a bit of character description because why not? Did he help me grow? Maybe. He definitely made me want to date men with money. Did he help me lose some erotic virginity? For sure.

When Levi laughed, he bent forward from the hips. Sometimes when he spoke he put his hands on my shoulders and peered down at me like a coach would to his protégé. He smelled faintly of burnt toast and mildew. I was strangely drawn to the smell as it reminded me of the town where I lived at various parts of my childhood, Camp Meeker. It smelled like the semi-poverty from which I had sprung. Not pleasant but pleasantly familiar.

I was still on my manic post-Spain high so everything was wonderful and breezy. It was not a time of discernment but a time of taking pleasure in pleasure itself.

Harper still came round from time to time. She treated our separation like a bad cold I was having, one that I would get over. She was so vulnerable to me that it broke my heart all over again. It put me in the terrible position of reminding her again and again that it was over. A decade later she would say: *It took you forever to get over me.* I guess two people's memory immediately diverges from its original source.

Levi didn't have any money. I only had some humble savings after Spain so I overlooked this. I knew I would become gainfully employed again. I started teaching one belly dance class a week in Mom's converted garage and doing tarot readings at Copperfield's bookstore. Even if people rarely sat down for readings I was happy to hang out among all my favorite authors, dipping into memoirs, novels, self-help, and cookbooks.

Levi and I started hanging out. We often met up at the swing set of the school across the street. We swung back and forth between the freshness of youth and the pressure of adulthood. Note this swing set is obviously something we will use in the Netflix version of this steamy memoir.

I helped throw Celeste's 30th birthday party. I came up with the theme: Hot Cuban Nights complete with rum drinks and salsa dancing. The vibe was, in fact, hot. I was flirting with a short blond surfer, a zaftig barista with smoldering eyes, and some femme ladies. The rum was flowing. On the dance floor my sisters were dancing with a potpourri of friends. Everything felt loose and easy in the way alcohol can soften the edges when you are young and open and stupid. I looked sexy in my skin-tight maroon dress and I enjoyed the glances I was getting.

I went into Levi's room. He was sitting on a drum stool playing a slow beat. I came over and looked him in the eyes. My dress was very short. He moved his hands up my thighs. It was a bold move for a virgin; oh did I mention he was a virgin? He caressed my inner thighs. I liked that he started with touch instead of a kiss. I wanted him in a different way than my robust lovers. Levi was not robust but sort of feminine. I leaned down and he kissed me and pulled me into his lap.

I led him into my bedroom while the laughter of the party trickled in. His hands explored my whole body as he undressed me. I felt the power of being the one who knows, the one who initiates. He was on top of me, dry humping, getting used to the mechanics of sex, all the thrusting men have to do. I got a condom and lube. Lube was something I was hearing more and more about from sex-positive Celeste and friends. There was some mythology floating around that you should create your own wetness or you weren't turned on. All my hippie herbalist friends insisted the more lube the better. I lamented all the times I had sex in high school without lube. No wonder it was painful.

Levi, of course, had no complaints. I slipped the condom on and lubed it and my vulva up. He looked into my eyes. I guided him inside me. He put his arms down straight as if to do a yoga plank. I wrapped my thighs around him. We grooved for a while.

"I can't come like this yet," he said. "It's just so different than what I'm used to." It was hard to figure out how to end things so I faked an orgasm for the first time. Back sliding, I know! He knew it instantly. He was very intuitive and sensitive to betrayal. I apologized and vowed to never do it again.

I had tried to explore the world by moving to Spain. The world spit me right back to my home. Now I wanted to explore something more intimate. Levi was the perfect laboratory to experiment in. Since his only experience of sex was masturbation and porn, I could try out all kinds of things and he didn't need to know he was the first lover I was trying them with. I could also design sex around my own desires, passing it off as gospel.

I watched the episode of "Sex in The City" where Charlotte is dating a man that can't orgasm unless he grunts expletives into her. Though my private fantasies involved all kinds of imagery and words it was jarring to see it bluntly showing up in pop culture. I asked Levi about talking dirty to me. He protested on a feminist platform that I couldn't argue with, but I offered another option. Before he entered me, could he sometimes say: *I want to hear you beg for it.*

Though I genuinely cared for Levi, I wouldn't say I fell in love with him. Up until that point, the only man I had ever truly loved was my hunky high school boyfriend Troy.

Aha! Ready for a rom com flashback?

Let's visit teenage lust, shall we?

Celeste and I were at a high school party at Simon's house. Simon was in Troy's band. Simon's mom was there: young, blonde, shapely, and sexier than any of us could ever hope to be. I was 16 and hated beer but I took it in long gulps, waited in hefty kegger lines, drank until I felt that spark of possibility that made everything loose, attainable, and blissful.

In the quiet peace of a bathroom I enjoyed intoxication most of all. My thighs spread out on the cold seat, a view of the mirror, Simon's mom's earrings hanging from mesh on the bathroom wall. I saw her pads and tampons and other requirements of womanhood. I gathered my forces to rejoin the party from this sanctuary of tile.

We played a loud drinking game that involved pounding on the table and chanting call and response style:

"What are we playing?"

"Thumper!"

"How do we play it?"

"Quietly!" we screamed.

By midnight I floated in an ocean of Miller Lite. Troy and I danced in the kitchen, he a towering golden corn stalk and I a short dark bonsai tree. He was tan and muscular with a happy-go-lucky smile and turquoise eyes.

These boys of my youth all had long cockrocker hair, tight blue jeans, and T-shirts of their favorite bands. They all hated Nirvana, which they pronounced in a whiny, nasal slang. Everyone else was playing drinking games in the living room. Troy's dancing involved a lot of knee bending, foot stomping, and forward arm waves. We kissed. His lips were soft, pillowy, shapely. The kiss was perfect. This was how relationships started in Sonoma County: a party, two people, just add beer, just add kisses. Some last months or years, some result in marriages, some divorces. Most end but imbed themselves in the heart, changeless, preserved in the amber of youth.

Downstairs we made out on Simon's bed. His sheets and covers were a series of flannel in gradations of brown and maroon. It was all very innocent and above the waist. Troy had the chiseled body of a Greek statue. But his penis was still attached unlike actual Greek statues which have been viciously looted. He smelled like the ocean and goat's fur. I was smitten.

He said: "I'm agro to your motif." This was huge in surfer-speak. There's no logical translation but it is akin to, or even surpasses, love. After school or on the weekends we went to Austen Creek in Cazedero to a swimming hole flanked by trees. We put our towels down, laid back, and the sun blanketed us. The second we were settled we both reached our hands out and clasped them together. Everything was new.

Troy would sit with his wide-open drummer mouth, blonde hair flying and thump on his kit, his muscular legs working the snare drums. I watched four different incarnations of his band, from the front row with all the girls wearing tight jeans and Wonder bras.

I loved going to his house on the river where he lived with his mom and sister. He had a rigged-up truck and a VW van. The soundtrack was usually Rush and The Steve Miller Band, but our song was U2's "Mysterious Ways." Troy never pressured me to go all the way. We dated for months subsisting only on long, passion-infused kisses. I was the one who kept bringing up the subject. I didn't know at that time that it would have been really helpful to have an adult to discuss all this with. Perhaps a worldly, queer aunt.

But I was the lone gatekeeper to my temple / amusement park and I alone had to decide who to let in and when.

Troy and I made a plan for our first time. I was housesitting in a country mansion. It looked like a hotel with its enormous king bed and original paintings framed in gold. We kissed and touched for a long time as always. His long heavy body was all sweaty on top of me. Then he slowly moved in and out moving deeper in with each pump. It hurt and I bled. Penetration was painful because I wasn't warmed up, didn't know the ways of the clit, and we didn't know about lube. *I didn't know about the clitoris!* This is just wrong. I wasn't a masturbater, probably because I shared a room and bed with my big sister and had no privacy.

I didn't know what to ask for sexually. I didn't know that I could ask to be caressed, restrained, licked, crushed, teased, spanked. I didn't know there were words that could make me weak. And what about going a layer deeper and thinking about how I wanted to feel: loved, cherished, desired. I clutched onto Troy but didn't move my hips. Our sex ended with him finishing.

After months of this he said: "How do you think I feel? You don't make any noise, you don't come. You barely move."

I was flushed with shame. Suddenly I was concerned about our sex life not on my own behalf but because I had disappointed him. I didn't know the secret tricks of womanhood. His brother suggested we put a pillow under my hips to improve the angle, as if it was all about getting the penetration right. Why hadn't his brother known about the clit? It's not okay for straight teenage boys to not know about the clit.

I asked Troy what he thought about when we had sex. He said he thought of images from magazines and porn. I was crestfallen. I thought I was the only stimulation he needed.

This little clue Troy gave me unleashed my inner fantasizer. To this day, to orgasm I need a scenario—often frantic jump cuts from one fantasy to the next. You've already heard all about this. This is where it started! Sometimes five different couples are involved. Much of my sexual life has been a struggle to accept that I must fantasize and that the imagery is far from politically correct. Much of it is variations on the theme of control and surrender.

This might be another place where I changed and grew. Maybe by the end of the book I'll stop feeling shame about my fantasies. (I won't).

Despite our sexual failings Troy and I were crazy about each other. I could draw his portrait from memory, right down to the beauty mark on his cheek. We were the kind of public smoochers that the phrase "get a room" was invented for. It was an enchanting power to have such a tall, stunning, specimen of manhood in my arms. In all his immensity he could be hurt by me and wanted to be loved by me.

Troy and I started to fight frequently about things so stupid I can't remember them. I emoted, I flirted with others, I tested him though I didn't do it consciously. After one of our fights Troy described a scene of hugging his sweet Mom in the kitchen while sobbing about me. "Why?" he asked her.

"Girls can be mean," she said.

Troy and I had a series of breakups and makeups that involved alcohol and sobbing. The breakups were all initiated by me. At least that's how I remember it and Troy won't even read this so we'll never know for sure.

My reasons for the breakups were that we fought so much, we didn't mesh sexually, I knew I wanted a future of travel and adventure and sexual exploration and I knew he wanted a wife and kids. We were in his bed for the final breakup. Even though we kept breaking up we still kept ending up together in bed. We were having one of those honest conversations you only ever have when you are breaking up.

"Why do you even want to be with me, we don't even have good sex?"

"It's not about that, April. I love you. I don't care about that." Dear Goddess as my witness, and you gentle reader, has any sex-crazed teenage boy ever in the herstory of the world ever said such a thing? Troy was special. In the rush of contradiction that is teenhood, he suggested we have breakup sex.

The year after Troy and I broke up, my high school friend Sam and I went on a research mission to discover the Female Orgasm. Sam was tall and solid with freckles and fierceness. She had lived on the mean streets of Oakland and she blew the roof off our quiet hick high school. Her home (featuring her genius-brained progressive parents) and her heart opened up a world to me. We looked at her parents' Mapplethorpe book of black and white images of Black and white men with large veiny cocks in provocative S&M positions. Sam said: "I take the bi way to the highway." So much can be gained from declaring your identity. And yet, this time of just experimenting by making out with my female friends—without naming it anything—was incredible.

We didn't practice orgasmic techniques on each other but we discussed our progress. We asked friends for tips. We asked out English teacher if the earth moved when she had sex. She claimed it had. We looked at Sam's enormous copy of *Our Bodies Ourselves* with its scientific diagrams of vulvas. But I lacked the patience to read about sex. I just wanted to know.

Sam asked her ex-boyfriend what he had done to make her come—or at least she thought she had come. He said he worked the clit, then went just to the side of it, then came back and got it all swollen, then backed off, teasing it some more. Okay, that sounded doable. Sam said when he did that, she felt this humming all around her clit, like it had a little heartbeat all its own.

Hoping to discover what she meant, I stroked away—but it was itchy and frustrating and inconclusive. I can't recall the exact moment it happened. There were several times where I thought it might have. Then finally I decided it had. And then my orgasms slowly got more intense under my hands.

I kissed my female friends in high school. We didn't demand to know who was queer and who wasn't, we just enjoyed the experiences. There is a gracefulness in the ambiguity of not declaring your status. Yet so much has been gained by coming together as queers: we have a voice, a movement, visibility, flags, parades, and legislation.

Our friend Helene, who was in her 20s, said she always cried when she had sex with her boyfriend. It wasn't sadness exactly, but a culmination of all emotions, as if he plunged her very depths. Helene had rich brown skin, big breasts, and a small waist. She was the ideal woman. Her boyfriend was sensitive, masculine, thin but well-toned.

I knew I was missing out. I wondered if I would ever find a lover who could make me cry. In a good way, I mean.

Now let's fast forward back to my exciting late-20s sex with a virgin.

Instead of the quiet prison sex I was used to, with Levi I let sounds come out, heavy breathing, whimpers, moans. First tries were like acting. It would take time before it became natural. It added another dimension to orgasm, this release in my voice. What I didn't know but certainly felt was that the throat, chest, cervix and uterus are connected through the vagus nerve. It spirals through our body like a vine wrapping around all it touches; low, resonate sounds in the abdomen stimulate the vagus nerve and increases pleasure.

At night I would light candles and change into red lacy nightgowns that clung to my figure. Or I would dress in my belly dance outfit and give him a private performance. As I undulated my body Levi lay on the bed very still, forgetting to breathe, leveling his enormous green eyes on me.

Each act was new to him. He laid me out on my bed so I was displayed before him. He looked at me carefully as he inserted a finger in, then massaged my clit, then back to the finger, and back and forth until he easily made me come. He really looked at and listened to my pussy. I thought he might turn his ear to it like it was a seashell while it whispered the pussy wisdom of the ages to him. That was the vibe.

When he told me he had been a volunteer firefighter I instantly integrated that into our role playing. He was coming into my room, flames licking the windows and heating up the floorboards.

But he always had time to fuck me on all fours before we both jumped out to the trampoline below. Sometimes we acted out the stories, other times we just talked about them while in missionary position. He was surprised I found the firefighter thing such a turn-on. He had actually volunteered to be a good citizen, not to become inspiration for torrid fantasies.

"What turns you on?" I asked.

"Girls coming."

I would ask him this question again from time to time. I knew he must have created a rich fantasy world through all his celibate years of watching porn.

"Girls coming," was all he said. I liked the purity and selflessness of it.

Levi and I took luxurious showers together. He had long thin arms and legs. He masturbated in the shower with round green bars of oatmeal soup. I got on my knees and took him in my mouth. I asked him to come on my face so I could see what it was like. The fact that I suggested it gave me agency instead of just playing out a male desire trope. He did so dutifully. He pulled me up and washed me off.

"I didn't like that. I'd rather be kissing you than doing that," he said.

Did I like it? I liked that I was trying new things. As for having the warm liquid on my face it would depend on the dynamic. Clearly it wasn't right with Levi.

Levi was on high alert when I was on my period. He eagerly went to the store for pads or ibuprofen. He asked what I needed as if we were sharing an endeavor as serious as pregnancy. I would drape my thighs over him while he sat up and massaged them looking into my eyes. I was queen for a day.

Levi chopped green onions on his knees at the kitchen table. When I wrote he looked over my shoulder totally absorbed and in communion with my creativity. And we played word games.

Me: I'm going to say a word and you say your first association with it. Ready?
Me: Raspberries
Levi: Vagina
Me: Astronaut
Levi: Vagina
Me: Tom Hanks
Levi: *Daddy*

I was with Harper for so long before Levi that I forgot the dangers of heterosexual sex. Little details like you must pee after intercourse to clear things out. I got a series of painful urinary tract infections. This was the beginning of the end. The way we connected was through sex and it became painful to even try. My UTI would seem to go away and then come back. I began to wonder if my pussy was rejecting him. Also, it's only natural that when someone gives you a UTI but doesn't have one too, you want to kill that person. It's just biological and stuff. I did my best to not kill Levi.

Levi's poverty was also losing its charm. He had a crappy car that broke down all the time. When it died he simply started riding his bike. My financial situation wasn't great but I was eager to improve it. I was doing tarot readings at a local book store (I know, I know) and learning to be a bartender. This was before YouTube videos so I just mailed away for a kit, took a test and they gave me a certification. Levi wanted to live off the government as both my parents had, especially my dad. This triggered all my memories of growing up with a dad who was either manically happy to spend other people's money (his parents, the government's, money he stole from my sisters and me) or in pain about spending his own money.

One evening Levi and I took a drive (in my car) on Highway 12 and I casually mentioned that my friend had a psychic dream about me.

"That couldn't possibly have happened," he said.

"Well it did, and why would I randomly lie about a psychic dream?"

Such are the conversation one has in Nor Cal.

"I don't know, but you are lying to me. This makes me really uncomfortable. I don't know if I can trust you."

I figured out what Levi was doing. Relationship was all new to him. He was testing me. I was his first love so he was playing out all the fears, tests, and games of fifth grade, high school, and college. I was his laboratory.

He was sweet and intuitive and then randomly cruel. One afternoon he was looking at a flyer of a dance instructor who taught ballroom, samba, salsa, swing, and merengue. He looked it over and said: "She's a *real* dance teacher." At the time I had closed my dance school of nine years to travel. I was teaching one class in our garage. But I was and am a belly dance teacher who has poured a singular devotion into teaching the joys and nuances of the dance.

My drawbridge went up. There was a subtle cruelty in his statement that I couldn't tolerate. That combined with other times he had been casually cruel and the bizarre fight about the physic dream led me to believe I couldn't continue. But I still had trouble breaking up with him because I knew how badly he wanted it to work. I discussed it with Allegra.

"How would you feel, if someone was staying with you just to not hurt you?"

"Terrible," I said. That simple reframe gave me the courage to let him go. (Note: I am the big sister and it's unfair that Allegra is always dropping the fricken sage advice.)

I would miss him. He was a quick study. Our fusion during sex was complete. Complete enough to grab my full attention, keeping me thrust into the moment. That feeling of being filled up, completely, like I knew why I was here and it was for this.

7: PRINCE CHANNING

Okay, aroused reader, let's talk about Prince Channing. From the moment I met him, which you will read about below, I gave that fucker too much attention. What you are about to read, which I should have just cut out of this book with scissors, is shorted from a whole damn book I wrote him. But, lucky you, when I wrote this I was going for a kind of peppy literary tone with a dash of *Sex in The City*. Will someone please make more SITC-type shows but all BiPOC queer people? Please?

I woke up with a resolve and called Celeste to tell her I was coming down to meet her in San Francisco for drinks.

"You never drink," she said, all accusation and intrigue.

"I know, but I want to find a man. And men are in bars."

"What's gotten into you? I thought you were happy enjoying the single life."

"People only say that when they want to focus on their career and get things accomplished. It doesn't last."

"Okay, where do you want to go?"

"Where men have good jobs." I was ready for a serious relationship after the pain of Spain and the sexual escapades with Levi, who was always losing jobs, driving an ailing car, and encouraging me to get food stamps. My criteria now included solvency.

"You know Aunt Bea always said, 'You can fall in love with a rich man as easily as a poor man.'"

"Exactly. I'll be there by five so we can catch the after-work crowd."

"Jesus you sound like..."

"... Every other 29-year-old, I know, it's pathetic."

I put on a white cotton blouse. Then I did something I have never done before going out: I ironed my skirt. I put on my Austrian crystal earrings that almost looked like diamonds and subtle pink lipstick instead of my usual bright red.

I drove south on the 101 in my tiny Corolla, past brassy fields of grass and sweeping hills. The strip malls of Marin beckoned with their promises of hot coffee and cold ice cream. Then the vermilion golden gate bridge welcomed me back to the city where I was born.

I picked up Celeste and we drove down to the Financial District. "So where are we going?" I asked.

"The Cosmopolitan. Kind of chic, overpriced drinks, should be what you're looking for. Sven's meeting us there." Sven was Celeste's best friend and trophy / platonic wife.

I should quickly explain that not only are my sisters and I are all queer, we also have platonic wives. Allegra married hers when she was 12. I married mine when I was in my late 20s. Wells! She has since tried to divorce me but I don't grant divorces. Celeste now lives with her platonic wife Sven as she has four previous times. You know how you grow up and realize your friend relationships were better than any other but you are following a societal script so you move on and suck dick and have kids and get wistful? Yeah, you don't have to! All women, all people really, need wives. Email me if you need help finding one.

We walked through an odd cement walkway and found Sven near the entrance in sharp black slacks highlighting her curvy body, heels and a white blouse. The distance between her eye and eyebrow gave her the look of an exotic bird. She took a drag from her cigarette.

"I'm glad you guys are here, I don't want to face this place without you."

"Is it that bad?" Celeste asked, taking a drag of Sven's cigarette.

"No, it's just not a place you want to go to alone."

Sven identifies as an international sex club party girl. Go see her one woman show of that same title.

We entered the full bar and took the only table left, a booth by the door. We ordered cosmopolitans and appetizers. I scanned the room. The central bar was raised up like a canopy bed with a rack of glassware crowning it. The bartenders were tall and smartly dressed in black and white; attractive in an unassuming way. A cluster of men in casual suits drank and talked at a corner of the bar. They were very white and bland looking.

"What about the one next to the bearded guy, he looks kind of cute," said Sven.

"Yeah, he's okay," I said.

Just next to us were two Filipina girls, mocha skin, sparkling eyes. One of them had a very impressive set of breasts that appeared younger than the rest of her. Also at their table was a thin black man holding a flute of champagne. He was simultaneously entertaining the women he was with, talking into his phone, and sipping his drink. He spoke in an English accent and appeared to always be on the verge of a satisfying laugh, as if the world were a great joke that he could tell perfectly.

(I wish I could say to my younger self: "He's a cad! Run away. It's not worth it." But it kind of was.)

I motioned towards him.

"That's who I want."

"He's gorgeous," said Celeste.

"He must be gay, right? I mean he's handsome, well dressed, charming and sipping champagne."

"He's definitely gay," agreed Sven.

Another half hour passed and the cocktail waitress walked over and asked if we wanted another.

"To tell you the truth," said Celeste, "we thought someone else would be paying for them by now."

"I know what you mean, in an hour I will be getting off and hoping for the same thing."

"I'll take another cosmo," I said.

"Sure, another round," said Sven.

"Svenny, are you more attracted to men or women right now?" I asked.

"I'm more interested in my genitals then anyone else's."

The restroom was very big with pale yellow walls and cushiony seats. Three women were primping in a mirror so big it might as well have had a neon sign that said: "You should spend the evening in here fussing over yourself instead of out there having a good time and loving yourself just as you are." I asked them for dating advice. They said online is the only way. It was still pretty new at this point, at least to me. Here I was, primitively trying to find someone face to face.

I exited the restroom looking down. When I looked up, the English man was directly in front of me.

"Well, hello there," he said, taking my hand. "How are you?"

"I'm fine, thanks."

I could barely focus on what he said. I was fixated on the BBC perfection. I regarded his oval face and winning smile. My sister and Sven were manically cheering directly behind him. He was still holding my hand.

I remembered my mission, to find a man, not a new best friend.

"Are you straight?"

"One hundred percent. Are you single?"

"Yes." We asked each other the wrong questions but by the time that was revealed, it was too late.

"Well good, right, I'm going to the bathroom, where are you sitting?"

"Next to you."

"I'll see you in a minute and get your number."

He moved past me. He wore tight black pants that clung to his legs and accentuated his round behind. I almost ran into the cocktail waitress on my way back to the table.

"What happened?" asked Celeste.

"I think he asked me out."

"Is he straight?" asked Sven.

"He said he was."

He appeared and we stood next to each other bordered by Sven and Celeste and his two friends.

"I'm going to see Erykah Badu tonight, but are you free tomorrow?"

"Yes."

"Great, how about brunch?" None of the hicks, surfers, or hippies I dated in Sonoma County even knew what brunch was.

"Perfect."

He gave me his business card, and I gave him my belly dance one. He read my email address. These were the days of the zany email addresses. Mine was aprilgoddess18.

"So you're a goddess, are you? Okay I'll call you tomorrow."

"Great."

He got up and left with his two friends.

"Did that just happen?" Sven asked. "You came here to meet a guy and you did. That's just weird, you're my new hero."

Our mission complete, we went to a funky Hawaiian bar called Sneaky Teaky and ordered grasshoppers. They came in tall goblets and tasted like mint ice cream milk shakes. Oh to be able to drink mint again. I have acid reflux now, don't you? Anyhow. All the conversations floated over my brain like petals on a river. I couldn't wait until morning.

Channing and I met at a café at Lincoln and 9th Street. He was sitting at a small table where he had placed a novel. I had never dated anyone who shared this habit of bringing along a book to stave off boredom. Channing complained that his cappuccino was hollow. I learned that he was black by way of South Africa and grew up in England. He told me he was in advertising and asked what I did for a living. I edited out tarot readings and belly dancing.

"I'm finishing my BA in Liberal Arts at the Santa Rosa Junior College."

We strolled into Golden Gate Park all the way to the tunnel on

Haight and Stanyan. It's made to look like stalactites are hanging from the ceiling, muddy candles turned upside down. For a brief moment I felt scared; horror stories of dates that turn dangerous danced in my head. But I didn't sense any real danger. Still, stepping into the tunnel felt like crossing some invisible line of intimacy. Halfway through Channing stopped.

"I've been told that you should get the first kiss out of the way. So you can just sort out right away if the person's a good kisser," Channing said, looking intently at me.

We leaned towards each other, our teeth hit lightly and then our lips found only softness. Someone who looked just like me was kissing a gorgeous man with a sexy accent in a tunnel in Golden Gate Park.

We kept walking until we reached Shakespeare's Garden with its velvety roses in every hue. We sat down on a patch of grass near the forest.

"I'm afraid the lipstick I wore doesn't taste very good. If you don't like it, I could wear a different kind, or none at all."

"Well I'm not quite, sure let me check." He leaned in and kissed me. After several minutes: "Still checking."

Channing and I spent the whole day together until it bled into late night. "Come home with me?" He narrowed his eyes, looking flirty and vulnerable.

"I'd like to come home with you but not tonight, I don't feel fresh."

He tried a couple more times to convince me. Later, much later, he told me that if I had slept with him that night it would have been a one-night stand. This was a red flag—the old "slut test."

I crashed in Celeste's bed. I dreamt that I saw Channing walking along Haight Street, a little ahead of me and I was trying to catch up.

A week later I drove to the city for our second date. I entered the Spanish lobby of his apartment building, ornate with lavish tile, heavy yellow sconces, and high ceilings. He greeted me with a peck on the cheek.

"Right then, shall we go to dinner?"

We went to Rose Pistola in North Beach, the Little Italy of San Francisco. I foolishly ordered the crab cioppino. He sensibly ordered a fillet of fish. My dinner arrived looking like a terrible murder at sea: all red sauce and claws. It also blasted me with a steamy garlic and tomato facial; none of the shellfish was precracked so I had to MacGyver it all myself.

"I can't believe I ordered this," I said wrangling a claw.

"It's very amusing really. Something I would usually do," he said, carefully cutting bites of white flesh with his fork and knife.

We drank the better part of a full bottle of wine. Though I hadn't been a big drinker since high school I imbibed to stave off nervousness and to accept an unwritten rule to dating. A real date involves wine.

We got on the subject of chefs and he said: "All the best chefs are men, that's common knowledge." I let it slide though it was clearly another red flag. I was thinking of an Ani Difranco line: *You gotta try to understand the grandness of a man behind the petty crimes. And let him off easy sometimes.* Channing did not deserve to have Ani save him but I was young, reader, very young.

He paid the bill and we left. I was tipsy, heading down the rabbit hole. On a dark street of Chinatown he pinned me against a wall. He kissed me and touched me between the legs. I was aching for it and yet I was nervous. I felt so lucky to be with a continental man with an accent. I worried that I wouldn't be able to please him sexually. I still believed men were complicated.

His hips pinned me against the side of the building. His perfumy cologne invaded my nostrils so that I could barely find myself in all of him. On the ride up in the elevator he pinned me again as we kissed passionately.

In his living room the pace slowed. He lit tealights around the windows. He brought out two glasses of wine, which we set on the floor because there was no coffee table in the sparse living room. The bustle of Nob Hill reached us through a series of windows facing the street.

He motioned for me to join him on the floor atop a furry white rug. He climbed on top. We kissed and touched. I was in a dream state. He was not at all what I was used to with the hikers and bicyclers I dated. I had switched from rice cakes to truffles. All the new textures of his skin, the sound of his breath. I tried to stay in my body, but I wandered and watched myself. He brought me into his bedroom. It was minimally decorated with the shades drawn and a white duvet on the bed. He comically flopped down on it and said: "Take me now!"

This wasn't what I wanted to hear. It kind of killed the build-up for a moment.

"Oh no, we're both bottoms," I said. But luckily, he didn't hear me. His warm hands were all over my hips and breasts. My hands were on everything I could reach, especially the muscles in his arms. He climbed on top of me with our heads at the foot of the bed. Then he moved behind me so he was spooning me. He deftly put on a condom. He began thrusting into me and came with a series of breathy moans. Then he promptly fell asleep and snored into my back.

I thought that only happened with older married men. But no. He fell asleep still inside me. And I smiled. So proud I made this gorgeous man orgasm. Like this was some kind of miracle. That is how naïve I was about men, how few of them I had for anything more than a fling.

The next day I drove back to Sebastopol. We talked on the phone. I kept sinking into grins at every sentence because they were dressed in his rich, sexy accent.

I went into the bathroom. When I sat on the toilet the condom spilled out of me. I was suddenly furious at his negligence. I went to the Planned Parenthood clinic and got the morning after pill. I called and I told him what happened.

"All I can say is sorry," he said without sincerity. But I was already hooked.

I started meeting Channing at his place in Nob Hill, sometimes referred to by locals as "Snob Hill," a mixture of fresh, sleek

California vibes festooned in the Gothic flourishes of a more antiquated place. Cable cars, moving like a child's toy train, traced their familiar tracks up the steep hills, giving the neighborhood a Disneyish quality. At the door he greeted me cordially, as if I were an acquaintance that just happened to drop by. Just the peck on the cheek. I had to re-introduce myself to him each time. I looked forward to the time that he was mine and we wouldn't have to go through this routine. He had me in his game. He always offered me tea. It was rich and creamy and sweet served in big black and white mugs. We sat in the sparse living room.

Every time I entered, I understood that I was entering another world. This was not my life, this was Channing's life and our secret life. I didn't know it was a secret, but he did. In the evening he lit tea candles all along the living room. We sat a few feet from each other on the couch; a distance he chose, as if a parental figure might appear at any moment to make sure the door was open and everyone's feet were on the floor. I moved closer. I could make out his sleek muscular body under his tight clothes. I saw his dark face, bright impassioned eyes, the smile that shot into me. He chatted about some of his friends that I had met. He mentioned a couple of them we might see this weekend and where. He made all our weekend plans, as I had not established myself in San Francisco yet. This was something he teased me about.

"Come on now, you're a local. Aren't you going to show me around?" Although I was a native of San Francisco, I hadn't lived there as an adult.

I moved closer. I had set my overnight bag near the door. Since I never knew how long I was staying I didn't dare put the bag in the bedroom. I was embarrassed of the bag because it implied pre-mediation on my part. He had just invited me out for the night, but I lived over an hour away so I had to pack my bag just in case. He cleared away the tea and came out with chilled wine glasses filled with Cabernet.

"I know they say you are only supposed to chill glasses for

white but I like it this way." Since he didn't make any moves I put my hand on his leg. He smiled at me. I was making it past the small talk, the re-acquainting. He was remembering that I had been in his room, slept pressed against him in his bed, and heard him snore dead asleep, satiated and still inside of me.

We had a little game about who would kiss who first. This was an unspoken rule that Channing made. It was a chess game. Showing the first desire is a sign of weakness. I didn't care about winning though. I just wanted to kiss him. I wanted the weight of his body on me and to hear the series of high brief womanly cries he made while coming. And for it to be all over so I could hold him quietly in the darkness when all the tests were done and he was mine.

Finally he took my hand and led me to the bedroom. When Channing entered me, he fit perfectly, filling me up like nothing existed but this fusion between us. With Levi I had practiced making sounds during sex: moans, whimpers, saying his name. I continued the practice of opening up my voice as Channing thrusted into me. One time I tried calling out "Daddy" several times as I came. Afterward, he said with disdain: "I was surprised you did that."

Sex with men is lazy sex. Our torsos pressed against each other. My offering is to be entered. I don't have to be away from their faces in my own actions while they receive. I offer the entrance, I pulse with them. There is an ease to this. But it lacks the delight in doing actions only for the other, in living in their sex, in that world of tastes and scents, to watch them closing their eyes and going other places while you work at their most intimate parts, obliterating yourself in an act of giving.

He said he was getting close. I tried to meet him by touching myself while he was inside me. He came too fast. He held me while I finished with a series of moans. He never made me come by his own doing.

"Do you like when I make sounds?"

"Yes, then I know you like it, it's like applause."

We went to dinner parties at restaurants with his friends, then to bars for cocktails. Sometimes to brunch, sometimes to outdoor raves, sometimes to house parties. He took us to house parties in mansions where we never met the host. I strolled around on top of the world, feeling like a peahen dating a peacock.

"All my friends like you so much. They are all charmed by you. Always complimenting you. I am a little jealous actually." This gave me a thrill. I was so invested in being accepted by Channing. For the first time I began choosing my outfits carefully to look refined, trying to say clever things, hiding parts of myself I thought he'd dislike.

I didn't tell him that my mom and I were both tarot card readers. I thought Channing might be in the category of people who thought tarot was low class, a charlatan's trickery. Allegra was horrified by my editing myself to fit into his world. She was onto me. But I was not close to my family or my friends during the Channing period. I only cared about him and obsessed about him and plotted how to be wonderful for him.

In the morning I took in the whiteness of his comforter, his walls, and furniture. His long body curled up away from me. Every word and phrase was a delight for me because of his English accent, his word choice, because of the wonderful derivations our shared language experienced divided by the seas.

We chatted in bed. When I got up to use the restroom he insisted I wear slippers so I wouldn't catch a cold. We listened to the radio.

"You would be good on the radio," he said. "You have that soothing voice."

"I've never thought of it."

"You should do," he said instead of saying, "You should try it." I loved that.

At these moments I thought *he really sees me*. He can tell I am not living up to my full potential. He nudged me about getting this job or that, something in human resources maybe. Then I fretted that he didn't know me at all. Human resources? Weren't they responsible for firing people?

The surfers, artists, the women I dated were not retreating in their emotions. I knew how they felt about me and that they wanted to be with me. Not Channing. He gave no reassurance, no sense of calm or security and I bobbed around trying to remain poised when really I wanted to fall at his feet and beg for a glimpse of something solid between us. I become a bridge and tunnel person, commuting between my world at home as a student, tarot reader, and belly dancer and dressing up preppy for my romance with Channing.

My life in Sonoma County was *Groundhog Day* in shades of grey with only a few sparks of color. Everything heated up when I saw Channing's handsome face, everything was new and alive.

I called him from my little yard at The Blue Witch House.

"Okay, what are we going to talk about today?"

I found this the oddest question. It made conversation seem so stark and calculated.

"How are things in Sonoma?" he asked like an uncle might ask.

"The same." I scrambled to think of something to say. I mostly spent my time dreaming about my weekends with Channing. I told myself that I was in transition. I was finally completing my 11-year plan at Santa Rosa Junior College culminating in an AA; a degree so rare that many have never heard of it. At this time I was doing tarot readings and occasional Thai massages. I sometimes danced with my sisters in our troupe and taught one weekly class. I've actually never cared about the total self-worth that comes from one's career. Celeste noted that I thought Channing was better than me because he had a proper job. She encouraged me to value myself.

All I could think about was my mom trying to make me eat oatmeal with her every morning. Oatmeal became a measure of our connection. If I declined I could maintain my own identity. If

I said yes to oatmeal we were a unit, I was her daughter, and this was our life together.

When friends spoke, I snapped back into the conversation from a memory of Channing. I was building dreams on shaky ground but I didn't know that. I thought I was investing in my future with this grand man. Everything made sense when Channing's hands were on me. When he was inside me there was nowhere else I needed to be.

I dressed fancy and changed my style. I bought a black push-up bra and silly silver necklace in the shape of a heart.

I brought him to my belly dance performance in Santa Rosa at The Restaurant Capri—high ceilings, shiny orange cement floors, tall exotic plants in oversized urns. He sat with my parents. Something wasn't right about that. I knew he didn't deserve to meet my parents but I was floating 20 feet above it all, in lust with him. My sisters and I all scrunched into a bathroom stall and changed clothes, repeating our mantra: *dignity always dignity*. One of them thought she might be pregnant; she struggled to get the bra over her breasts. My sisters held hands and we did our little pre-performance circle.

I felt giddy thinking of Channing see me perform with my two sisters. We made our grand entrance shimmy-walking with our arms raised high, a flutter of gold, teal, and white satin. I was engrossed in the music, watching my sisters for cues, catching the warm faces of clapping audience members. I could smell that irresistible combination of tangy tomatoes and dreamy basil coming from the kitchen.

Finally I started looking out at Channing while facing him and circling my hips. His eyes weren't on me. Whenever I dared to look at him from behind my sparkling costume he was smiling and talking to someone. I kept up my choreography, tuned into my sisters and fully enjoyed myself. But afterwards, back in the bathroom, I was sad at his disinterest.

I came and sat next to him.

"Well that was just lovely as I'm sure you know," he said, as if he felt it was his duty. We were served big goblets of Pinot Noir, we shared pasta and pizza dishes. My family is always lively around the dinner table after the heightened energy of a show. My mom flirted playfully with Channing. But I couldn't shake the idea that he hadn't really seen me.

That night I brought him into my bedroom at the The Blue Witch House for the first time. I had moved from the tiny room to the converted garage. I was embarrassed about the shaggy rugs, raw wood ceiling, belly dance mirrors leaning against the wall.

But despite the shabby setting what took place that night was a major shedding of my erotic virginity. With my requests I set the theme of our sexual encounters. I wanted to explore kink. I wanted to explore the dynamic of dominance and submission. I had tried to explore with Levi but his feminist ideals wouldn't let him just as my feminist ideals had once stopped me.

"Talk dirty to me," I whispered.

"What do you want me to say? I don't want to offend you."

"Just try it; I won't be offended."

Later I would wonder what our connection would have been like if I asked for more loving, sensual sex. This would become an ongoing dilemma for me. Turning men or women into beasts and then wanting them to return to gentleness. After I had them calling me a slut and a whore for a while, part of me would say to myself: *But you love me, right? You cherish me, right?*

He gently thrust into me missionary style and said: "I own you now. You have to obey me." This sent incredible aches and tingles through my pussy.

"You like being my little, whore, don't you?" He was looking right at me. I arched my back and closed my eyes, letting a moan come out. And then he thrusted into me forcefully. He made it clear that he was in charge and I couldn't complain or stop him. With each iteration he became more forceful. He had endless

positions for me and endless energy to thrust himself into me. I was getting sore but I didn't want to stop the dynamic that was coalescing. I could tell he liked it from the noises he made when he came. I didn't orgasm but I felt very satisfied. I felt a little shy having never done anything like that with anyone. Letting myself be taken completely. Letting someone call me names. After we fell into blissful sleep.

Those little sentences stayed with me for years afterward, so erotically charged that I used his narration when I touched myself.

I own you now. You have to obey me.

So that became our script. No *I love yous.* I was supposed to do what was asked of me.

The next time we had sex was at his SF apartment. We never returned to my place. Once inside of me he said:

"Would you do anything for me?"

"Yes," I said.

"Say it."

"Anything."

"Say you're my slave."

I thought *He is Black and I am white.* I wondered what the word *slave* meant to him. But I never asked those kinds of questions. That was another unwritten agreement of ours.

Channing and I never had oral sex. He didn't really like to receive it. One time when I tried, I asked if he could come that way.

"That's a rare occurrence," he said.

I wasn't into receiving oral sex at that time. My pussy had her cycles and she wasn't into that. I'd had enough of the type of sex where your torsos weren't touching. As far as going down on me, he quoted his mother's advice: "Black men don't do that."

In Channing's kitchen there was a wall of photographs. Channing with a group of friends at a bar. Channing with a gorgeous black woman. Channing in Egypt. Channing in Spain. There was a recurring theme of Channing with a voluptuous woman with long black hair.

"You're with so many beautiful women in these pictures," I

said. Channing appraised each picture pointing out how they were friends or someone else's wife or girlfriend or sister. But he never mentioned the black-haired woman. The two of them in fancy dress out on the town. One of her in shorts and a tight shirt, sitting on an immaculate bed with flowers on it. Beckoning.

Later I asked about her again. He said they had broken up when he moved to America for his advertising job.

On my drive down to SF from Sebastopol I hoped it would be warm as I wasn't wearing much. But the SF chill hit me immediately. I wore a black tank top, short skirt, garter belts, and Spanish leather boots. A wind blew up my skirt and I pushed it down as I bent to refasten a garter. A heavyset man in baggy clothes rode up on his bike. His eyes were enormous hazel orbs. They had a deep seriousness like he might be well caste in an edgy noir film about a disillusioned officer.

"Are you waiting for your boyfriend?"

"Yes."

"Is he late?"

"Just a little."

"If I was your boyfriend, I wouldn't be late, I would make sure to be early." He moved his hand along the stubble on his chin and looked at me with open lust.

"I like watching you straighten your skirt."

I saw Channing crossing the street towards us.

"He's here, he's coming just now."

The man didn't look back, he just said, "I hope he deserves you"and—sped off.

"Making friends are you?" Channing asked. He wore tight black slacks and a black button-up shirt that sent little firecrackers going off in my lower stomach.

"Trying not to," I said.

He gave me a peck on the cheek.

"Right wadja want to do? Hungry?" He asked.

"Yes, Absinthe is nearby isn't it?"

"You like that place."

"Yes, don't you?"

We walked down Hayes Street toward the swank brasserie and tucked into a booth. We sipped Champagne with a splash of Courvoisier and a twist of lemon peel as the oysters came out on a big tray with thick strands of seaweed and ice under the grey shells.

I hadn't been drinking much until Channing came into my life. Intoxication came over me quickly.

After dinner we entered his apartment and I set my bag down by the door in his bedroom. I usually left it in the living room but I was slowing moving towards Channing via the placement of my stuff; last weekend, I forgot to repack my toothbrush. He hung up his coat in the closet. He came back into the bedroom.

"Do you want me to take off the boots?" I asked.

"I like the boots."

I walked into the kitchen. I took the placemats off the table and put them on the counter. I leaned my stomach, breasts and head to rest on the table.

"You look good like that."

He moved his hands up my legs until he got to where the flesh was. He moved my thighs slightly more apart. He stood behind me and slowly opened me with his cock. He moved faster.

"I have to punish you." He was pulsing into me. My head was turned to the side, breasts pressed against the table. Just beyond me was a window that had no curtain.

I moved my hands behind me and touched his hips feeling their heat and motion as he forced himself deeper in. He grabbed my wrists and pulled my arms back.

"You need to be punished, you're my whore, I am going to fuck you so hard."

I was in his grip, giving everything of myself to him. He turned me over to face him and bent my legs to let him in. He was standing over me with his eyes closed moving in and out and in. He never opened his eyes during sex. His muscular chest was taught; he was working into me with his thin strong body.

He moved me into his bedroom and onto the bed. He was on top of me, thrusting. As he came inside me he said, "You're just a hole for me to fuck."

It was hot and problematic in all the ways that hot things are problematic. I knew a line had been crossed. But I wasn't offended by it. I was fascinated. I knew I was not just a hole for him to fuck. I knew I had started our role playing and name calling. He was expanding the territory, testing its limits. When I was in a higher state of arousal the dirty talk was the most titillating. Because it was sexy, because I had initiated this language, it was mine and I saw that when he came saying it, he was the helpless one.

Channing and I had a big weekend in the suburbs with his friends. We ate Filipino foods and had sex in the children's room where we spent the night. Two of the Filipina women Channing was with the night we met were our hosts. They were dating very tall, very muscular black men. Channing looked so different from them: a little otter among powerful whales. After thanking them for a wonderful time we went back to Channing's place. We had sex at his apartment and I drove home.

Later that night he called me and after the usual niceties he said: "I have a girlfriend."

"And she's coming to visit?"

"Yes."

"Are you serious?"

"Yes."

"So that's it. I won't see you again?"

"I thought that's what you'd want."

"I could feel you were withholding something but I didn't think it was this."

"Well, you get ten points for perception."

"Why didn't you tell me when we were together, we spent the whole weekend together?"

"I wanted to but it never seemed the right time and then you left early."

"You still managed to have sex with me, I noticed."

"Well it's hard not to do that."

"Goodbye, Channing."

I hung up. The day's light perished during the call, leaving only moving grey particles floating nowhere. I looked out but not at anything. My body turned to stone and thoughts moved slowly through my head. The conversation repeated itself. The thought that he had known all along repeated itself and I heard myself saying "Goodbye, Channing."

He always knew this girlfriend was coming. All the photos of the woman with black hair came back like a frantic flipbook. She was watching over us the whole time. Waiting for her turn. I had just been something to pass three months' time with. He was always going to leave me. I entered a low-level depression. I was absent-minded with friends, my thoughts still billowing backwards into all the moments I had shared with Channing. I wondered what he told his friends about my disappearance.

My therapist, the same one I went to with Harper, said, "It sounds like there is a mystery here that you can't let go of. And because of this you can't let go of him and move on."

By this time several months had passed. I walked out into the yard that was blooming with pink roses and lavender. I called him.

"Channing is there something you aren't telling me?"

"I broke up with Anya before I came to San Francisco. Then she told me she was pregnant. I didn't know what she wanted to do about it. At points she didn't want anything to do with me."

"What do you want?" I said.

"I want you and the baby."

When I hung up the phone I felt relief. I believed that he really wanted me, that what we had was real, that he only chose her out of obligation. But I was shocked at how high the stakes were. A baby. We saw each other a couple of times. He never contacted me but was always eager to see me when I contacted him. We had sex in the back of my car. Our relationship, which had spanned the whole city, was now confined to my backseat. I found a condom discarded there a week later. He had just tied it off and left it.

I stopped calling him for months but couldn't stop thinking of him. I knew I needed to break away, to stop trying to see him, but I couldn't let it end. I needed to prove I existed, and chose a dramatic way to do it, something he wouldn't forgive, something to force an ending.

I called his apartment knowing he would be at work and his girlfriend, the mother of his child, would be home.

"Hello, this is April. I'm a friend of Channing's but I'm calling to talk to you. Channing hurt me by lying to me. We were seeing each other before you came and he never mentioned you."

"Why are you calling?" she asked, in a very civilized voice. I heard the faint coo of a baby, machinery like white noise, wind even. When I called in the past his apartment was as silent as a movie set.

"I thought you had a right to know."

"I think I know Channing pretty well and he wouldn't be with me if he didn't want to." She had a strong resolve but her curiosity took over. "So he was seeing you?"

"Yes, he was seeing me for about three months before you got here. Then he broke up with me a week before you arrived, saying he had a girlfriend in England. He's been trying to get back together with me and telling me he loves me. Is that what he tells you?"

"What do you look like?" she said.

"I'm short with long brown hair."

"I see."

"I've seen your picture," I said. "You look very sweet. I wish you the best, I don't want to be with Channing." This felt true at the time but in the big picture it was false.

"I'm going to go see about the baby," she said. "Goodbye."

8: THE TURKISH PALM HOTEL

So yes, Channing was a trash can fire. But he had a perfect cock, so what can you do? And believe it or not he will make another appearance! Let's get out of the cold blue city of love and go to the Mediterranean.

Up in the air over the Atlantic I was again seeking the geographic cure to let go of Channing and find myself again. When our affair ended, I wasn't as strong as I used to be. I was not like Peter Pan, whose shadow was captured. Mine grew to great heights, it followed me, strangled me. I couldn't shake the ugly grayscale it cast on all my interactions.

I found a job working in a hotel in Turkey. I would be part of an "animation team" hired to entertain hotel guests with classes, performances, and activities. The fact that there was no picture of the hotel, only an architectural blueprint, should have been a warning, but I had just turned 30 and was too restless to pause.

After staying some nights with a friend in Istanbul, I took a bus to Turgetreis near the town of Bodrom. After 13 hours I looked out the windows to see palatial hotels and arched whitewashed villas. Bougainvillea climbed up latticed walls. The cerulean ocean rippled and sparked like a mosaic. On the street Turkish women glided by with flowing scarves and glittery clothes. This part of the Turkish coast was only a 45-minute boat ride to the Greek Island of Kos.

I met the eight men and five women on my team, half Turkish speakers, half Russian. Because The Turkish Palm Hotel was under construction, we stayed at a small nearby hotel they called a pension. I was assigned a neat room with a single bed and a big window.

I woke up in darkness to a man's voice chanting prayers, the sound emanating from the two white minarets of the nearby mosque, distorted through an aging P.A. speaker. This would happen four more times each day. Harper and I had heard the same prayers on an island in Thailand. She would close her eyes and lip synch the words, cracking us up with the sacrilege. Here, the prayers would become a ritual anthem jarring and comforting in their regularity.

To attend team meetings, we walked through the damp tunnels of the Turkish Palm, dodging the sparks of electric wires. We skated across puddles and ate where the floors were damp and the low walls were windowless. I took a photo documenting my team waiting in line for the food that was served on silver prison-style trays. The Turks, Russians, and Ukrainians accepted our paltry conditions with grim stoicism. I pretended to. After a month, I had only spoke to one native English speaker. My sentences became shorter, my vocabulary stripped of its colors. I relied on gestures, smiles, emphasis. I hoped my meaning would come through my eyes, the movements of my hands, and my naked desire to be understood.

As the skeleton of the hotel was filled in, we had eight-hour dance rehearsals on dirty tile floors with amused construction workers watching us. Other times it seemed they were learning the dances and that one fine day they would throw aside their brooms and drills and we would all break into a rooftop dance together, Bollywood-style.

A layer of white dust covered everything. It clung to our jackets, stuck in our throats, made us cough, and eventually everyone got sick. Out the windows we watched palm trees carried and arranged like sticks for a fence, the symbols of paradise carefully falling into place. The newly appointed pool was a depressing swampy green, but one day it was suddenly divided into three symmetrical circles of aquamarine. When waters turn from muck to crystalline, something in the human animal is deeply satisfied.

A Ukrainian named Ivan choreographed all the group dances. He constructed dances in his mind, his body still, as the music beamed through the earphones he always wore. I was asked to lip-sync to the Shakira song "Whenever, Wherever." Leyla, a stunning woman with huge eyes and lips who was dating my boss Balian, watched my dance and lip-sync and told me, "You're moving around too much." She suggested I do simple powerful moves and exaggerate the words by opening my mouth wider. I should have grown up with a drag queen brother; surely he would have taught me this.

The Ukrainian women were packing an artillery of hair dryers, hair sprays, creams, nail polish, and carry-on makeup kits. I didn't even bring deodorant. They were always reaching into their vast purses and pulling out hairbrushes to tame their long hair. I felt like a peasant tomboy in their magnificent presence. They tried to teach my how to blow dry my hair by starting at the roots, not the ends. Leyla took me aside and told me that I needed to shave my legs, pluck my eyebrows, and cover the gray on my hairline. "We are entertainers," she said, "we must remain forever young." Sometimes the Ukranians did my makeup and painted my lips into a wet sparkling blow-jobesque glow. Allegra saw a picture of me after their ministrations and said it looked like my evil porn twin.

In my little room I journaled excessively, jotting down observations like this one: "If it's so great being a straight man, why do they spend most of their time trying to get inside women?"

On a dance practice break I walked up to the balcony of the roof bar overlooking the Aegean Sea. As in "my birthday party" had already passed, it was here that I crossed the long bridge from 20-something to 30. An odd thing happened as I stared out at the sea. A deep calm passed over me, as if the world was suddenly made up of oatmeal cookies and chamomile. I felt okay. I felt comfortable with myself and the choices I had made thus far. For the first time in my adult life I wasn't worried about the future. I savored this moment because I knew it wouldn't last.

I was still many years from sourcing my identity and truth from my deep self. I still needed to prove myself. This solo trip, like my previous ones, was proof that I deserved adventure and was willing to throw myself to the Fates. I knew many of my peers were trying to prove they were marriage material. I had other things to prove.

The preceding paragraphs are very memoiresque and reflective, don't you think? Our protagonist is learning and growing, her character arc rising up like the arches of Turkish doorways! She is going from needy to content. Or lost and confused to learning to lip sync to Shakira.

Finally, the Turkish Palm Hotel was in full swing. That meant 16-hour work days seven days a week. The Turks and the Ukrainians took to it with their usual stoic resolve—this little hippie American, not so much. The day started with a morning meeting at eight. Next we ate breakfast at the hotel buffet with the guests, chatting with them and letting them know about our activities. They were surprisingly friendly about our interruptions partly because Europeans are kind and partly because many of them were familiar with animation teams. Then we had another meeting. We split up and taught various poolside classes. I taught yoga and belly dance. Mostly the guests wanted to be left alone to sleep tits out in the sun.

Midday, we gathered around the pool and did our flashmob to "Life is Life" by Opus. This usually culminated in us jumping in the pool with the guests. Then we ate lunch with them. After a short break, we met to practice our dances, skits and lip-syncs. In the evening we performed on a big outdoor stage. But that was not the finale. We went with the guests to a swanky after-dinner dance room off the pool. Our boys danced with the older Danish and German women and the Ukrainians and I let their husbands twirl us around. I decided to think of it more like an amateur rendition of "Dirty Dancing" as opposed to light sexual surrogacy. It was actually very innocent as the husbands were respectful and treated me like a glamorous dance star.

Around this time of night I lost the capacity to think or walk but the work went on. We were required to go to the late-night disco until it closed at 2am and dance with the guests, making them feel good. They played The Village People, Turkish songs, Tarkan, and Euro Pop, but I didn't know it was Euro Pop until I got back to America and never heard those songs again.

I recognized a Swedish couple that had attended my belly dance class that day. The muscular man with a square jaw whispered in my ear, "I swing and so does my wife." I feigned ignorance, mumbling something about swing dancing. The woman was zaftig with wispy blonde hair and loving eyes. In some ways I longed for the comfort of being pressed between their bodies though they weren't really my type. But if I was caught slipping into their room, or out of it, I would be fired. I knew the slutty Turkish boys were scoring in a wide range of ages, but the old double standard applied. When my boss wasn't looking, I snuck out of the disco an hour early. Back in my room there were TV wires sticking out of the wall but no TV and I had to use a wrench to turn the water on and off. I put a plastic tub in my shower and soaked in hot water, my muscles relaxing after hours of dancing.

I assessed my situation. If you do just about anything in America for 16 hours a day, you can make a decent wage. I was making $500 a month plus room and board. I was left out of the social stratosphere of my team due to language and cultural barriers. The Ukrainian girls were sending most of their meager earnings back to their impoverished families. I could tell they resented my Americanness and the solvency it implied. I started entertaining the idea of an escape from this crazy workload. But where would I go? Back home Celeste had moved to San Francisco and Allegra had just graduated from Bard and was living in New York. I had no intention of going back to the Blue Witch House and eating oatmeal with my mom. I loved being in Turkey but wasn't sure what my next move should be.

Balian, our fearless leader, sensed we all needed a treat. The next evening he took us upstairs for drinks at the roof bar where an older gentlemen summoned me over to him. We weren't allowed to talk to anyone unless they spoke to us first; Turkish business is very hierarchal. Faris was a Syrian businessman and silent partner in the hotel. He was 14 years my senior with a handsome Golden Age of Hollywood face, tan skin, and a potbelly. The staff treated him like royalty. He had lived in America where he had many successful businesses before moving to Turkey. He loved American culture and was delighted to speak English to me. I could see my team was surprised, even envious of my conversation, which they wouldn't be invited to join.

He caught glances at my body as we spoke. He had a handsome face. But my attraction to him was more about his status, his power, the fact that he had stock in the hotel. I was literally elevated from the damp basement where we had our meetings to the right hand of a Syrian God on the rooftop. The bar might as well have been Mount Olympus. We talked about the things he missed in America. What he missed the least was cereal. Turkish breakfast is a gorgeous affair of fresh breads, olives, several kinds of homemade feta, cucumbers, hardboiled eggs, tomatoes, and cooked eggplant salads in olive oil. He saw it as a sign of defeat that his Turkish friends were eating *those darn cereals.*

A week later, I arrived late to one of our famously tedious meetings. As Balian was about to dole out the punishment for this behavior, I shocked myself by saying "I quit!" Once I said it, I knew some part of me had felt it building for a while.

I cleared off my make-up tray and departed. I checked back into the pension we had stayed at before the hotel was built. Balian found me sitting on a stretch of sand I called Unemployment Beach. He came to try to woo me back. After all I was his investment. It had taken countless emails and phone calls to get me moved out of my California life and into Turkey.

"What can I do to get you back, I'll do anything. Is my girlfriend bothering you? I will have a talking to with her. Anything, just tell me." His sincerity was disarming. I let loose my complaints:

"Inna and Marina get to do all the fun sexy stuff. It's as if I'm an ugly klutz. Inna and Marina can do the tango, Inna and Marina can be the cage dancers, Inna and Marina can be the prostitutes. April, you can play the tourist in the khaki shorts."

"You want to play the prostitute? You can play the prostitute."

"You're missing my point."

My next suitor at Unemployment Beach was Faris. (Not going to lie, I loved all this attention.) I greeted him in my bikini. He smiled broadly, then twitched his face into a question. I have only seen this gesture in Turkish people. They approach you and make a questioning face, leaving you to speak first, explaining yourself. Faris was a problem solver. No one actually bowed before him but almost. They lit his cigarettes, parked his car, brought him his sports coat, gave him Turkish candies and other gifts, and refused to charge him for various services. I had never met anyone like this: able to solve problems by simply opening his wallet.

He moved me off Unemployment Beach and into my own apartment overlooking the sea. My first time living on my own. When I went to the open-air market to look for a postcard so people could see where I was living, I found one with my very apartment on it! I strolled through the bazaar streets covered in triangle tapestries casting shadows of light and dark over the spices and scarves. On either side of the stores was the Marina with white boats with red Turkish flags. The shops were filled with rhinestone bathing suits and beaded candles; everything had a preponderance of tassels, fringe, glitter, roses. The clothes were as girlie as possible and I wanted them all.

Shoppers floated by leaving echoes of Turkish, French, German. I found a small shop where nice ladies cooked eggplant, tomatoes, and zucchini they kept chilled in a small case. When I didn't visit them for a few days they'd say: "Where have you been?" I felt at home as I ate the soft, green eggplant in olive oil. In fact, I felt at home in Turkey. People assumed I was Turkish. I had a sense that these were my kinfolk. They had an effortless elegance tempered with an earthy, felicity and readiness to laugh.

Faris got me a job working on a tourist boat. I wasn't really attracted to Faris, except maybe his face. But I was mesmerized by his spending power. I felt all the bohemian ideals my parents had so carefully instilled in me slipping away.

I resisted the temptation for an entire month. During this time he took me to lovely seafood restaurants where the desserts arrived on a bed of flowers and the wine goblets were as big as my head. He drove me to his farm and his many luxury hotels. We went to one of his houses that had an Olympic-sized pool with Jacuzzi jets. As we toured the many upstairs bedrooms I heard myself saying, "My family will be very comfortable here." He smiled good-naturedly. This was my big chance to take one for the team. Faris tortured me by saying how he had bought houses for his previous girlfriend's family members, installed them in well-paying jobs, invested in their businesses. Nobody in my family was flush at this time. Celeste was getting her Master's, Allegra was jobless and strapped to student loans, my mom was a tarot reader, and my dad a nanny earning 18th-century wages. I grew up eating government cheese; cereal was an appetizer, entrée and dessert. Clothes came either from Mervyn's, the flea market, or a big garbage bag full of our cousins' discards. This was my family's chance to pick ourselves up by Faris's bootstraps. Here was a man who wanted to spoil me in a way I had never been accustomed to. When I said I wanted a sushi dinner he offered to fly a chef in from Istanbul.

There wasn't a plethora of dating options in the little Turkish town. It was Faris or an army of Turkish man-sluts who slept with enough tourist women to impress Hugh Hefner. As he slid his credit card at The Metro, Turkey's version of Costco, I looked at the three bikinis and the sandals and dish set and socks and underwear, and something clicked. Three bikinis! At once! I had been sporting the same black faded number since the Reagan administration. I kissed him right there in the store. We went back to my place, a gorgeous one-bedroom apartment with white tiles that spilled out onto a little deck overlooking the Aegean. The view was so perfect I had taken up painting again.

I tried to focus on his handsome face and ignore the bags under his eyes and the hair covering his body, oh the hair. Faris was a sweater. Sweat dripped down his double chin and all over me. His grey and black chest hairs curled in the afternoon heat. He bit his lip and closed his eyes as he pumped into me.

I grabbed a towel and tried to mop him off but it was futile. He moved me over him and accidentally knocked me off the bed. Any sane person would have used this as an excuse to say "time out," but I climbed back on, accepting his apologies and stroking his ego. He sweated and grunted and made the "Oh" mouth. I emerged feeling like a huge genital covered in his discarded hairs.

We "dated" for another three weeks.

"April, I can't marry you, I'm done with marriage, but I can offer you a great life," said Faris, grandly. He would have a beautiful younger girlfriend and what would I have—other than sweaty coitus on the regular and riches and splendor to share with my entire family, I mean?

"Listen there are women with much better bodies than yours (Jeez!), but there is something about you, I'm so drawn to you, I'm crazy about you." I'd like to say something was lost in translation, but his English was perfect. A young man came up and served us a fish platter and refilled our red wine.

Faris and I remained friends. When I left, I had to choose whether to ship my clothes back or my paintings. I chose my paintings. Faris said he would send them. They never arrived, which pains me still: a terracotta vase like a woman's body, and a portrait of my friend, her hand raised up like a jazz singer. Faris kept emailing me for over a year, asking me to return.

I went back to Istanbul where I started my trip, staying with my friend and her Turkish boyfriend. I didn't know what to do or where to live. I didn't want to move back into The Blue Witch House. I was unemployed. I didn't want to take advantage of my friend's kindness by staying indefinitely. I called Allegra and made a plan to meet her in New York. But from there my future was a mystery.

Allegra swooped me up in a taxi from the airport. This was an extravagance for us. I launched right into the story of Faris wanting her to help absolve me of the guilt I felt for my brief stint at as a GOLD DIGGER. She shocked me by saying: "You left the Syrian Millionaire behind?"

"Possibly Billionaire."

"Are you insane? You couldn't learn to love?" She was joking but there is a little truth in every joke.

Allegra and I walked the muggy skyscrapered streets wondering where our future would take us. It was fun to be lost together for a moment, her post-college and my turning-30 crisis colliding into the splash of possibility that is New York, New York. Celeste called. She had heroically found Allegra a job at the place where she worked, the Center for Research on Gender and Sexuality. We got on a one-way JetBlue flight to SFO.

For a while, I lived in the backroom of my Nepalese friend Mohan's import store on Haight Street. Most shops on Haight don't crack their doors until afternoon. The sky was always grey and the air always cold. I ate Thai takeout and Middle Eastern platters at The Blue Front Café. Mohan and I reminisced about Nepal in the front of the shop with all the masks, jewelry, and textiles.

Soon, my friend Julie and I opened a store behind Mohan's shop called Healing Traditions. I did Thai massage and tarot reading, thus finally living the dream of owning a curios shop on Haight Street. Julie encouraged me to get my Swedish massage license so I could practice legitimately. I took a two-week intensive. I never meant for it to be my career, but it became the perfect side hustle to support my love of travel, belly dancing, and the arts.

With our new shop taking up the space behind Mohan's where I used to sleep, I moved in with my friend Rafael on Treat Street near 24th in the heart of the Mission District. Nearly every building in the neighborhood was covered in colorful murals depicting mythological stories of humans and animals larger than life, one fantastical image bleeding into the next: totems, talismans, rainbows, goddesses, symbolism delighting the eyes, bringing us all, momentarily, into dream time.

I landed from some great distance of the Ottoman Empire onto the streets of San Francisco. I could have just driven one hour from Sonoma County, crossed the Golden Gate bridge, *et voilà*.

But no. I chose to go by way of a 26-hour hour round trip flight to Turkey.

9: KUNAL

In my Mission District apartment I had a little bedroom with a big windows that was available while Rafael's girlfriend went off to find herself in Italy. He was tall and a great hugger. He would look me in the eyes, nod his head, and say "I know you are going to have another relationship with a woman."

I denied his intuition completely. I didn't want anything to do with the lesbian world. I wanted a sexy San Francisco boyfriend to explore the city with. Harper was the only woman I had had sex with. During our time together I didn't know myself as a sexual person so my associations with lesbian sex were skewed. I had been so vanilla, so earth mama feminist, and lacking in any erotic freedom.

Channing had already gotten all the best out of me. I had belly danced for him, massaged him, cooked meals, drawn baths. I tried to sound witty and cultured. I was just a deflated shell of my former glory. I felt unsure at every turn.

One weekend I helped my dad's friend sell jewelry at a gem show. In the queue for coffee I saw a striking Indian man behind me. He was a specimen: broad shoulders, impossibly sensual lips, chin-length black hair, Shah Rukh Khan eyes. He had tasteful Elvis sideburns. He was wearing black slacks and a blue collared shirt. Struck by open lust for him I initiated small talk. When he spoke his face remained still as a statue, which made me want to listen to each word. We chatted pleasantly.

"I'll come and see you at your booth in a bit," he said. When I walked back to resume work I noticed he was only two booths away, practically my neighbor. As I approached he was outlined by glittering gemstones of every shape and color. A gaggle of middle-aged Indian women cooed around him.

"I'm not trying to flirt with you," one of them remarked. "You actually remind me of my son."

"I am trying to flirt with you," I interjected. I wasn't sure if he heard me or not. He was busy so I walked away.

He came over to my booth later and gave me a jazz CD. I hate most jazz and wondered if I should cut things short then and there. The atmosphere would be wrong with him, it would be full of jazz. I smiled and thanked him. My dad's friend engaged him in an elaborate gem conversation that I couldn't break into.

"Thanks a lot, why don't *you* date Gemstone Guy," I said after the object of my lust had returned to his own booth.

"Sorry, I didn't mean to steal his attention."

He came over one more time and Dad's friend quickly excused himself. We chatted. We exchanged cards. His said "Kunal Bhalla." Kunal! Remember him from way back in the beginning of the book when you were more invested and there was a threesome? And you were like why did we just leave the threesome story to go to Nepal? *That* Kunal. I set it up this way on purpose because Literature!

Kunal asked me out the next night. I was driving to a dinner party so I had to decline. He was going back to New York and said he would be doing another show in two weeks and asked to meet up with me then. I hung up the phone thinking this was the perfect way to ease back into the murky waters of dating. Since he lived on the other side of the country there was no fear of starting a relationship or getting attached. It could be the perfect makeout session. Failing that I would at least get a good dinner, and Allegra, my dating guru, insisted this was very important to urban survival.

I went all out in my pre-date grooming: nails polished, hair blow-dried, contacts in, and skin covered in a sheen of lotion. I slipped into a short skirt and long boots to finish the look. Rafael sat back in shock. He was used to a makeup-free girl in glasses and jeans. Kunal picked me up in his rental car and we sped to a

California Cuisine restaurant in Noe Valley called Firefly.

I sat down across from him and I was in the ring once again. Instead of boxing mitts I had cutlery, instead of a coach encouraging me and feeding me water through a straw I was handed a goblet of blood-red wine. First dates are supposed to be flirty and fun, but usually they aren't.

Why couldn't I bring a sister or friend to encourage me and help me sound witty and charming and funny and cute but not too serious or political or apolitical. But I was alone and he was talking incessantly. I tried to listen but felt unengaged by the wall of words. I tried to remember who I was and what I did and what parts of that would be interesting to my opponent. He was smiling and getting drunk and talking and talking. I ate a chanterelle mushroom drenched in a white creamy sauce. I knew I should just break in and say something but I felt frozen. Plus he never paused to say, "You know?" or "What do you think?" or ask any questions. An older student I went to college with once told me: "When men talk about themselves that means they like you." That perspective did nothing to make me feel better.

Still, Kunal was very handsome and I wanted to kiss his cupids bow lips. So the talking man and his mute date exited the restaurant.

"So, who was your last boyfriend?" Kunal said and now the focus was on me.

"I dated a guy named Channing, and before that Levi. I had a longterm relationship with a woman named Harper."

"So that's hot. Have you ever had a threesome?"

"I've made out with two people while drunk in high school, but no not really."

We landed downtown at an Indian restaurant and bar called The New Delhi that advertised itself as "the kind of Indian Restaurant Columbus was searching for." Kunal ordered a single malt scotch and I nursed a frothy Guinness beer so I could sip on it but not actually get drunk. The talking continued. I listened feeling bored and scared that I had forgotten how to date. I was scared that I was wasting my time with a man who wasn't asking me about myself. I was mostly scared to be hurt all over again.

The conversation got political and I heard myself trying to say something clever. Suddenly the attention I had been craving was focused on me. He was responding to what I said.

"What do you mean California's votes don't count? It's one of the biggest deciding factors in the race."

I felt humiliated. Inwardly I vowed to read *The New York Times* every Sunday and listen to NPR. "Um, I guess I meant that it didn't count in the last election (of Bush the Lesser), but I guess nothing did, ha ha." Very close save. It's not that I don't know about politics. I have a deep-rooted understanding of the world we live in and the world I would like us to create. But I have never been good at memorizing facts, figures, and statistics. I don't enjoy debates or banter.

We walked towards his hotel to get his car so he could drive me home. I asked him if he was okay to drive. He innocently asked what other choice we had. I was horny and lonely, a deadly combination. He said he wanted to get a coffee before driving me home.

"Why?" I asked.

He said, "It's just something to do." I could tell he was stalling; he didn't want our date to end. We headed towards the coffeeshop and I overheard myself saying, "Let's go up to your room and watch cable."

We pulled a walking U-turn and headed for his room. We passed a white man holding hands with an Indian woman. The woman and I exchanged knowing looks which the men didn't notice.

The Union Square Westin was gaudily decorated but pleasant. He insisted on cleaning up before I came in. I looked at the bed and edged over to a credenza and leaned against it. He turned on the TV and we both pretended we were going to watch it. Bright lights blared on us from the bed lamps and the ceiling. Kunal looked me in the eye and came towards me. Although his pace was fast and determined I felt like I had an eternity to feel his approach. I liked that he came at me like this, full of desire and confidence. Finally his lips met mine, switching me on, our bodies colliding. He pulled me on top of him on the bed. The room sparkled with new lust. We kissed and rolled around and discarded clothing. He tried to get my underwear off and I tried to keep them on. We dry humped for a while in a swoon of kisses, with hungry hands grabbing all they could reach. Eventually he got my panties off and put his face between my legs. I didn't orgasm but I passed out feeling satisfied, the long months of being touch-deprived finally over.

The next day at breakfast, he talked and I listened. We had dinner at a snazzy downtown vegan place called Millennium, where he launched into a discussion of the contract of marriage. He had no problem with the ceremony but the paperwork was bogus. I was sure that marriage was an off-limit subject for the second date. I squirmed uncomfortably and sipped my organic wine. I felt trapped and afraid. I had never had a panic attack until I moved to San Francisco. The dimmed lights brightened and there he was, a perfect stranger that I had recently had sex with. He was waxing maudlin about expensive divorces. I wanted to leave. I wanted to nestle back into my soft bed with the white fluffy feather comforter. I wanted to put the sterile hotel room with its nylon blankets and loud air conditioner behind me.

"Sorry, I guess I was babbling."

Was he talking to me? I was already miles away in the safety of my own room and my single roommate. I wanted to be mean and make it his fault. His fault that at age 30 I was scared of relationships and intimacy; his fault that I didn't have the answers to the big relationship questions around monogamy, marriage, and living together. My parents separated when I was nine. What did I know about marriage? But what did that matter? Outstanding and doomed relationships loomed all around and their successes and failures were as mysterious as the Electoral College. I took a gulp of wine and re-grouped.

I am a middle child and we are ultimately a self-reliant group. When you aren't the first or the cutest you sometimes just have to fend for yourself. But I still wanted some backup so I went to the bathroom and tried to call my sisters. Ornate restaurant bathrooms have a soothing effect. I didn't have cell service. I calmed myself and decided not to sabotage the date. I thought about chamomile tea and oatmeal cookies. When I got back to the table, he ordered a trio of vegan tortes and I ordered crème brulee without the crème. I tapped my spoon against the orange-black roof and dug in.

Back at the hotel he made a valiant attempt to seduce me. I tried to respond but had no verve as we had barely slept the previous night. He bounced around me like a personal trainer trying to motivate a coach potato. I lay limp as quiet waves of sleep beckoned me. In the morning he said he would never take me to a vegan restaurant again. *Oh no. Did my anxiety attack freak him out?*

"The crème bru-tofu was really good," I stammered.

"Yeah, but you fell right to sleep afterward," he said, smiling his cute smile. I liked to watch his long black eyelashes and his full pink lips.

Fast forward to day three. With his plane leaving in an hour, he was at my apartment, figuring we still had time for sex before he went on his way. My room was a tiny little sunlit number with a huge window and a huge bed. He excused himself to the bathroom. I stripped down to my skin and jumped under the covers and tried to think of what expression I should have on my face when he walked through the door. I considered turning on my side and casually turning over when he approached. Then I could have an "Oh it's you," look on my face. He walked in while I was still deciding.

"Wow, you're in bed." He jumped in and took off his clothes.

We thrashed around as midweek bicoastal lovers are supposed to do. He was dry-humping me when I noticed an odd third party had joined our session. My teddy bear had come between us.

"I was fucking the bear?" he said, as we dissolved into hysterics. He put me on all fours and mounted me from behind like they do on the Discovery Channel. It was the end of my cycle and I wasn't turned on enough. I barely made it through. Moans, some of pleasure and some of pain, issued forth. Finally, I said the words a man hates to hear: "I'm sore."

He came out and towered over me as we both stroked ourselves. His swim team jumped out in white blobs onto my stomach. He laid on me and I continued circling my clit with my index finger as I fantasized that he was married and I was his mistress. That did the trick. Afterward, we showered and washed each other. I thought about how amazing it was to shower with Channing. And how terrifying it was to shower with Faris. And how there wasn't anything spectacular about showering with Kunal. But give it time.

After he left I had some time to reflect. I had a feeling that Kunal and I weren't entering a new relationship as much as about to have a lot of sex. I have an ongoing relationship with casual sex. I enjoy it if I am feeling strong in myself. Or if my horniness takes over. I'm attracted to and repelled by it. There is a sensual diva in me that wants to try everything and there is a sensitive woman in me that can't handle the intensity of such closeness with no umbrella of love or a planned future. Slutty and sensitive is a difficult way to be.

"Oral sex is strong enough for a man, but made for a woman," said Allegra. We were chatting during our sister belly dance practice. We also used dance practices to eat and gossip. She had several friends who were porn stars. One of them told her that it was just wrong for a man to go down on a woman. Woman to woman was the only natural course of things. This same woman was plotting her retirement from porn and starting a woman's colony.

Up to this point, I had only sporadically enjoyed receiving oral sex. This is a source of disdain and embarrassment for my sisters. Usually at the first sign of disinterest on my part, my male partners give up entirely on trying to lick me. Not Kunal. He was visiting me regularly, every couple of months. Slowly I relaxed into the utter invasion of having him between my thighs. There was no limit to the time he would spend on this endeavor.

"I like being lost in there, in my own little world, everything else disappears," he said.

I especially liked it when Kunal got stoned and lost all sense of space and time. At first, these attempts felt okay. Then really good. Eventually I was turning ownership of my yaya's over to him completely. He was the only one who ever took that extra uneven layer of flesh into his mouth in worshipful appreciation, like he wanted to taste all of me, like he fully accepted all of me. I waxed myself for him. My exposed pussy seemed coy and oversexed. Whenever I caught of glimpse of her she looked ready for anything, lips in a perpetual bawdy, knowing smile.

Kunal pressed his lips against my labia, head shifting side to side, eyes closed. "I'm a Pussy Man," he said proudly. He was the most sex-positive lover I ever had. He was willing, carefree, playful. He had no hangups and exuded the idea that sex is the best thing in the world.

My sisters were relieved that I finally understood what all the fuss was about. "If nothing else comes of this relationship, besides a healthy desire to receive oral sex, than it was worth it," Allegra said.

Kunal flew me to a gem fair in Sedona, the nexus of the Woo Universe. He convinced me to have sex sans condom. The true definition of manhood is to be able to convince someone that your disease wand is not in fact a disease wand.

He had me belly down, legs against the bed, feet on the ground. He spanked me hard for a long time, until I was all rosy and longing for tenderness as temperance to the pain. He entered me standing, going deep and hard. Then he sprinkled himself on me saying, "Pearl necklace bitch." The dirty talk was always my idea. This is because I can't orgasm without something torrid playing out either in my words, their words or in the layering of fantasies playing in my mind. I wish I could have a tantric, vibrational, body-centered orgasm stimulated by sensation, feeling, presence and love. But I can't. Right before the orgasm there is the just-right sensation coupled with the just-right image or idea, and then I let go. So instead of feeling ashamed when men say these things, I feel satisfied that I got my way.

We started plotting to have a threesome with a woman who worked with my sisters. He called these brainstorm sessions "organized crime." It never materialized, mostly because we had so little time together.

Somehow, almost a year went by with me seeing Kunal exclusively. We had a big New Year's Eve planned with my sisters and their partners.

After a fancy dinner at Farallon, Kumal and I take a livery to the Kat Club in the Soma district. Kunal pays for coat check. This is the first time I won't have to bundle my jacket in a dark crevice where it will inevitably hit the floor in a beer puddle. The '80s theme resulted in netted shirts, Cure-esque hairdos, checkers, and polka dots. It is exactly 22 minutes until midnight. Kunal and I crowd surf through a throng of sweating drunk people in search of my sisters or their beaus.

I spot a distinct mocha brown balding head: Dante, Celeste's long-term date. With him are Celeste, Allegra, and Stavros—Allegra's high school sweetheart who wasn't particularly sweet but had other qualities. I wave frantically as if this were an airport reunion even though I saw them yesterday. I dart towards them, reaching my hand backwards to link my fingers with Kunal. Everybody hugs and kisses. Dante is in a suit and Stavros looks like a 80s aerobic instructor. He's famous now and probably will not appreciate being thrown into this book so I've changed his name. Also he isn't Greek. Twelve minutes to twelve.

Kunal orders a round and hands me a vodka cranberry. Five minutes to midnight. Perfect music plays and I am lost in a swirl of nostalgia as the lyrics of Modern English play. They remind us to be in the moment, to stop the world, and to melt into now.

I think of all the people I've kissed and melted with. I think of the movie *Valley Girl* and the rawness of the couple's love and how the main character's parents had a hippie restaurant. Oh, how full of angst I was when watching it and living in the eighties. And now I am not a doe-eyed teenager. I am a woman in my thirties able to make conscious decisions about who I date.

But dating Kunal is like one prolonged lack of decision. He is a sexual partner, a companion, a way to spend some time. These days I am just rocking myself, soothing myself about being thirty and unattached and still feeling a little heartsick over Channing. I suspect I would profit from just being on my own but then Kunal comes bounding into town to take me to fancy dinners and ravish me in hotels. I am a sucker for beauty and Kunal is beautiful.

Two minutes to midnight and the go-go dancers take off their tops. Single guys roam around predatorily. My sisters and I position ourselves eye to eye with our men. Thirty seconds to midnight. I look into Kunal's eyes. His eyebrows are intricate lines creating a pattern like ancient carvings on a bone. Our lips are six inches apart. We whisper ten, nine eight, seven, six, five, four, three, two, one.

Kissing and kissing and more kissing his huge soft lips, against my small lips. Biting and tonguing and kissing. We emerge from our private lip ritual back into the energy of the crowd. We hug and kiss wishing everyone a happy New Year.

Dante smiles mischievously at me and motions towards a nitrous balloon in his coat. Oh how I miss the time when my sisters and I were wild. Now they eat weed and drink, but just quietly at night to help them sleep and recover from parenting. I lean down, ostrich style, and suck in the chemically plastic air. I emerge in a momentary acid daze, tangible joy pulsing in my brain. Particles distinguish themselves around me as buoyant laughter ushers through my body. I lean back in a slow motion like I am doing a team building trust fall, am caught by my sisters, my mouth full of giggles. I somehow knew they would catch me without having to ask.

We all take turns breathing in nitrous and Kunal buys endless shots of lemon drops, gimlets and tequila. I feel loose and full of possibility, bodies in motion dancing and pulsing as one, united by 80s nostalgia, whippets, firewater.

Celeste and I spot a male fantasy lesbian couple. They are impossibly hot: tawny skin, dirty blonde hair flecked with highlights, tight jeans, exposed jeweled thongs, painted on tanks and pop-up breasts. Their faces soft and pink and their eyes dove-like and sweet. Two of us, two of them. Fueled with the alcoholic power of irrational belligerency I stampede over and deliver a mildly slurred "Happy New Year."

They say it back all smiles and giggles. Celeste joins behind me.

"So, my sister and I were wondering if we could kiss you," I say.

"Oh, thank you but we're just here with each other."

The hot girls start dancing with each other very close. Perky breasts against perky breasts. Heterosexual women convert to gay before our eyes. Straight men stand and openly drool. My sisters and our partners dance a while with each other and the people around us.

Eventually two bartenders, one male, one female, are planted in front of me. "You need to pay for those drinks," they say. The blonde lesbians are kissing each other. Men are practically falling down around them.

The hottie lesbian couple are dancing in our periphery. They smile in our direction. And by some bisexual magic this time they initiate a smooch-a-thon with us. Then Celeste and I switch women and kiss some more. Kunal comes over, ever the opportunist, and my gal kisses him too.

"I like kissing you better..." she whispers to me afterwards.

Drunk beyond reason, Kunal and I trip into the cold night and a cab. We order a pizza and eat it in my bed. We lie down with our feet in the pizza box in a hurricane of cologne, cigarette smoke, and stale alcohol. We babble for a while. He tries to start my motor but I am beginning to doze off.

"I'm so in love with you," he says.

I remain perfectly still like a spider playing dead at the bottom of a bathtub.

"Well, that shut you up."

Fade to black.

Kunal left me ravaged. A layer of the skin on my chin continually rubbed off from his abrasive facial hair. My breasts tender from all his grabbing. My stomach roiling from all the rich food and acidic wine.

Why wasn't I falling in love with Kunal? He was handsome, well traveled, a passionate lover. Was I still too broken after the dramatic betrayal of Channing? There were little deal breakers. Like when I told him I was a tarot reader and he dismissed it as fake. He also seemed like a mama's boy who wanted to be taken care of. He pouted sometimes.

I wondered if it was possible for me to fall in love with a man again. Here I was half a year with Kunal and to me we were still just dating. Then again, I didn't have any desire to get married—though I was excited by the prospect of someone *wanting* to marry me. I didn't want kids, so there was no desperation to settle down. I didn't want to settle down into the path I saw most traditional relationships taking: move in, marriage, kids, divorce, death. But I did want love, and deep communion, and I wasn't getting that with Kunal.

On his next visit Kunal sent me to a lingerie shop in the lobby of the Westin for something to entice him with. I picked a black sequined bustier with thong panties. It wasn't really my style, but it fit and I handed over his credit card and they accepted my signature.

I would forget each time about my post-Kunal hangover and invite him into my life and bed each time he came to town. When he left, I'd curl up on my soft white bed and write in my journal.

In transition. A popular phrase to describe the chaos we are always in. All will be replaced. I am not fully comfortable with

Kunal, just as I wasn't with Channing. With Harper I was completely comfortable. Our love was a soft round thing that we both protected. But there's this: There is a place of discomfort in our daily lives that sparks great passion in the bedroom. That place of discomfort becomes exciting when my hands are held down and I'm called dirty names and I want to please. Crawling inside of that embrace I find ecstasy and surrender and passion. When it ends I have the fabulous sweaty spoon snuggle. Then the non-sex life starts again and I am unsatisfied.

My love with Harper was never reassured by sex. It was constant, invisible, perfect. Channing and Kunal smell like cologne and aftershave, like man. Delicious. Intoxicating. Their scent does not relax me. It makes me want more more more. Eventually seven or nine months pass and I have excellent sex and nothing to fulfill my full heart. What is lacking is the comfort of softness and the smell of home. At the Cat Club a tall man with curly hair and a slightly goofy look asked me to dance. We were already on the dance floor. "Okay," I replied with a laugh. The song ended. A new song began. "This is our song," he said. "We'll play it at our wedding."

He said wedding and my heart leaped. Women are so easy to manipulate. Then the song skipped.

"What does that mean?" he asked.

"A bad sign."

10: QUINCE

Subversive reader, you are in for a treat. We are getting back to Quince, she of Chapter 1. The memoir should be *all* about Quince, it should have flashbacks and flashforwards built around our relationship, but unfortunately I didn't get around to writing that version—yet.

Kunal was coming into town less often. If I hadn't been fired from my job (don't worry about which job, it's not important), I would have never been at that Fourth of July party. If I hadn't gone to the party, I never would have met Kensington. And thus I never would have met Quince.

The party was in a cramped apartment on Clement Street. We played some flirty drinking game but I didn't kiss anyone. I gave Kensington my number mainly because he asked me for it and sometimes I have trouble saying no to men. He asked me out to lunch and I forgot about it. When he called wondering were I was, I ran down the street to meet him. He mentioned an informal soccer league he'd joined and I perked up.

"Can anyone join?"

"Sure, we're meeting at 5 this evening."

I put on my favorite black tracksuit and walked over to Dolores Park. Gay men were sunning themselves in Speedos on the ledge known affectionately as "the fruit shelf." Just below, families played on the swing set, hipsters drank coffee on plaid blankets with their bikes tangled around them. At the tippy top corner where Church Street meets 20th, there was a fantastic view of the San Francisco skyline and the high baroque dome of Mission Dolores.

I searched the park for Kensington and the soccer players under a white sky. Near the tennis courts, I saw his tall figure clad in a black t-shirt and tight black jeans. No one but a High Holy Hipster would wear such an outfit to play soccer.

He and several other players held cans of beer as they kicked the ball around. I remembered the rugged joyful days of soccer where everything smelled like cut grass and lemonade; the only place in my young girlish life where I enjoyed aggressive athleticism. I hadn't played since I was 12.

I decided to don a super-outgoing persona and introduce myself to everyone as we played. All the girls were dressed informally in sweats and shorts. One girl with amazingly muscular legs was extremely fast on the field. Her raven-colored hair was arranged into two ponytails on either side of her neck. I noted her androgynous vibe and that she was not courting the male gaze. She seemed to be an adversary that would have to be addressed if we were to win this game. I decided it would be my mission to fearlessly guard her.

"Hi, my name's April."

"Quince," she said quickly and then we both sprinted off after the ball. In five minutes, I was winded. As I chased the elusive ball, I noticed muscles that hadn't been used in years.

"We need team names!" I heard myself shouting.

Tomas, a short handsome Latin man said, "Okay, what's our team name?"

Nobody answered.

"We'll be the Menstrual Cramps," I said.

Danny, a gay man with long legs and a goofy personality, rushed to get the ball and bounced it off his chest, sending it toward me. I sent it to Kensington. He scored! Kensington asked for an instant replay of Danny's spectacular chest bump. Danny ran for the imaginary ball in slow motion and then made a burlesque of hitting his chest against the ball. We all cheered.

"Anyone want to go for drinks?" Kensington asked after the game. Some people were already mounting their bikes. I was tired and kind of wanted to go snuggle into bed. But the whole point of organized sports as a post-college thirty-something is the bonding afterwards. Six of us agreed to get pizza.

We ended up at Valencia Pizza and Pasta Company, the diner that time forgot. In the midst of the high-concept trendy ethnic food orgy that is Mission cuisine, Valencia Pizza and Pasta stayed loyal to its mashed potatoes and gravy, "skinless chicken breast with mustard cream sauce," and the décor of plastic plants hanging from the ceiling.

We sat around a big booth and Kensington and I ended up far away from each other. I had run out of the house with no cash so I sheepishly asked him to cover me.

"Sure thing."

"So, what are you into?" I asked Quince.

"I take tons of dance classes and yoga classes. In the fall, I'm getting my teaching credentials to teach elementary school. What about you?"

"I have a shop on Haight Street where I do Thai massage and tarot readings." The truth was that shop was barely operating. Because we were located in the back of a store we hardly had any business. I was too embarrassed to say I had been fired and was mostly unemployed.

"Thai massage. I've always wanted to try that. Could we do it sometime?"

"Sure."

"So how did you meet up with these soccer players?" she asked.

Just then the waitress brought three enormous pizzas.

"I met them through Kensington."

I had a good feeling about this Quince character. She was fun and spontaneous. We chatted effortlessly. At some point she said, "This conversation is more interesting than any one I had in the last year with my ex-girlfriend."

On a piece of scratch paper I wrote "Your soccer buddy" and my name and number. Later, this piece of paper would surface from time to time in the chaotic waves of Quince's belongings.

I had tried to make new friends many times in the city.

Usually nothing came of it so I decided to take an extra measure.

"Don't let this just be one of those numbers you take down and never call. Okay?"

"I'll definitely call you when I get back from the Michigan's Womyn's Music Festival."

I walked home that night feeling satisfied, my muscles stretched, my social circle expanded. My only disappointment was that I didn't get Quince's number. If she didn't call, I'd never see her again.

A month later Quince texted me: "Remember me? Your soccer friend."

I called Quince and left a message telling her my sisters and I were performing a belly dance show at Philz Coffee, a funky café in the Mission near my apartment. She said she would come.

Philz wasn't set up for dancers. We had to move furniture aside. We changed in a dingy bathroom. Our feet were quickly stained black.

"Dignity, always dignity," said Celeste.

As my sisters and I shimmied into our finale among old couches, large plants, and bewildered looking coffee drinkers, I noticed Kensington and Wells (remember Wells from Chapter 3?) smiling near the door. No sign of Quince. My sisters split and my friends and I headed towards an art opening. Then I got a text from Quince:

"At the Lex, does a girl want to meet me there?"

I convinced Kensington and Wells to go there instead.

The Lexington at the corner of 19th and Lexington was San Francisco's queer/lesbian/bi/trans bar. It was small, dark, and crowded, with one pool table and a stacked jukebox. It was a dive bar with chandeliers. Gay men had their selection of three-story discos, intimate lounges, and piano bars, and we had this. And sometimes I hated the Lex because there was so much posturing and sceneyness. This is how Audre Lorde described lesbian coolness in the '40s: "In those days gay girls were usually not very sociable outside their own little group." Here we are 60 years later and it's still cliquey, Audre! Is there to be no progress?

I spotted Quince wearing a red and blue plaid shirt, cargo jeans, and a pink Holly Hobbie hat of all things. We slid past girls that looked like boys, girls that looked like girls. Lesbians, trans men, genderqueer all exuding cool.

Quince and Kensington did a high five. Kensington chivalrously took our drink orders. He came back and handed Quince a beer and me a vodka cranberry. I didn't know anyone there but Quince fit in and gave quick hugs to a couple of women. Kensington was the only straight guy there and he towered over all of us.

"If you all don't have plans later, there's a lady party a couple of blocks away," said Quince.

"Kensington, you up for a homo party?" I asked.

We were flung out into the crisp, cold city air. I was thoroughly tipsy at this point and with superhuman powers of speed and immunity to the weather. Women were spilling out of a two-story building. Smokers were out front talking about smoking. A beer bottle was hurled from a window and landed two inches form my head. Despite this, we went upstairs where the theme of the party was stated in a long banner: *Ugly is the New Pretty*. San Francisco was certainly going through this phase. I had never seen such a conscious effort to showcase freakish hair, faded jeans, expanded earlobes, blurry tattoos, and naked faces.

We forged our way to the living room where a DJ was spinning and clusters of women danced. A slow song came on.

"Let's dance," I said to Quince. With an arm motion, she invited Kensington to join us. We enjoyed a three-way slow dance. I was plastered against Kensington's chest but wanting to be closer to Quince.

The song ended. On the way to the kitchen I spotted a real eye smoothie with yellow silky hair and blue eyes, a version of of Meryl Streep in her glorious youth. I was not usually into femmes but this woman got me all melty. I wanted her clothes off. *Did I learn how to look at women from men or from myself? Is anything pure or are the conquerors always teaching us how to conquer?*

I got a drink and struck up a conversation with her in the hallway while I waited for the bathroom. An oafish man stormed out and I went in. A small sign said: *Ugly in Pink.* I popped out and she was still there.

"Go ahead, it's all yours," I said.

"I wasn't waiting for the bathroom," she said.

"Oh," I said. She smiled.

We leaned our heads against the wall and talked. Most San Francisco parties are long railroad hallway events.

"Are you a local?"

"No, I'm from Alabama."

I wanted to date locally, but I was drunk and she was lovely so no harm.

"So how do two femme girls ever start kissing?" I asked her. We kissed and it was soft and luscious and sent tingles through me. It feels more taboo to kiss a femme than a butch because there's no heteronormative masculine-feminine dynamic to imitate.

I felt bad that I'd ditched Quince and my friends but the alcohol made me loose and spontaneous.

We all ended up on the street. Quince appeared, looking adorable in her pink hat. "I'm taking off," she said touching my arm quickly and leaving. I took the pretty lady home and tried to go down on her but she stopped me, which was for the best.

The next day I left voice messages for Kensington and Quince, apologizing for my disappearing act.

"Well at least I know you like the ladies," Quince texted.

I didn't want to date Quince. I wanted to be friends. Kensington, Quince, and I would go to bars, swim at Lake Anza, watch movies on his bed. Kensington's one-room apartment was hipster edgy featuring a terrifying picture of Jack Nicholson in *The Shining,* insects pierced and displayed behind glass, and Wonder Woman posters. His fridge had beer, mustard, and a lone package of Jarlsberg cheese.

After we all hung out, Quince would come over and snuggle in my bed. I didn't think we were going to date. Or maybe I didn't notice that we already were dating. I was the last to know. My sisters knew, of course.

Quince helped me move out of my small room with Rafael to a bigger Haight Ashbury place. In fact, suddenly, Quince was everywhere I was and it was wonderful. We packed up my room. She had a box covering her face.

"So who do you have a crush on these days?" I asked.

She slid the box down revealing her huge eyes.

"Well there is always someone."

I took a load of boxes from the Mission to Haight. I saw a couple putting a decent mattress on Haight Street and I got my new roommate to help me move it up the four flights of stairs. Our apartment was right next to Janis Joplin's old place, the one that reeked of pot every time you walked by. I expected Ms. Madrigal to show up any day and slip a joint under the door.

Quince and I were spending all our time together as "friends." Our bodies were drawn to each other. We were always picking up each other's hands, grazing our hips against each other, hugging when there was no greeting or farewell.

Two months into our friendship we went to Shamrocks on 9th and Lincoln. It had cozy couches and tons of board games and free popcorn. We were with Allegra and a bunch of friends. Quince and I kept finding excuses to touch each other.

We went back to my new apartment. We faced each other lying on our sides on my bed in my new room with its yellow walls and odd ceiling angles. I kissed her ever so softly. And she kissed me back. The thing that's so great about hot queer love is how we find each other. For straight people it's just the norm: boy meets girl. But for queer love we climb across the unknown through centuries of shame and silence, and yet we find each other, a spark of recognition and the spice of taboo. After a while I started to unhook Quince's bra, an act that already felt performative.

"It's probably been a while, do you remember how to do that?"

she teased, knowing I was still seeing Kunal.

I did. We entered those blissful moments of early love where you are looking at each other and feeling the same things, the same notions, without saying anything. Love's invisible language. In the beginning of our relationship I didn't have lofty goals. I basked in her company and the fact that she was my person. It was the dream of having a girlfriend and best friend all in one.

Quince was sleeping with a beautiful woman who had obsidian hair and dark brown eyes. We all showed up at a party. This lover was clearly peeved that Quince and I were spending so much time together. I told Kunal about Quince. During what turned out to be our last visit with him as my lover we had passionate sex but I wasn't as into it as I'd been before. He extracted his punishment by leaving me with yet another UTI. Kunal moved to the place of the purple hills you leave behind on a road trip to somewhere new and delightful.

After the shock of Channing's lies and my guardedness with Kunal, Quince got deep inside right away. I trusted her. Our first months together were liquidy, effortless, dreamlike. I didn't care what we did; I just wanted to do it with her. I would kiss her and she would say, "Again."

She had a birthday party early into our courtship at Bissap Baobab. This is where I met Athena with her long, shiny black hair, oval face, big smile, small frame. She would become one of my close friends. All Quince's friends were queer, artsy, many of them gardeners, teachers, nannies, visual artists, and musicians. It felt so natural and right to be among them.

Whereas Harper and I became a homesteading lesbian "married" couple, Quince showed me the sexy, youthful aspect of queerness. Living in the city I saw much more of my queer self reflected. In the countryside of Sonoma County, Harper and I were an accepted anomaly. Only once did guys in trucks drive by us yelling "Dykes!" Of course that is still once too often.

But San Francisco was the gay capital of the world and we were going to suck the vegan marrow right out of it.

Quince and I went to the Lexington bar, baked fresh cakes for the Fuck Off Bake Off, brought sketch pads everywhere. We went to healthy potlucks our friends put on in their home called Queer Food for Love. We had picnics in Dolores Park. I got all glittery and femmie for Hot Pants dance party at the Cat Club and she wore a t-shirt, tie, and jeans. Quince looked good in pants. This was universally acknowledged. Everywhere we went there were beautiful and handsome queer women to hug, to dance with, to drink and laugh with.

Quince always said, "All the prettiest girls are gay." In San Francisco in the aughts, there was evidence of this everywhere. Underneath all the tattoos, uneven fades, flannel, ripped black t-shirts, and body piercings, exceptionally attractive people shone through their shells. She helped me find myself again in the queer stratosphere.

Quince's 17th Street house was all hot butch women who had gorgeous mostly femme girlfriends. There was no lesbian bed death. They called the place The Lighthouse because it was perched on a hill and when you returned to it you were safely inside the arms of your queer family.

Everyone had company in the evenings and everyone woke up freshly fucked, eyes twinkling, winding their hands in their girlfriend's fingers and hair, smelling faintly of sex. We made big brunches with tofu scrambles, potatoes, salads, coffee, tea, cheese on everything, soy sauce and nutritional yeast as condiments, crepes with sweet or savory fillings. We all wanted to go see *Brokeback Mountain*, as everyone agreed that gay man sex was hot. That year for the Pride Festival, Quince made a shirt that said, "In my movie the gay cowboy lives."

I loved Quince's Save-the-World kindness. Restaurants that were empty at dinner time made her tear up. She came up with the kind of wealthy parents that teach you to do good through volunteerism and daily choices around recycling. Quince and her roommates were supporting a young girl in Africa through her schooling by sending monthly checks.

We would chug down the 17th Street hill with the grand view of the Bay in her wagon she called Sally and chat away about anything that came to mind. There was always so much to say. Though she had grown up wealthy in Ventura, Quince's presentation was funky: She wore paper thin t-shirts and jeans faded and molded to her shape. She supplied the soundtrack to our relationship. Her selects were very emo: Cat Power, Iron and Wine, Modest Mouse, Sigur Ros, Eliot Smith, Badly Drawn Boy. They were all songs tinged with melancholy. She made me CD mixes that she put clever titles on like:

blanket hot sage
girl you give me the tingles you magical being
i kissed a girl she blew my hair back
i love her
your brush has angel hairs in it

I loved to smell Quince. Her neck, axilla, loins, everything smelled good to me. When we had sex we dove at each other at once. She was a gymnast so I liked to see how far I could stretch her legs. Quince was very quiet during sex. If she wanted me to put two fingers in, she lifted two of hers up to show me.

Quince's room was always in flux, with wooden boxes and clothes everywhere, white faux fur on the wall, and a huge bookshelf overflowing with toolboxes, art supplies, clothes to be mended. Her closet was filled to the brim.

One Saturday Quince and I got ready to go out. In ten minutes, I had scrambled on my pants, shirt, sweater, and jacket. I put my hair in a ponytail without brushing it and smeared on my only lipstick.

"I'm ready," I told Quince, standing behind her so we were both looking in the mirror. She was moving sections of her hair around. With a small pair of scissors she cut little clumps off. I sat on her bed and thumbed through a magazine.

My keys, purse, and ID were all in place. She had on a tie, a vest, and striped 1940s style pants.

"Which tie, babe, this one or the blue one?"

Without looking up I said, "The one you're wearing is good." She noticed another stray hair and snipped it. I couldn't think of anything to do with the empty pre-departure time except get more impatient. Then she rummaged through her drawer and pulled out a sock. She cut it into a band and put it on her arm. She created a new item of clothing or accessory for each departure. She changed her tie and shirt to ones that looked exactly the same as her first choice. She kept with the same vest. Instead of a bra she put two pieces of tape over her nipples.

I ambled into the bathroom and begrudgingly brushed my hair and my teeth. My toothbrush was covered with lipstick. I walked back in and Quince was still looking in the mirror with another armband on, different shoes and a knitted yellow cap. She glued the hem of her pants together with rubber cement.

"Are you about ready?"

"Yeah, do you have the keys?"

"Check."

She leaned over and took a big swig off a bottle of Patron tequila she got for her birthday. I would be driving. We were heading to see a lesbian movie at the Castro for Frameline Film Festival.

She double parked on Castro Street so I could run up and get a pass for the movie. Allegra and I curated the bisexual film night so I had access to any tickets available that day.

I ran up the carpeted stairs and got some coffee. I got our tickets and turned around to find a short balding man in his early fifties blocking my way.

"Excuse me," I said in a rush to get back to Quince. He looked at my badge but couldn't read it.

"Are you a filmmaker?"

"Yes I am, but this is my curator pass. I host the bisexual film night."

"Oh well I have a husband," he said backing away as if I was about to hit on him.

I was so shocked I didn't say anything and just bounded back down the stairs. But the story stayed with me. That someone in my community, a gay man, was thinking that just because I was bi I was attracted to everyone, every man; even a short, balding gay man. I was a threat to his marriage. He had physically distanced himself from me as if he didn't want to catch what I had.

Quince didn't feel confident in the kitchen. She does now, I'm sure she would like me to add. She probably is reading this. She disliked having to babysit the food for longer than five minutes. Usually she wandered off, letting things overcook or burn. If I ever mentioned buying anything like a shelf, bookcase, towel rack, or planter box she quickly offered to make it herself. She was a thrift store hound who bought secondhand towels. Toothbrush care was the only domestic area I saw Quince take a keen interest in. She had an almost superstitious fear of the goop that gathers at the bottom of toothbrushes when they sit in cups on the bathroom sink. I would go into the bathroom and see the clean jar, hung upside down, the brushes lying about like shipwrecked sailors.

She didn't like square or geometric designs, especially when it came to linens and bedding. Plastic made her come undone. She preferred everything to be made of wood, moss, fur, old metal.

She didn't like seafood, which was my favorite food in the world. She was fascinated watching me eat muscles, oysters, clams. "That sure looks like a pussy," she said as I devoured them.

Quince was all black curlicues and ringlets, big blue soft marble eyes, round breasts, supple skin. And they had powers over me, those eyes. They manipulated me to their desires with the double authority of beauty intermingled with inevitability.

Our sex was delicious, languid, healing. Her strong legs and round breasts were perfection to me, eliciting a helpless desire. Quince had a friend who worked at a dildo factory so she had four different strap-ons. Harper and I hadn't experimented much with this. Quince would put the strap-on in a cup of hot water first. The sensation of her smooth, sleek feminine skin against mine, her breasts pressing into mine while a hard cock dove into me was delicious. My layered desires all being met at once.

Sometimes it was enough for her to come. I was fulfilled by her pleasure completely, by my handy work and tongue, by her peaceful stillness.

When I wore the strap-on I quickly became sore and winded in the arms, legs, and hips. A deep respect bloomed in me for Masculine of Center women, butches, tops, and cisgender men. They had been working their biceps, rectus femoris, and quads for years in order to sustain themselves while driving rhythmically into me. Let's hear it for the boys/bois.

I'd have her face down and whisper in her ear *you need it*. And who was I in that moment? Was I man or woman, neither or both? I was completely focused on her, listening for her breath, as she never made audible sounds. Quince and I didn't role play or talk dirty. We made love.

There is nothing like the feeling of making love to your person, your partner, your future. This principle underlined and scented all our sexual exchanges and filled me with delight and comfort. I never got bored of Quince's perfect shapes. I always wanted her, I always wanted more.

She taught me how to be in a sustainable long-term relationship. I would fret when we didn't have sex for a week, fearing we would get into the pattern Harper and I had found ourselves in. The ever-leering Lesbian Bed Death. But she would remind me that desire ebbs and flows, that we were women run by wise natural cycles. One night we snuggled so blissfully she texted me the next day from work: "We had some nice holds."

One night in her sleep she turned to me as I got back in bed and said: … *with my skin and my bones*. I didn't hear the first part of the sentence exactly: *I love you with my skin and my bones,* but I felt it.

She was athletic and aggressive but socially could be suddenly shy and even blush when speaking to a group at a party. When she cried she always said: "I'm not crying for myself, I'm crying for all the homeless people (or abused children or battered women)." Her therapist and I tried to get her to focus on herself and not get so panoramic. Her pain was always linked with the universal.

She sent me texts like: "Let's do take on the world, Beauty."

We had our six-month anniversary at an Asian fusion place called Ponzu. Just as the mango sake was marinating my thoughts, they brought us a champagne toast, showing us a much respect as they would a grand old heterosexual couple celebrating their 50th. The drinks, the surroundings, the company made me delirious with joy. I felt so lucky to be with Quince.

I took two lovely photos of her. One was at the restaurant with her hands together and her shoulders lifted like a shy mime and a smile full of promise. The other was in the stairwell of my apartment. I stood above her. She was wearing a maroon velvet jacket, a tie, plaid pants, and men's shoes. She looked up at me and into the camera resulting in a picture of perfect androgyny, neither man nor woman but also the most beautiful man and woman. She looked to be in love.

Years later, after our split, she will use this photo as her profile picture on OK Cupid. Her caption will read: "It's the year of the rabbit and I'm a free bunny."

Sometimes I would call her and she would answer the phone by saying "I love you."

11: IN THE HOTEL

Quince's roommates were moving out and she was tired of getting new ones all the time. The Butch Shangri-La that she had for years slowly disappeared as each roommate moved to New York, Seattle, in with their girl, or to Oakland, the new affordable San Francisco. We had been together for three years and the conversation of living together had come up from time to time.

I was living in an apartment that we called The Velvet Temple. Allegra had found it for me on Craigslist. Its best feature was it being kitty corner to her apartment. I was touched by two sentences in the add: "We all like the ladies and sometimes we do each other's dishes out of love and not martyrdom." I had been living there for a couple of years when Quince moved into the adjoining room to mine and we opened up the pocket doors. It was, however a very low-risk move in. It was nothing close to marriage and we didn't get our own apartment. We didn't even choose to share one room. We were doing commitment lite. But still it was a step that I was thrilled to take with her.

We were getting along great despite occasional rumbles between us about my bisexuality. The old "will you leave me for a man," story. Quince found me writing about Channing (for this damn memoir) and it upset her. She was more amused than jealous about stories of Kunal.

The next time he came to town she wanted to meet him. We met him at his hotel in South San Francisco. We all shared some drinks at the hotel bar, took a hot tub, and hung out a bit in his room. I felt a sort of flirty vibe between the three of us.

A couple of months later he was coming to town again. Quince's room was always in need of cleaning as she had so many clothes and art supplies. I was hanging up her shirts.

"I think I want to have sex with a man so I can know what it's like for you to be with men. It will make us more equal."

"Like without me?"

"No, I think we should have a threesome with Kunal."

"Really?"

"Yes, I think it will be a bonding experience for us. And somehow it will make me less worried that you will leave me for a man."

"I don't want to leave you for a man!" I said, turning away from hanging up a plaid shirt that looked exactly like the other plaid shirts in the closet.

"It will just help me," she said. "And I guess I am kind of curious about having sex with a man."

For some crazy reason I agreed to this idea though we set up no clear boundaries about what we would or wouldn't do.

I called Kunal as I walked on Sutter Street in downtown San Francisco to the Aveda Salonspa where I gave massages. I like to think that in our split screen, Kunal was walking through Central Park.

"Hi there, Kunal."

"Hi babe." He still called me babe. Years after we breakup, Quince will still call me Baby Lou. And Harper, after never giving me a nickname even though I gave her a hundred of them will start calling me Nup Nup. Draw your own conclusions.

"Are you coming in the fall to do a Gem Show?

"Yes babe, I sure am."

"Quince wants us to have a threesome, interested?" Here I imagine Kunal tripping over a pigeon, spitting out his latte and then composing himself.

"Of course."

"Okay we will talk closer to the time."

"Hot."

I had a dream that Quince and I were having dinner at a restaurant inside a big moored boat. Then suddenly the boat was unanchored, floating out on the bay, unprepared. I felt panicked that we were traveling on the sea when we had only just sat down to dinner. I finally accepted that solid ground was receding. The boat had a comforting motion like a slow rocking chair. And I wanted to be on that boat with Quince.

It was time to get ready for the date. I was lying in bed having just finished *Bridget Jones' Diary*. I slipped the bookmark out of its pages and into *The Diary of Anais Nin, Volume 1*.

Quince declared we would both don sexy dresses and makeup though she never wore dresses or makeup except sometimes at straight weddings. Normally Quince presented as an attractive androgynous person; all dolled up she became a beautiful femme. Allegra said she looked like a young Angela Lansbury (meow). As we walked into the hotel restaurant together in heels, short skirts, and makeup, it was clear we held the most combined power in the room. There was also a sort of hooker vibe about our entrance.

We greeted Kunal and ordered heavy, oily foods and lots of Champagne.

At some point during dinner Kunal turned to Quince and said, "How about a kiss." And kissed her. He was all in, but I could tell Quince was not. It was weird seeing Kunal imposing himself on my girl. But it was only a kiss, if there ever was such a thing.

We took all our conflicting desires up to his hotel room. And what was in it for me? I was going along for the ride. I liked that we were being experimental. I felt at an advantage as I felt safe and trusted both of them. I knew I had chemistry with both of them. But I couldn't quite picture how the night would unfold. I didn't expect that panicked moment where Quince disappeared. Kunal and I left the room to go and find her. Then ... more about this in Chapter 24.

Quince wanted children and I did not. It was always lingering in the back of our minds, in the place you push trouble to so you can get out of bed, the blessings of compartmentalization. Mom tried to reassure me, saying, "Don't try to figure it out now, just trust." She had been reassuring me about life's mysteries in this way my whole life and I clung to her pagan optimism. Maybe she hoped, as most mothers do, that I would decide I did want to break my vagina as she and hundreds of my ancestors had broken theirs to make my life possible. "Trust the universe," she said.

In the 2008 recession I wasn't particularly solvent. Though I was a mostly self-employed artist, unscathed by the ebbs and flows of capitalism, I had to admit I was a little cash-shy. We had been together about four years. Quince was doing okay as a teacher. She wondered how I could help support a family with my meager earnings. I wanted the two of us to be a family. She said it was only a family with children.

"Pet children?" I said hopefully.

"No. Not pet children."

I have consistently not wanted children my whole life. I have never had the desire for a takeover of my body, for breastfeeding, sleep deprivation, and for the lifetime of sacrifice that children require. And there are other reasons not having to do with sacrifice and impingement on my freedom. For one, I don't want to witness a child lose their innocence, which every parent must do. Only in the next few years will I begin to warm to the idea of being a stepparent.

Things that scared me about traditional marriage and having children were numerous.

My parents had called the whole thing off when I was nine years old.

My mom left with her boyfriend, first to Yelapa, and then moved to SF which was an hour away but a lifetimes distance for a child.

I've been scrutinized for this choice all my life. In my 20s older, earthy women regularly informed me that the mysterious biological clock would take me over like the moon eclipsing the sun. Sometimes I feel estranged from the majority of women who have all chosen to be mothers. But I also like the anomaly of it. I have no idea what this biological clock business is about. It makes me feel somehow androgynous. Don't be fooled by my feminine exterior, deep down I am a man who seeks sex for its own sake, never for procreation. Or maybe this makes me an indifferent gay uncle. Or maybe not wanting to have kids is the most womanly thing about me. Wrap your brain around that!

I've been the recipient of a rather withering look when I tell someone I don't want to have children. Like they are searching my face for some insufficiencies. They see I've been poured into the shape of a nurturing woman. I long for a world where all parents want to be parents and all children feel wanted. I would consider being a stepmom or adopting an older child if there were actually a village to help me raise them. I have seen so many of my women friends cloistered in homes doing all the childrearing on their own, their husbands referring to their shifts as "babysitting," and the dreams they once had for themselves stifled.

In Golden Gate Park Quince and I sat on the slant of Hippie Hill to review our relationship.

"I was always taught to work hard and your lifestyle isn't like that," she began. "I'm jealous of your lifestyle but it's not my way. Also, you write movies and study film. So why don't you do something with it? Why don't you go to NYU and go to film school?" This spoke to an impatience that she suddenly had with all my renaissance arts. Why was she trying to ship me off to New York?

Then she brought up her desire to have kids. I said we should break up. What choice did I have? She disapproved of my career, my lifestyle, my finances, my arts, and I didn't want kids. There was no ground left for me to stand on. She had ushered it all away. Neither of us saw this coming. We got up and walked along the field that borders Hippie Hill. Quince stopped and hugged me.

One month later we got back together. We had a second honeymoon; I felt Quince wanted me again, loved me again. We had lots of sex. Another thing looming in the back of our relationship was my bisexuality. I adored Quince, she was my person and she turned me on. But because our sex was more loving than hot, raunchy, or aggressive, I did miss men at times. I still hadn't experienced a super butch aggressive female lover at this point.

We were in my narrow, sunny kitchen and Quince brought up a subject we had long since abandoned.

"Why don't we open up our relationship? That way you can sleep with men and I can explore other women and maybe find one that wants to have a baby with me." This was years after the Kunal threesome that happened in the beginning of our relationship.

In the moment I was scared and excited. I thought this was a weird chance to have it all. To explore the bodies of men but still have the love of my life as my partner. I also wanted to explore with other women, I am a greedy bisexual. Show me a more naïve pair than those two women in my kitchen on that ill-fated day. I wish I could shake them and scream: "Stop. You're going the wrong way!"

Just two days later I got drunk at Reverie Café and went home with an Arab guy who lived in the Outer Sunset. I was high on freedom. I texted Quince I wouldn't be home that night.

We got in the shower, where all my pubic hair demoralized him. He mowed it so fast with an electric shaver that I didn't have time to stop him. In bed he lost his erection. We didn't have sex. I lost interest in the whole ordeal and got in a cab and went home. Quince was gone. Instead of easing into our new arrangement, I had been a headstrong Aries with the help of alcohol, my firewater. When I came into our living room the next day Quince was seated by the window, unable to look at me. The profile of her face was white as chalk, her body shook.

"I can't believe you just went home with someone so soon."

She left again to get some space and I went into a shame spiral. What I had done was so careless. I called a friend who said, "It was open so you acted on it, you don't have anything to feel bad about." But her words didn't ring true. I should have entered into it with clarity and diplomacy instead of rushing. Was I secretly sabotaging us? Was it an attempt to gain freedom? A fool's search for who else might be out there? It was a turn I couldn't correct.

A week later we returned to some sense of normalcy. We were in my room across from her bedroom. I took off my pants and she watched me, flirtatiously, like I was suddenly her stripper. I took off my panties and she looked horrified instead of excited.

"Did you shave for all your new lovers? You never did that for me?"

"No I didn't." But I couldn't go into the details of how it got shaved. I didn't want to talk about that night.

In a panic I met up with Allegra.

"Did I ruin my relationship by getting drunk at Reverie?"

"No, that's reductive," she said.

Quince and I were lost for a while. Then we both started exploring other lovers. A couple of months into our don't-ask-don't-tell open relationship I got an intuition she was seeing someone. She left her phone on the bed and I knew by some witchy sense if I looked at it I would find out who she was. I picked it up and the last message was a nonsense word with an exclamation point. Something like "Razzle!!!" I looked at the name and it said Claire. Claire? Claire who lived across the street from our apartment? Claire whose bedroom window I could see from my bedroom window? Claire and I were even friends on Facebook. Across The Street Claire! The claustrophobia of it took my breath away. I didn't say anything to Quince. In the morning I found out that Wells knew as did some other friends. I wasn't a cuckhold but I felt like one.

I approached Quince as she was on my bed, writing belly down on her computer. I implied that I found out through a friend instead of admitting that I looked at her phone.

"I understand this is upsetting babe," Quince said. But her tone quickly shifted as though she didn't at all understand. Quince's non-reaction to my pain was such a raw terror. It was like she was a cat I nurtured from kitten to adult suddenly, inexplicably biting me until I bled, then looking at me in that distant cat way as if nothing unusual had happened. It made me wonder if perhaps in year five I had finally discovered a mean bone in Quince. After every incident in our open relationship we just went back to normal as best we could. We stuck to the plans we already had in motion.

This lurked in the background as Quince and I rode the shuttle from the Grand Rapids Airport with a carload of festies going to Michigan Womyn's Music Festival. I looked out the window and saw elegant green branches, so green that all the tender feelings of all the summers of my life were evoked.

Once out of the bus, friends from all over the country and world hugged in reunions only this festival provided. The warm, soft air caressed our skin. We kicked up dust as we walked. The requisite butches directed traffic and loaded our gear onto trucks. "Welcome home," said everyone in greeting. We waited in various lines and walked our belongings to our site under the trees. We signed up for our work shifts. Work shifts are a very lesbian women's festival thing, everyone chipping in, even though we paid to be here. The controversy of Mich Fest was trans folks weren't included and so they had their own camp in protest. This terrible restriction was ultimately the undoing of the festival whose gates closed in 2015.

All the fashion that had died off in other parts of the country was alive and well here: Crocs, fanny packs, overall shorts with side boob, rat tails, waist high jeans, mullets, matching extra-large tie die T-shirts, knee-high parachute pants, feathered hair, feather and bone amulets, dream catcher and labrys tattoos, nylon jumpsuits, onesies, one piece long johns, boots with a slip dress, boy shorts with a belt and t-shirt.

The women's / lesbian / queer community is all about fairness, inclusivity (except for trans women!), and rules. The food line had sections for moms with kids, and crafts women. No male voices, recorded or otherwise, were allowed. Topless women walked around boasting breasts that started at their sternums and ended just past their belly buttons. I loved seeing the voluptuousness everywhere. I wondered where all these women lived. I didn't see them in my daily life and there is no trace of them in movies or advertising unless they are set out as a crude example of who not to be. I overheard a woman say, "I didn't realize how unsafe I felt in the world until I got here and felt safe."

Every now and again some self-possessed young girls of about 14 walked by in small groups. They were extraordinarily pretty. The zombie fuzz of TV was not present in them. They had bright open eyes and their confident carriage implied the presence of parents who read to their children, bought healthy snacks, and encouraged art projects.

In the afternoon of the second day, Hilary and Athena joined our camp, and we made a sign that said: "We support camp trans." Hilary and Athena will come up more and more, dear reader, because they will become my besties! We all attended a class on The Clit, despite first protesting that we knew all there was to know on the subject. Quince and I sat next to each other on the grass. The teacher was a hot, young butch. She drew vagina diagrams on a white board. She said: *If the clit gets over stimulated you can slowly, gently lick it until it calms down. Then you can start again.*

The next day Quince and I took a sexuality and spirituality workshop. The teacher was tall, jovial, and sex positive. She said: "We are designed to receive touch." She gave a Sexual Activities Checklist to fill out. You rated each activity based on if you have tried it, if you want to try it, if you didn't want to try it.

She also suggested a game where one partner was the director for five minutes. You do exactly what the director says. And you always have to say yes to their requests (within your boundaries). Hot. I wondered if taking these classes with Quince would bring more spice into our sex life. I hadn't felt desired by her much since we opened up our relationship.

Later that afternoon, right in the heights of the Mich Fest joy, our crew was out in the sun listening to the Indigo Girls play as a woman came running through the crowds shouting that Prop 8 had been overthrown. Gay marriage was on the road to legalization.

I had thought my open relationship with Quince might give me the chance to fulfill my occasional desire to be with a man again, to feel muscle, be thrown around, see that raw male desire in his eyes. To perhaps have a man and woman at once. Here I was at a feminist utopia—a world of tents, music, workshops, communal food—longing for a man. But make me walk into a typical straight bar for a night, where everyone is conforming to outmoded gender norms, and I'd rush right back into the arms of my lesbian lover.

Being gay was once called the love that had no name. For me, bisexuality was still the love that had no place, at least no place that felt solid. Just a pendulum, constantly swinging.

I found Quince sitting on a rock by the dusty road near our campsite. She had a look on her face I hadn't seen before. Far off, lost, sad.

"What's going on?"

"This isn't the life I imagined for myself. I love it, its magical and amazing. It's also just so weird and different."

Quince grew up in a fancy part of Southern California where she was groomed to marry a doctor. It was also encouraged that she become a doctor, lawyer, or scientist. Her upbringing was supposed to culminate into a conformity she hadn't surrendered to. Growing up she had luxurious golden wavy hair in a halo around her blue eyes and a perfect gymnast-sculpted body. She looked like the heterosexual Girl Next Door. When I met Quince she had pale skin and raven hair. She cut and dyed the locks, let the tan fade, wore secondhand clothes, drove a funky blue car and moved to San Francisco to be a barista with a Stanford degree. She had cut all the threads of expectation that her parents carefully wove into her. Being queer was leaping across a far wider chasm than I had to, given that I grew up on a hippie commune and every single member of my family was bisexual.

But some part of the authentic Quince really did want a more conforming "normal" life. She wanted kids. And I was really excited to live a childfree life.

I now know that opening a relationship requires many discussions, perhaps some written guidelines, and an experienced couple's therapist. But we were optimistic; we thought our bonds were strong. The open relationships I see that work were open from the beginning, involving people who are calm about jealously and possessiveness, or at least willing to do a lot of processing. There is really no way to generalize about any of this. But I will say that I see many relationships open up just as the ship is already capsizing.

If only Michelle Tea had already written *How To Grow Up*, her wise words could have warned us: "Unless you are a free-spirited Polyamorous Polly at heart and you've always wanted to live in a nonmonogamous manner, flinging the bedroom doors open on your LTR is just procrastinating its demise, and guaranteeing that it will be much more painful and dramatic." Later, when I saw friends doing it without true preparation, I thought to myself *Welcome to hell.*

I could have stayed on and gone with Quince and Hilary and Athena to a queer wedding in Vermont. But instead I went home and had a terrible threesome with a younger hetero couple I met at my massage job. Trust me, it's not worth your time, so we'll skip the details.

In the midst of all these dumb moves, I went a step further. I contacted Channing. I know, right?

I picked him up downtown and we drove to Golden Gate Park. We ended up at the entrance on 9th Street across from what had been our first date. The café that had once housed rotating art installations and creative performances was now just a chain fish restaurant. The color palette was navy, pewter, ebony, and the darkness seeped inside the car. He was too cheap to pay for a hotel. "They fleeced me," he said of his wife and kids.

"My wife and I are both on antidepressants. I don't want you to think I'm some sad, old man." By now they had four children. All I could think was how the mighty had fallen.

"Are you going to show me your knickers now?"

"You want to have sex? Where?"

"It wouldn't be the first time we did it in the car. Come and straddle me."

I refused that offer. I was no longer the woman who was obsessed with Channing. I went into the past trying to find two lovers who no longer existed. We both had our seats in reclined but it was nothing like lying side by side in a bed. I wanted to just drive us away. But if I did, I would burn a whole chapter of my life. He had been my obsession.

While I was lost in this psychological storm, he began to masturbate. He still wanted to have some sort of sex. I looked out onto the field where my mom played baseball the day I was conceived. I was glad she wasn't witness to this tawdry scene. Channing stuck his cock inside my mouth and his hot semen filled it. I opened the door, staggered out, and spit it into the muddy grass.

"I'm surprised you didn't want to swallow that," he said when I came back into the car, like he was talking to some porn version of myself he had invented. Maybe that's how he saw me. We barely spoke as we drove home. I wished I could have just ended everything when he told me about the pregnant girlfriend. Channing was nothing more than a ghost. It took this rapey humiliation for me to finally realize it.

I found Quince in her usual position belly down on my bed working on her computer. I said I wanted to talk and she rolled over.

"I want us to recommit to each other. I don't think this open relationship is working."

She stretched her legs out and folded forward on them. She liked to multi-task by stretching as she spoke.

"We can't do that. It's too late." She got a far-off look.

"What do you mean? You make it sound like we signed something, like it's out of our control."

"I don't want to close it."

But the more I tried exploring other lovers, the closer I felt to Quince. Everyone seemed imperfect compared to her. She was so kind and loving. Her body so supple, malleable, hourglass shaped. She looked good in clothes. She looked good in pants. She looked better naked. When I said I wanted to do something she said: "Let's do it right now! I'll help you."

In the hunting, the lead up the pre-date, I was less present with her. After I had sex with a lover I was thrilled to get to return to her arms. I wanted her and I wanted her to want only me. I only had the courage to spiral out into the arms of others because she anchored me.

I started making breakfast for Wells and Quince every day. I was trying to pull our disparate household together into some sense of domestic rhythm. But I knew the days were numbered for this configuration of our apartment. I made tofu scramble or pancakes with veggie sausage. I boiled water for tea and coffee. Wells usually helped with preparation and Quince cleaned up. We sat down to eat and Wells did most of the talking, Quince mostly listening.

At night we held each other like everything was the same. I looked into her blue eyes and saw my sweetheart, like always. Then we remembered we had sullied the purity. We let other lovers into our arms. Nothing was clear anymore.

How did I really know it was over with Quince? When I came home, she stopped acknowledging my presence with a hug or a kiss. She was unhappy with our roommates. She said Wells was too loud and boisterous. They used to be friends, always exchanging massages with each other. Now they inhabited the same space with no warmth.

We had recently tried a new therapist; a larger lesbian woman with a serious nature. She said I needed to re-establish boundaries with Quince. She suggested Quince move into her room for real, sleep there and only come into my room when I invited her. I liked her bold directive.

One night I returned from my women's group and stood in the pocket doors that separated our bedrooms. Quince was standing by her loft bed, her room in its usual post-hurricane state. Her hair looked frazzled and she was wearing sagging yoga pants. I couldn't believe I would be losing that beautiful face, the one from which I divined my life. She looked at me with a little smile, a hint of the big ones I used to get, but her eyes didn't widen like a surprised cartoon as they used to. The smile made everything harder.

"There is work to do," I said. "But I am not going to do it with you. I want you to move out for good, and for us to break up."

"Really, babe? That's what you want?"

She was still seeing Claire from across the street. That knowing hovered somewhere. Was she feeling some glee in having the freedom to be with Claire? I didn't shut the door between our rooms. Nothing so dramatic. I just knew it was time. Of course, I regretted it since. What I regret most is that post-breakup, to my great surprise, Quince and I will not be friends—only friendly.

12: THAT WAS THE BEST

I sat on a blanket at Dolores Park, the same park where I met Quince six years ago. Celeste looked at her phone while I recruited her husband Dimitry and my nine-year-old nephew Devin to practice wrestling with me. I wanted to learn how to wrestle with my new date Finn. I asked Celeste to go to the bathroom with me. We have a long-standing codependent trip-to-the-bathroom thing. She didn't have to go, so I went alone. The ladies' line was long as usual.

I caught sight of my friend Stuart and went towards them to say hi. As I approached I saw Stuart was sharing a blanket with Quince and Claire. Claire looked pleased, like that cat that swallowed the goldfish. This was the first time I had seen them together. As if they were a couple and that was normal instead of The Worst Possible Thing that could happen to me. I waved at them cheerfully while something heavy sunk inside me. I stood around, shifting my weight.

"Awkward," I mumbled. Stuart valiantly got up and hugged me. Then Quince walked over and hugged me. She and I walked to a spot below the playground equidistant from my family and her friends. And Claire. We chatted. She still had curls peeking out of her hat.

"I almost cut them all off," she said.

"You are always about to cut them all off," I said.

She told me about her relatives and their ailing health and their bravery in the face of it. She told me about a howler monkey she saw in Nicaragua.

She said her family was doing some volunteer work together. I was reminded that she was raised with a do-good innocence and

I was raised with the weariness of radicals and the mania of hippies. Her family volunteered and wrote checks—my family was more likely to chant and scream in the street.

"How's life at the commune?" I asked. After she moved out of our apartment she moved into a commune with 19 people.

"Its fine, but some of the men are persistent in hitting on me."

She lifted up her arm and I noticed her jacket had a big tear in the elbow. She wore the same jeans she'd worn for years. She always had a love for clothes in elegant decay.

We talked until I noticed Celeste waving her hands in the air in a signal of departure. I took a sip of Quince's beer.

"You hate beer, "she said. We hugged. I pressed into her. I let my hands feel into the shape of her back. I didn't want to let go but eventually I did.

That night she texted me at 5:57pm: "That was the best."

When feeling lost, in transition, unsure, I try to affirm myself. The breakup with Quince put bricks on my heart. At night I would remind myself I was an artist. I had already lived so many lives. I studied feminist witchcraft in my early 20s. I followed the old tradition of studying for a year and a day and was ordained by a priestess. You can also proclaim yourself a witch simply by saying, "I'm a witch" three times. Go ahead, try it.

Or you can take a Slut Pledge. All of this is easy, if you know how. I can't trace backwards, I can't be a virgin, or not a witch or not a slut. Words and actions have alchemized me into the woman I am.

13: COSTA RICA

Here's what one editor said about this chapter: *Sometime around your trip to Costa Rica, your character starts to feel like someone who's just out to fill a hole in her life—like your search for the next relationship is a little unhealthy. She becomes less sympathetic in these moments. I don't know what the answer is to this; but I'm calling it out in case it's useful feedback.*

If only I knew how to integrate "useful feedback," I would have finished this book a decade ago. But let's pause for a moment and imagine that I *did* know how to integrate it. To what purpose would I try to convince you, dear reader, that I am not someone trying to fill a hole in my life? I mean, would you even believe me? I think you're smarter than that. I think you know I am trying to fill a hole in my life—a restless longing for adventure, experience, love, connection, meaning, purpose, bliss, happiness—and guess what: so are you. Some of us fill it with law degrees or marriages or babies or real estate portfolios. I fill mine with art and dancing and my sisters and friends and a whole lot of lovers.

I feel closer to you having come right out and confessed about that and now I am ready to take you to Costa Rica. Just because you've been a patient reader I am going to share this chapter in short flash-nonfiction snippets—you're welcome!

Why

Headed to a small Surfer town in Costa Rica called Dominical with Celeste's friend Zhiva to get over Quince. Was super sad for much of the trip.

Tarot Reading

Zhiva and I sat at a picnic table by the beach to give each other tarot readings to hail in the New Year. Zhiva turned over the Queen of Wands for me: a woman seated on a throne of fire with a leopard obediently at her side. She heard hesitancy in my voice, dissatisfaction with myself as I described my life in San Francisco to her. Nothing I described matched that woman on fire.

"April, you have an amazing artist's life, why are you trying to talk me out of that?"

Yet Another Threesome

We went to bar to find some guy to have a threesome with. And we found one! He was a young hot Portuguese dude. He and Zhiva had more chemistry and I felt left out. This is when I finally admitted that threesomes need a choreographer.

He did touch both of our pussies at once and say: "This is why I have two hands." So that was clever. I got my period. The whole thing made me feel lonelier for Quince than ever. I don't think anyone climaxed. Maybe Zhiva. The moral of the story: Why didn't I just have sex with Zhiva! We almost did but got interrupted. She was very feminine with long wavy hair. The femmes intimidate the shit out of me.

Steady

I met an English bloke and his three funny, chummy friends. We had breakfast with them. I said to one of them, let's call him Mike: "Mike, you should have stayed up later with me last night. I wanted to make out with you."

Mike banged his head on the table again and again and again.

His friend said: "Steady."

I love that dry Brit humor.

Running Naked

A bunch of us from the hostel went for a night swim. We all started walking towards the shore. I took leave by jogging away, naked, knowing all the men behind me could see my figure cutting a white streak through the night air. The voice of one my yoga teacher came to me: *We are always running away from ourselves. Try to run towards yourself.*

I ran through the shallow water. I ran across the damp sand. I tried to imagine how I could be myself and run towards myself at the same time. I'm having trouble tracking this metaphor but I think it was about self-love.

Tits Out

I walked into the hostel with one boob in my shirt and one boob out. My English friend Pip said: "April, tits out."

Tan

Before I left for Costa Rica, Quince texted me that she wanted to see me on my return "a woman transformed." I texted that I would come back "a woman with a tan." That's all I could promise anyone. She mentioned the transformation several times until it enraged me. She had a girlfriend. It implied she had moved on and I was just wallowing in the past, pining over her. This was exactly true but it struck me as arrogant for her to point it out. Do you think there's a connection between the Queen of Wands and A Woman with a Tan? Something for you book clubbers to consider.

Dreams

In Costa Rica I mostly dreamed I was elsewhere. Once home I knew I would dream of Costa Rica. Under the San Francisco night, thick with screams and sirens, I let these images dance through: huge shiny avocados, fuchsia ruffles of bougainvillea, endless water cascading over rocks, lines of sea meeting lines of sky, sweet plantains resting on white rice, strangers from everywhere gathered on a bus, a palm tree creating tropical shapes, upside down monkeys. Let me dream of what tore me apart and what mended me back together.

I wish could I sew all my patterns into one quilt. Wanting a sugar daddy, wanting a wife, wanting to be a slut then wanting to be loved tenderly, wanting to be unfettered, wanting to be claimed.

Flashback

A couple of months after our breakup I was at the Lexington Bar playing '80s music on the jukebox. I went outside to get some air and was suddenly surrounded by Quince and the friends I had met through her—Hilary, Athena, and others. All our mutual friends were doing their best to negotiate social etiquette since our split. I was relieved Claire wasn't there. Quince pointed to my neck.

"That's my scarf. You keep wearing it everywhere," she said good naturedly but firmly. She had mentioned it the last couple of times we ran into each other.

"We've been through this," I said. "My mom gave it to you for Winter Solstice, you didn't want it and gave it to me. Don't you remember?"

"I never gave it to you. Maybe I lent it to you once."

The scarf was generic gray and black and could probably be purchased at Walgreens for $3.99. I pulled it off my neck and handed it to her with a mock flourish.

"Fine, take it," I said.

"No, I don't want to take it *right now*."

She put her hands on the end as if to rip it.

"Go ahead," I said.

"No, no. I was just kidding."

I took a hold of the narrow side and so did she. With our friends around us we ripped it in two equal parts down the middle. Then we laughed. Everyone laughed.

She put the scrawny scarf around her neck. I put the other half around mine. I wasn't laughing anymore.

"It's better," she said. "I like it better this way."

14: ROMANTIC OUTSIDERS

Myself in flux, San Francisco in flux—lost lovers, closed restaurants and art houses; relationships that no longer exist, on to the next dance. Marlena's Drag Bar, The Lexington, Osento Women Only Bath House, The Red Victorian Movie House, The Cosmopolitan, Reverie Café, all gone.

In San Francisco there were two conversations: How the city was changing with the tech industry, sending rents through the roof and making evictions commonplace; and how humans were changing because of computers and phones.

My life in transparencies, intersections, double visions. My life in unequal dualities, overlapping dizzying pleasures. Sometimes I long for an anchor. I long for a reprieve from this spinning.

In Costa Rica I was just my own woman out in the world. When I got back to my Cole Valley apartment I compared myself to my sisters. I saw our adulthood as a game of musical chairs. Somewhere in our thirties the music stopped. Allegra married Shellie, a wonderful woman with whom is she is incredibly compatible. They lived across the street from me. Celeste married Dimitry who shared her life, her business, and made her a stepmom by bringing my wonderful nephew into our lives. My sisters were married with children. And I was not. When the music stopped, all the chairs were taken. In my most self-loathing moments, which attacked me late at night, especially in winter, especially when I was pre-menstrual, especially when I was unpartnered, I'd think it's because I am bisexual. I was all the stereotypes packed into one lonely body: indecisive and faithless. I wanted too much. I longed for men when with women and women when with men.

I wanted passionate sex and a long-term loving relationship.

The years after Quince made me whip smart, bringing me searing hot sex, romps, and ravishes but they didn't bring me a girlfriend or at least not for long.

I didn't date much right when I got back from Costa Rica. I was mad at myself for not signing up for film classes. I began doing research on being a life coach. I was naturally enthusiastic and always encouraged friends to follow their creative dreams. I had experience working one on one with clients doing tarot readings. But I wondered if it was just another thing that I would have to self-promote like tarot, belly dancing, and massage.

I found a school called IPEC and despite their very corporate wording and stock photos I had a feeling it was right for me. I enrolled in Life Coaching school and immersed myself in its tenets. I finally knew there was a reason I didn't take more film classes and that the free time in Costa Rica had opened up a space for me to find this calling.

The weekend modules were each a condensation of a lifetime of therapy. Layers of my ambivalence and self-doubt were peeled away. I got coached about Quince on the insight that I needed to just mourn and not date right away. I got coached on my low self-esteem that Zhiva had noticed during the tarot reading. Inside of me were tired stories I no longer believed. So much was unearthed, soothed. Simply putting nurturing attention onto all my issues by being truly listened to was so healing. During my weekly coaching sessions I learned how to speak tenderly towards myself instead of listening to the critic. I signed up to forge a new career where I could help others and along the way I transformed myself. But I was still lonely.

It took over a year to get myself back. The self-love was stronger than ever. I would never love the way I used to. That was of a certain age and time. I vowed not to lose myself in a relationship again. How did I lose myself with Quince? It was subtle; it was a hundred little adjustments to get the love I wanted. I think some people don't worry about this. I worry about it because I am an independent artist and being true to myself and my art is my life.

In many ways I blossomed with Quince but there is nothing like standing alone for a while to remember yourself.

I vowed to hold my love of self and love of the earth and sky deeper than any one person. I would.

Allegra and I always run into each other because Cole Valley is like a small town. We recreated Occidental in our own way. I was getting in my car to run an errand and I saw Allegra and Shellie beaming down Cole Street holding hands.

"Homos," I yelled.

Without missing a beat, Allegra yelled back: "We're free."

April and Allegra when they lived across the street from each other in SF (above)

April and Allegra at their Annual Bi BQ (below)

Celeste, April, Allegra all dressed up for Winter Solstice

Allegra, April, and Celeste in their Three Sisters
Belly Dance costumes

April's parents,
Marc Hirschman
and Magick

15: DESTINATION LESBIAN WEDDING

On the flight to Tulum I had time to reflect on my breakups. For the two years after Quince and I split my heart was heavy and my game was off. I dated here and there but I really wasn't in it. Then, one evening that actually was enchanted, I met a celebrity. We dated for five months. I saw what it was like to be in love with someone famous, who I had a whole other separate concept of before meeting them. I also got to see the reactions of my friends, the best of which was Wells jumping up and down on her bed with glee. Through my relationship it was as if the peasants were finally made visible, out of the margins, and in proximity to royalty. Our time together could be a subject for a whole other book.

But the actual dive into quick and deep love was epic. I saw such a future for us. The breakup was swift and I was prone to unexpected fits of weeping. I hoped this destination wedding would be a good distraction for my winter blues and my breakup sadness. I felt a wave of optimism in the Tulum Airport bathroom. I put on makeup and changed from my shabby travel clothes into a flowery dress and platform sandals. Hilary and Athena smiled approvingly as I emerged all fancy into the sultry air.

An acquaintance once said, "Every time a friend gets married its like a tiny funeral for our friendship." I know this won't happen to my friendships with Athena and Hilary, though it had happened with others. The tiny funeral usually happens when my friends have kids. But in the coming years many of my other friends will retreat into pairs. They will build their worlds around each other and their friends that don't intersect with me. I will need to make new friends.

We arrived by night into the grand villa that overlooked a pool and a semi-private beach. All the queers fanned out to examine sleeping arrangements and prepare for the awkward ritual of choosing rooms.

I got first pick so naturally chose a room that mirrored the bridal suite. I would be sharing it with Wells and Finn. I'd share the mammoth king bed with Wells. It faced French doors out to a private deck overlooking the pool. Finn and I both pretended that sharing a room was no big deal even though we'd had many dating near-misses. At this point we both happened to be single.

I noticed Finn sitting on our deck as night was falling. She wore frat boy shorts and a knock-off Izod. Conversations from the pool below trickled up. We looked into each other's eyes and then away. I moved closer to her. I hoped she would make a move but she didn't. We all slept in the same room, with only a distant hum of desire interrupting my wave-lapping sleep.

In the morning the Mayan Riviera shimmied into the windows, the sun brighter than at home, everything gilded. The water looked covered in gold and silver confetti, glistening, glinting, catching the light.

None of us were able to use our cell phones or email, ushering in a delightful present-momentness and making our villas an instant commune. Conversations flowed effortlessly around the stove, the outdoor table, along the pool, spilling onto the beach and into the great blue beyond. People were already kayaking and snorkeling on the beach. Coffee was brewed on the counter, half and half in the fridge. Someone had cooked breakfast; others cleaned up after.

We all seemed more glamorous on the Mayan Riviera under the Technicolor sun, frolicking and splashing about and sipping drinks. Like we were just the type of people that would get invited to a destination wedding in Mexico.

I tried to get Finn alone though I had promised myself that we definitely were not going to have sex during this trip. I was taking a break from casual sex. I thought I would quit it forever. Years later, trying my hand at standup comedy, I would blurt out my true sexual identify: *slutty and sensitive.*

Allegra coached me about Finn before our arrival. I referenced Olympia Dukakis in *Moonstruck* when a stranger asks her out after a woman has just dumped him. She declines his offer "...because I know who I am."

"I don't just want a fling," I told Allegra. She wasn't impressed with my theatrics.

"You're totally hooking up with her during the Mexican wedding."

I looked out an enormous wall of windows at aqua water that faded back into a deep ocean blue. I looked up to see Quince's new girlfriend reading on a sofa nearby. She was an earthy woman who usually had a soft smile on her face. By this time I had already hung out with her several times so there was no sting in seeing her. One time at a party where I saw her look at Quince with fresh lust—that hurt. But essentially, I liked her from the start. When they started dating, a friend casually mentioned that Quince had said: "My new girl and I can just get on our bikes and zip out all the way to Ocean Beach together." I never rode bikes, cautioned Quince about the dangers of riding in the city. I saw a picture of the two of them in motion, hair flying, laughing. Quince speeding on to her new, wild life. That was over a year ago. I still missed Quince and what we had. But I missed a different version of her, one that no longer existed.

"Here's where the nerdy introverts hang out," Quince's girlfriend said. I nodded in agreement.

Later, Hilary put on her workout mix and a spontaneous dance party started in the big open kitchen with the windows overlooking the patio and pool. Finn was killing me with her little dance moves. She wore a cream Guayabera shirt and board shorts.

Finn twirled Athena around. Then she two-stepped with Hilary and I cut in. We danced a two-step. I am usually a good follow but felt clumsy. Then somehow everyone cleared out of the kitchen and spread out around the pool. I looked into Finn's hazel green eyes.

The first time Finn and I hooked up, my friends sat in a circle under my curved windows in San Francisco, like that part of my room had its own pagan rites, like anything could happen there. We played a combination of Spin the Bottle and Truth or Dare. When I had the chance to kiss Finn, I knocked her over and Athena had to move out of the way so we didn't take her down with us. This kiss was hot and public.

Finn was in an open relationship with her girlfriend. I had never met her and Finn didn't bring her around much.

Hilary dared me to touch everyone's breasts. I looked around and no one objected. I went around the circle touching the breasts of seven of my friends. Many looked at me with an indulgent smile; some were small, some were big, some on butches, some on femmes, each set a round pleasing delight with their own merits. Finn gave me a bright frat boy smile as I touched hers. Then Hilary flashed her butt at all of us and it signified an "end scene." Everyone scattered, leaving me alone.

I texted Finn: "Where did you go?"

"Do you want me to come back?"

"Yes, I do." I changed into a red negligee and waited under the covers of my four-poster bed.

Finn came in and looked at me, her face still as a statue.

"There's no street clothes in the bed," I said. Once her pants were off, I noticed her large brown thighs.

Finn's weight on top was wonderfully heavy and soft and her muscular arms held me tight. She covered me. When her hand touched my thigh, chills shot up between my legs and goose bumps lined my arms. The first time with someone, I often get overwhelmed and my mind wanders off to being a spectator instead of co-creator. But I was able to stay present with her. We kissed softly. She looked down at me from her position above. She tugged on my panties

"Can I take these off?" she asked.

Back now to the kitchen in Mexico: Finn leaned against the kitchen counter. I could have left well enough alone. Noises from the outside pool party trickled in through the screen doors.

"What am I going to do with you, Finn?"

"I don't know, what are you going to do with me?"

I leaned in and kissed her soft lips. The kiss a quiet doorway. More kissing. Dancing too. She backed me against the kitchen counter. We kissed with all the scandalous pent-up energy we had been gathering over the years.

Finn looked into me with her relentless handsome eyes. As we kissed I pictured what we looked like; my round butt popping out of my small curvy frame in my red gingham retro bathing suit. Finn cut out from the space I left. Passionate kisses. Me pressing into her. Applause broke out from our friends around the pool. We ignored them and continued in our delights until the rush of passion ebbed.

"What next?" asked Finn.

"I'm going to swim in the cenote and then eat a seafood dinner. Join?"

Finn took my hand. I recalled my grandmother saying how she loved the innocent words of the Beatles song "I Want to Hold Your Hand." It felt incredible to hold hands walking along the beach when I thought I would spend the entire trip watching other couples embrace and perhaps holding my own hand, as I did in Spain.

My resolve to not sleep with Finn evaporated, and with it my hopes of not having casual sex. I put the emotional consequences aside as lust in the tropics came to the forefront. Plus it was a wedding. The maid of honor and the best man always hookup!

We stopped to kiss. Then we walked to the Blue Lagoon cenote. The sun slowly retreated as we swam around the clear and refreshing water, the kind of water that restores ones faith in life.

Afterward, we had a romantic candlelit dinner overlooking the windy sea. We shared ceviche. I had shrimp quesadillas and she had beef. The wind blew lazily across us. Her cranberry margarita arrived.

What's you're coming out story?" I asked, dipping a chip in the ceviche and tasting the lime, salt, and fish tingling in my mouth. I love hearing how women found their way to being openly gay in a world that projects heterosexuality onto everyone.

"I cheated on my high school boyfriends with girlfriends."

"Well done, poor boys, they must have been crushed." She smiled and ordered another margarita.

"My mom wanted a feminine daughter in pink, frilly clothes. We had blowout fights where she would try to get me to wear dresses all the way up into high school. We still fight about it sometimes." Finn had the body of a sturdy football player. Luckily for a femme like me, the butch loves all that was foisted on her but that she rejected: the dresses, the feelings, the femininity. Whereas the man loves all that he was told to reject but was never foisted upon him. Or as comedian Hannah Gadsby laments: "He hates what he loves."

On the walk back we found a beach that had no villa or hotel directly behind it. We sat down on a towel and kissed. I wanted to draw things out—the kissing and making out. Then her fingers were inside me. Just like that I was entered. We were having sex on the beach under the round bright moon. I am constantly titillated by the carefree way a woman can just enter me. It isn't laden with consequence like it is with a man, even with his fingers. Maybe it's because I celebrate sexual boldness in women, whereas sexual aggression in men can sometimes come with entitlement or abuse.

She enters when she wants to. Then she is inside, the ride has started, and I am stinging with the need to continue and be fulfilled by her, by the promise of release that the insistent pulsing into me implies. The night was a magic blanket of darkness lit up by a sheen of the spotlight of the moon. It was as if the lighting technician from the movie *Moonstruck* had carefully placed every beam and shadow.

Wells said we could sleep in the room together that night. The shower was spacious with dark brown tile. We washed each other under the flow of steamy water. I sensed she was uncomfortable. She wasn't a Never Nude but it wasn't her preference to be naked. "I think of myself as boyish," she said. "Then I look down at my body and I'm curvy."

On the bed passion spilled over, filling up all available spaces. She wiped sweat from her face. Her ankles and calves were thick. Despite her ambivalence about her curves, soft and strong was her brand and she knew it. It had power. She pressed into me, crushing me. My whole body was alive with desire for her. Her fingers went inside again, her eyes focusing, unflinching on me with that perfect combination of seriousness and a slight handsome smile.

The next morning at the pool Athena approached me. For the first time in our decade-long friendship, I heard sharp displeasure in her voice.

"You're moving out of the room. You'll stay with Finn now. That room needs to be for Wells and Navi. They feel displaced."

I felt like a harlot being punished for her sluttish ways, banished from the castle to some neverland without an ocean view. Athena was becoming Atlas, the weight of the needs of all her wedding guests bearing down on her.

"But, but, I'm not sure that's such a good idea," I said.

"You don't want to stay with Finn?" She said Finn was staying at the adjoining house and Navi would be joining Wells and me.

"Well, what if it all goes wrong? Then we are stuck in a room together, in a bed together. We will behave ourselves, I promise."

But we didn't behave.

The more we met up in our trysts, the more I desired her. Away from the bounds of our daily lives, for this week we are lovers, we are girlfriends, we are that special person to hold and to dance with. I give everything to her. I hold nothing back. I am fearless because I can be, because I know it won't last. I sense we lack some deeper compatibility. She carries me over her shoulder up the windy stairs and throws me onto my bed.

We talked about OkCupid. She tried to make me jealous.

"There aren't many butch women on there, so I do pretty well."

So maybe Finn didn't think we had a future either. Or maybe she was testing me.

My mood was buoyant. Here was a dream of impossible ease. The bed was made for us every day. Our piles of dishes and bottles were spirited away each afternoon. Birds told us the time of day. Coffee was hot and ready each morning. The fridge was stocked. Friends wove in and out throughout the day. At any moment I could be completely alone and soulful or in the presence of one to ten friends. I was glad to know myself again as a basically happy person. I had a full satisfying life, an amazing community, a harmonious rapport with myself. And yet I was jealous of all the couples in long-term relationships. They had each other's backs through life's joys and hairpin turns. I didn't think Finn could provide that kind of love. After my hopes were crushed with Quince and the celebrity I just wanted to be in the moment with Finn. It was easier to push away all thought of the future because the present was so sexy and fun.

Finn and I sat on pool lounge chairs. I was so at peace away from all computers or phones. The sun drenched us in Mayan effulgence; some floated in the pool, others dangled their legs in.

"Who do you think is more butch, April, you or I?" asked Athena.

"I think you are because when we were at the airport, you ran to find our friend at breakneck speed and I sat and waited. Also, you've been driving us everywhere."

"But you are saying it like it's better to be butch then femme."

Why did I think butch was better in that moment? Stronger? More like a man? Oh, these tired old stories.

The next night Finn and I were on the roof of our villa, a long, flat space with a raised stage-like area in the center. Finn pressed me up against the painted, blocky fencing. Her fingers suddenly inside me, my body wet and clenching around this nexus. After a while I laid out naked on the mattress on the raised stage. She remained completely dressed while I wore only the luminous moonlight, this power imbalance adding another dimension. Her hands working my body. Looking at me. A naughty sexy look in her eyes. My naked skin out in the world. What a sensation to be naked and warm at once under the bowl of night. Her risking nothing, fully clothed. I released while her finger was inside of me with my other fingers working my clit. Then we sat up. I got on my knees and said, "What can I do to please you?"

We pulled down her pants but kept everything else on. I licked her while putting a finger inside. I believe everyone's sex has its own beat and rhythm. If you are patient enough, quiet, you can hear it and play it. I found Finn's. It made me wet all over again to hear her come, thighs clenched around my face, a helplessness and surrender that I had initiated. We held each other.

"After the first time we briefly dated, I dreamed of you for months," she said.

The next morning Athena's childhood buddy told everyone of a delicious tryst he witnessed from his window, looking out on the roof. He said he quickly looked away out of polite respect. But he wasn't respectful enough to keep his mouth shut. By noon everyone knew. We were *those* people at the wedding. I felt no shame. It provided a backdrop of hilarity.

Finn and I kissed in the pool, on the deck chairs, in the kitchen, finding clandestine moments to touch and press and wrestle. Holiday madness. A stolen honeymoon. So good to have someone to touch. So good to have a place to put all my infinite love. We massaged each other. I stroked her hair and pulled it. We were foils for Hilary and Athena who were, at this time, in a sustainable partnership full of love and commitment, all the things of marriage. Finn and I didn't have these things and probably never would, but we had the fresh lustful passion, the kind that's impossible to have after seven years together because its fuel is novelty.

Athena, Wells, Navi, some other guests and I parted from the larger group and went to Posada Marguerita Italian restaurant on the beach. A candle-lit walkway speaks of entering a temple. Our feet steeped in sand, our eyes on wooden shelves lined with mason jars holding glowing candles. There were big earthen pots reminiscent of women's round bodies, exposed brick walls, fresh and dried flowers everywhere.

We dined on a long wooden table with Mayan mythology carved into its surface. This became a sort of hen night for Athena. I had *gamberoni al guazzetto,* the prawns were perfectly stewed in a spicy tomato sauce. Each time the olive-skinned server brought a dish, he made excuses to talk to me, holding my gaze. Men can spot fresh lust a mile away.

Afterward we all got naked and splashed in the night sea, surrounding Athena and blessing her nuptials.

Back at the villa, Finn, Hilary and the others had been drinking beer. I sat with Finn by the pool. She bragged again about her game with women. In quiet retaliation I told her of the servers naked lust for me.

"What do you think of that?"

"I'll tie him up and make him watch me fuck you," she said.

"How will you fuck me?"

"Every way."

That night we had sex on the upper deck of the room she shared with another. I could have moved in with her so we wouldn't have to sneak around. But then we wouldn't get to sneak around. When she was on top of me, I asked her to talk dirty to me. She called me her *good girl.* At first I wasn't sure how I felt about it. Then I needed it. Couldn't come without it. It made her sound older than me though she was six years younger.

"I'm gonna make you mine," she said as she drove her finger into me.

Being someone's slut turns me on. But then I wonder will that person ever love me? I have never had this kink dynamic inside a long-term relationship.

Back in my room, sleeping next to Wells, I went over all the sexy moments with Finn in my mind. But in the morning I woke up nervous. I was nervous each time I re-connected with Finn, wondering if I'd be rejected. I was pretty sure we were both enjoying this lustful plot as it unfolded, but still. I told myself I couldn't do casual sex. I gave myself a good talking to. Finn and I had been a story of missed connections, bad timing, and disappointments until now.

The wedding party gathered in a slanted sandy area cooled by short coconut trees just paces from the ocean. I was set to lead a wedding ritual, the handfasting ceremony. Wells went around with the burning herb of palo santo to purify the space. Fallon handed everyone silky multi-colored ribbons. The sunlight was that impossibly cheery bright spectrum that seems to only exist in Mexico and Italy and parts of the Riviera. We gathered into a warbled circle. I wore a big hippie priestess dress of Wells' with suns and moons in muted marmalade tones. The breeze shifted about and I felt the sensual line of my body, despite the big folds of the dress. I stood in the center with Athena and Hilary next to a simple altar. Everyone looked at me with soft smiles as I began:

"Today we gather for an ancient tradition called handfasting. Each of us will have a chance to tie a ribbon and say a blessing to Athena and Hilary. The handfasting symbolizes the weaving together of the tapestry of their lives with each other and all of you—their community. This is a spiritual and symbolic way of binding their spirits together and deepening their commitment to each other."

Hilary and Athena made their way around the circle as each person tied on a ribbon around their joined hands and spoke sincerely into their eyes. All blessings ended with a hug for both of them. There were many wet eyes.

After they completed the circle, I said: "You're lives are woven together for as long as you both shall love." Then we all joined in on a sing-a-long to *Islands in the Stream,* Athena and Hilary's wedding song.

The next day we all piled into the rental van. Athena, ever the dad, insisted on driving. The beach was long and wide and went on forever. We sat at a tequila restaurant on the sand. I couldn't resist having a shot. We bought many shots, then the waiters started bringing them for free. We made drunken toasts. Friends watched me closely. They knew that on the rare occasion I drink, I can go on a binge, prone to exhibitionism and bad decision-making. I don't like the taste of most alcohol. Sometimes I drink just to access my wildness.

"It's happening," I said. There was a man playing guitar by our table and I got up to dance with him. Then I sat on Finn's lap. She put her hand between my thighs. Someone suggested we go skinning dipping in broad daylight, the beach populated, the restaurant patrons within eyesight.

Finn kept her board shorts and rash guard on. Athena, ever cautious, held her swimsuit in case we got "caught." Everyone else wore nothing but the saltwater. I was emboldened and for once didn't fear the big waves; I stayed close to Finn in the troughs between waves. I felt sure I wouldn't be carried away or under with all my friends close by giggling and splashing about.

We had done what we came there to do. We danced, dined, and got the couple hitched. We packed up to go home.

On the plane we switched seats so Finn and I could sit together. I lay on her lap and tried to jack her off with my hands. We were impossible, feral, sex-crazed as if the whole world wasn't watching and waiting.

"I wish I could take you home with me," said Finn.

I didn't let on that this made me freeze internally. I was ready to be in my own self again. But by morning I woke up with a springtime twitterpation thinking: *someone likes me.*

"We just need to see if we work in the practical, real world, April," she had said. But then panic ensued. I didn't think Finn and I were right for each other. We didn't have much in common, or much to talk about. She was a bit of a frat-boy jock who wanted to play tennis all the time. I wanted to travel, philosophize, talk about art, explore tantric sex. She had a deeper side but didn't want to access it as constantly as I do. And she wanted to have kids—that ongoing saga that I can't wait to age out of though it seems that no one ever ages out of it anymore. Laura Linney was fifty when she gave birth.

A Lyft dropped me off in front of my apartment. A notion came through: *That's not my home, I would never live there with all that sidewalk and cement.* There was an eerie gray glow on the street. As I walked up the stairs, I sensed a familiar dread that was growing each time I came home from my travels. I didn't want to be there. There was no flow of inside and outside as we had no yard or balcony or porch. Lines from "Band on the Run" started running through my head: *If I ever get outta here.* I was a country girl at heart.

Finn came over for a date a few days later. We tried to have sex but I couldn't let go enough to finish. I made her come and there was blood on my hands. In the bathroom there was blood on the toilet paper but it wasn't my menstrual time. Something we did was too rough. All the shimmering beauty of our Mayan honeymoon reduced to the smell of iron. I asked her to leave, said that it just wouldn't work. As she closed the door to my bedroom her eyes had that little sheen of moisture like the tough guy in the movie. I remembered Finn saying, "I have never lost interest in you April."

I got her back and we dated again for months, periodically breaking up due to my panic attacks. One happened after we had sex. I locked myself in her bathroom and looked in the mirror. *Why am I having sex with someone who is not my girlfriend? What does this mean? Is this what I want?* I missed sex with the dimension of love. I missed relationships with a future. This wasn't the dream of the Mayan Riviera, I was wide awake. I walked into the kitchen, not able to join her in the bedroom. Finn found me frozen like a marble statue in a plaza no one visits. She looked at me with such sweetness.

"I'm still getting used to this casual thing," I said.

She held me and guided me back to the bedroom. I clung onto her to fall asleep. I felt good hearing her breath and feeling her heartbeat. But it was an animal comfort that didn't have a future sustenance.

Despite my freewheeling nature, part of me was looking for a wife, for The One, and I didn't think I should be spending my time with someone I didn't have a future with. Finn wouldn't let me constantly deconstruct us. She was a stable palm tree that my tropical storms periodically blew helter skelter. I respected her for that.

When we had sex, sometimes she would be in a mellow mood and I would get hyper, attack her, try to tackle her. Then she giggled and called me Taz, short for Tasmanian Devil. When I stayed the whole weekend, she said, "It was nice to have lady clothes hanging around my bathroom."

She had an enormous TV on which we watched *The Hunger Games*, romantic comedies, and well-chosen movies she found from genres I usually avoided like sci-fi and fantasy. We talked about scenes we liked in movies.

"I like the part where someone searches for things, sneakily, frantically in drawers and closets," I said.

She said she couldn't watch documentaries because they consumed her for a year. For a year she'd wrestle with the cause and how to contribute to it.

One time I came over and tried to press her up against the wall and make out. She stopped me. We were at the point in the love story where she wanted to know if there was something lasting here. Beyond the sex. If we could make it "in the practical." She climbed in bed and began reading. In my mind I thought: Sure, that phase will come but why hurry it? *Why can't we just read after sex?*

But we didn't discuss this turn directly. I felt that if I said outright that I didn't want a future with her it would kill the fun we were having. I wanted more time with her. Finn mentioned a pattern she noticed: she would break up with a girlfriend, and that girlfriend would marry the next person she dated. But it was Finn who got married after we broke up. She undid the curse.

In the fall she carried pumpkin spice in her backpack and put it on everything. She said she never developed a fashion sense because she fought so hard with her mom simply for the right to wear jeans. She never had the chance to bust out in her own splash. I made my way through her book collection: Dante's *Inferno, The Happiness Project,* and *Mating in Captivity,* a brilliant read with life-changing lines like this:

"Our partner's sexuality does not belong to us. It isn't just for and about us, and we should not assume that it rightfully falls within our jurisdiction."

We liked to tell each other about the bad dates we were going on from OKCupid. This was a first for me, casually dating and sharing our escapades with each other. During the end of my time with Quince I wanted the freedom to explore more relationships with men and women. But after a few short relationships with men, I wanted a female partner again. I wanted a wife. I was lonely. Both my sisters and almost all my friends were partnered.

I told Finn about one date I went on with a woman. We weren't a match. I told her I didn't want to see her again. She did internet research before composing a 10-paragraph email disparaging me. I refused to read most of it, but I did see this sentence: "Thinks she's an artist because she made some dyke films with her sister." I took a month's break from new dates after that awful interaction.

Finn told me about a girl from out of town that she never met that texted constantly and then threatened suicide. Through online dating you cast a net out into the universe and sometimes you pull up troubled souls. Finn taught me how to date and have sex but not let it all spread out into everything, into the future, into ownership, into deeper love.

"How do I think about Finn?" I asked a friend.

"Finn's a player. She's like a rainbow. Be stoked when you see it but don't count on it. It's not like the sun and the moon that you can see every day."

Then Finn had a good date. Then she got a girlfriend. And that was that. We ran into each other on Easter for the Sisters of Perpetual Indulgence's Hunky Jesus Contest. The Sisters are philanthropic drag queen "nuns," a San Francisco institution if ever there was one. Golden Gate Park was awash with queer folks in rainbow colors and their Easter best. A line of longhaired, open chested, very gay men lined up to strut their Jesus stuff.

I had just started dating a gorgeous woman and was flirting with another one that very day. I wanted a wife, but no one claimed me so I carried on under nobody's rules.

"We should always be lovers." I said to Finn. "Let's have sex again in five years."

"Five years. That's too long," said Finn.

"We should always date people that let us be lovers," I said.

"Yes, we should."

16: WE SHAKE THE EARTH

Finn had moved on, Quince had moved on. I was scampering, gathering, dispersing, collecting, discarding. So many fishes nipping at my hook but nothing caught and if it did it would be half dead. The bisexual life, the freelance life, the first-world problem of too many options, too many dizzying possibilities. Some days I was crushed. I wanted someone to tell me what to do.

Are you kind of wondering if I ever work—or do I just travel, have sex, fall in love, break up, and write it all down? For the record, I "cobble a living together," as Allegra once put it. In this phase it was mostly life coaching, belly dance performances, giving massages, and tarot readings. Later I will add sex coaching to my cobble because—why not?

I went on a date with one of my favorite local comedians, Marga Gomez, who texted from time to time. Men invited me out on Tinder. Some lady from LA on OkCupid wanted us to have phone calls. It was great to have this interest directed at me. But it was a lot of texting, swiping, searching, with little results.

During the early years with Harper, I had so cherished our domestic life; I enjoyed being so in love and safe. Chasing after Channing, I thought I wanted him to be my husband even though everything indicated he could never be. And Quince was going to be my forever person. But a child ran right in between us. I ran into her at a mutual friend's wedding, pregnant, holding hands with her girlfriend. She looked peaceful and happy. Everything had fallen into place for her. When the music stopped, she had her chair.

All my lovers had helped me shed my erotic virginity and

push my edge. Now I was ready to meet a girlfriend, someone steady who could become my wife.

Sometimes I got hopeless, fearful I couldn't sustain sexual interest with anyone. That there was no relationship or category for me and I was doomed to my own company.

I flew through a copy of the book *Girls Like Us* about Joni Mitchell, Carly Simon, and Carol King and briefly cheered myself up by casting myself in their lot, all vivacious artists who for all their beauty, genius and fame often had trouble making love stay.

Just when I would give up hope, a lover would give it to me real good. And I returned in kind. We'd hold each other in such simple bliss that I got hopeful again. I'd climb up on the carousel, on the camel that goes up and down with its fixed overly painted grin, and go for a spin. I'd watch the pretty colors so full of potential, even though the scenery was blurred and didn't vary much. The music cheery, the ride buoyant and breezy.

As Athena says: "At night the sharks are circling, in the day they're sardines on toast." In the light of day I remembered that there is no perfect relationship or marriage. That being happy, not being married, is the most important thing. Tracee Ellis Ross says "they teach women how to plan their marriage and not how to plan their lives." Actually my parents didn't teach me either of those things. But they did let me play.

I had a belly dance performance with Celeste at Bisexual Visibility Night at El Rio in the Mission. El Rio was iconic. We were all in the back patio with the big painting of Carmen Miranda, the twinkling lights, the avocado tree, the wooden tables and palm trees. Bisexuals are the kindest folks in the queer community. Natural outcasts, always ready to please. Mom had come to see us dance. The comedian Nick Leonard hosted, introducing Carol Queen as someone who has been "phasing so long." He also said people ask him if he is a top or a bottom and he says: "I'm off to the side or nearby." Celeste and I performed to an old-school CD player that skipped when we stomped too hard. They raffled off a vagina painting and Mom won it. A band of bisexuals called The Buds played a song called "Questions in My Head."

"It's the bisexual anthem," said Celeste. After we danced, I said goodbye to my mom.

"When's your date picking you up?" she asked.

"He's here now, I have to go."

"He? It's a man?"

"Yes."

"You have a date with a man?"

"Yes."

"Who is it?"

"From Tinder."

"Really April, a man. From Tinder."

"Are you really bi shaming me at this bisexual visibility event?"

"No it's just been a while since you dated a man. Have you met before?"

Was this the queer version of a madcap conversation Debbie Reynolds and Carrie Fisher might have, I wondered.

"Mom I'll be safe. Don't you need to go find a place to hang the vagina painting?"

"Go, go, I love you."

I was taking a risk having him pick me up in his car for our first date. I saw an older Corolla across the street and assumed that was my date. But the tired Mexican man in the front seat wasn't having any of it. Then I saw a BMW sports car where the real Yusuf waited for me with a huge smile. I was immediately disarmed by his voice—English, French, and Wolof intermingling to create a charming, innocent affect.

We sat down to dinner at Bissap Baobab. Yusuf 's eyes darted, only landing on me now and again. He adjusted himself in his seat and made big, goofy smiles. I kept the conversation humming as best I could all the while thinking *This is a man April, a man.*

He drove me home. We sat in the car and talked. Finally he put his arms around me, saying "How about a hug." He turned his lips towards mine—"and a kiss." I was surprised at how hungry I was for him, how good his cologne smelled. We came into each other's spheres, two strangers lit up, kissing with the patience of teenagers, kissing as its own theatre with acts, climaxes, denouements.

Later he texted, "Tinder did a good job matching us up."

We soon found a routine of going to dinner and then back to my place. Once in my bedroom we kissed and whispered in each other's ear.

"You want me to tie you up?" asked Yusuf with his French accent by way of Senegal.

"I want you to do everything to me."

Yusuf didn't need to put me in restraints. He quickly had my thighs locked between his knees, one hand clipped my wrists together and the other was playing a small beat between my thighs. Then he whipped me onto my stomach. He butterflied my legs up around his hips. His hands pressed down on my lower back, harder than I thought I could take. I was lost in the sensation of him inside me and holding me in place. He moved down, putting his weight on me, his hand pressing my head into the mattress, his shoulder pinning my shoulder, the heat between us leaving sweat on my back.

This was the type of sex Gloria Steinem was musing about when she said the sex of her youth was mostly gymnastic.

When I met Yusuf on Tinder, I was tired of self-pleasuring. I felt like one of those 1920s pianolas where the piano keys played themselves. All his daft handling of me felt like a reward for a job well done.

Sex is best when there are two or three points of contact. For example when Yusuf was taking me from behind, his cock inside, one hand wrapped around my chest pinching my nipples, and the other holding my head down. Later, we'd be out in the world together, at a restaurant, and I'd look at him and think of what positions we'd been in. The memory was almost as intimate as the sex itself.

The black nightie I bought on a shopping trip with Athena was a hit. At sushi dinner on Mission Street I showed Yusuf I was wearing the nightie from the picture I had texted him. He mock raised his hand as if to ask the waiter for the check right then.

Back at my place, after he had wrestled my dress off, he threw me and my nightie against the only available wall in my room, the door where my coats hung. He threw me three times, harder than I was expecting, but the coats muffled the blows. He scooped me up in his arms, making me feel that carefree feeling only the young know when a giant adult can elevate them instantly. Yusuf moved me quickly from one position to the next like a savvy dancer. I love when men get creative. He was a wrestler and a boxer so his maneuvers were seamless.

I took Yusuf in my mouth. The taste of semen on my tongue had a buzz of zinging energy to it like the fermentation on the top of kimchi. The buzz continued in the back of my throat, a substance that is not food but a piece of life itself, lingering there like a potion even though I didn't swallow.

Next he moved from inside my mouth to inside my pussy. I came first. My insides became sensitive but I kept going because bisexuals are people pleasers. After he orgasmed, Yusuf slapped me on the ass, a punctuation for the end of the sentence.

Afterward, Yusuf held me in his embrace all night as if that was the natural way for two people to sleep.

"Daddy, you're my woman," I murmured to myself. I guess everything is fluid to me.

In the morning he left quickly. I caught his goofy, sweet smile framed in my door and then he was gone. Yusuf was terrible at texting me back. I sent him a YouTube video of Billy Joel's "Tell Her About It" in the hopes that he would. Tell me about it. Tell me that he likes me. Or really just stay in communication.

My roommate cornered me in the hall.

"We were just talking about you," she said.

"Good things I hope."

"When you and your African King have sex the whole house

shakes—my bed, the living room, everyone's rooms. We all ran into the hallway. We thought there was a damn earthquake."

I had a loosely hinged four-poster bed that banged against the living room wall. The fixings need to be oiled regularly or a ratchety 1970s porn sound squeaked again and again. I texted Yusuf about our predicament. This time he wrote back right away: "We shake the earth."

I went to bars for queer nights and no women flirted with me, except my friends who are flirtatious by nature. Since the Lexington closed the nexus of queer woman and trans men shifted all over the city. A Facebook group Guerilla Dyke Bar was a pop-up queer convergence where we showed up at a "straight" bar and took it over.

Maybe all the sex I had in my bedroom was a continuum. Maybe I just switched the bodies. I was always the host. My bed the stage so the scenery, for me, never changed. But I did change. They transformed me under their hands. Some even confessed love. But mostly they said, "I own your pussy, you're my slut now." They said this because I told them to. This all started with Channing. I kept writing the same script and expecting something different to happen.

I texted Yusuf: "I need to be crushed under you with your hard cock leaving me breathless."

"Oh I'll crush you, I'll do you so bad until you beg for mercy." He was compact, goofy, sweet, though very capable of being serious and dominating me.

On Tinder, I was only interested in lesbians and black men. Don't judge me. We like what we like. And as you can tell it changes a lot for me. I'm usually not attracted to white men. I tried to match with femmes because I found them sexy. I remembered a friend saying she liked taking on the role of the butch aggressor sometimes, but couldn't maintain it. That rang true for me. How long could I maintain that role? I liked holding doors for ladies, putting on their coats, taking care of their needs. I imagined a femme in my bed. I would wrap my hands around her neck, then down to cup her breasts, kiss along her smooth stomach, bring my hands to her wet sex, stroke her thighs while kissing her and keep touching her everywhere, making her all breathy, not knowing where I would strike next.

Two years after her Mexican Wedding, Athena came over for tea. We sat in my living room by the big windows where the leaves get so close it's like a tree house.

"Hilary and I are breaking up," she said in her warm but stoic fashion.

I was shocked and not shocked. Even going into their stellar wedding they both had reservations. Still, they were such anchors as couple friends; they made me dinner and listened as I talked about my latest sexual triumph or heartache. They were younger than me but it still felt like Ma and Pa were selling the farm. Everything was up in the air. Who would live in their Mill Valley home? What would become of their dog, Indigo? Where would the future they imagined float off to? I felt so far away from the days we had all been couple friends together, Athena and Hilary and Quince and April enjoying dinners, vacations, costume parties, more golden things that couldn't stay.

17: HAND ME YOUR GLASSES

I met Ace at Oakland Pride. I thought she was cute but didn't feel an attraction. Or so I thought. Ace texted the next day. The recent concatenation of dates left me feeling bored with myself. Each one felt like a tiring job interview where I had to package myself all over again. I ruminated over it but didn't respond to Ace.

Hilary and I were really *on one* that summer. We headed to Fabulosa, a queer women's campout and music festival near Yosemite that was like a tiny version of Mich Fest but without the exclusion of trans women. As we drove to pick up our rental camper van we obsessively showed each other pictures of dates, potential dates, and terrifying people on Tinder.

The van was a big beast whose walls couldn't talk but nevertheless exuded a storytelling odor. I slid into a sauna of rancid boy cologne and cheap European cigarettes. I could hear the echoes of laughter of the Danish, Dutch, and German travelers that came before us. I imagined their Aryan eyes scanning the vastness of the American landscapes and highways. Hilary and I assumed our husband and wife roles, her driving and me in the passenger seat.

Hilary gets into riffs and repeats certain song lyrics and phrases when she's in a mood. Sometimes she quotes our favorite lines form *Broad City*, like when the two young women (Ilana and Abbie) go to the college frat house and an outsider throws up his hands saying: "You kids, you are all straight and you're all gay." She makes me laugh hard.

We tried to get to Fabulosa before sunset but it was dark when we pulled in to a table of eager dykes ready to check us in, put wrist bands on us, and tell us what to do. Dykes love to tell people what to do. It wasn't Mich Fest. No one said *welcome home*, but it still felt great to arrive. This time Hilary didn't have her wife Athena and I didn't have Quince. We were on the loose.

I rushed off to score us some dinner while Hilary parked the van. There was a mellow, hushed vibe around the pool. Fabulosa was situated in a dry landscape, some trees green and flourishing, others black and skeletal, humbled by fire. A latticed shady walkway lead to a pool and an in ground hot tub. My job for the weekend was to be the Singles Coordinator hosting flirty gatherings for queer women and trans folk to meet, as if these groups were open enough for something that direct.

In the morning we walked around in our festive wear picking out babes to flirt with. Yet we looked like a couple, which sabotaged our chances.

"Maybe this is good," I told her. "They will think they can't have us, then they will discover we are available. A couple, real or imagined, has a certain magnetism." I knew this well from observing my sister Celeste and her husband Dimitry and all their girlfriends. They said the desirability was whipped up to the most profound frenzy right before their wedding.

And yet somehow the hotties were able to resist Hilary and me. On day two I walked over to the pool in my shorts and bikini top and saw Ace. I walked right up to her. I had found out she was genderqueer and comfortable with female pronouns. She looked cute in the sunshine, with long brown hair, hazel eyes, floating belly down on a unicorn.

"Hey." She smiled warmly. I crouched down next to her. Though she had long hair she was clearly more sporty than feminine.

"Sorry I didn't text you back, I had gone on too many first dates."

"So you did get the texts?"

"Yes."

In the evening Hilary, Ace, and I sat on a hill watching the outdoor concert. I was warming up to the idea of Ace. When we went back to her truck to get me a sweater I thought we might jump in and romp around but it was covered in messy blankets and backpacks. This is the thing: in addition to being torn between my desires for domestic stability and novelty, I am also torn between holding out for love and the impulse to dive in and get sexy. Maybe these are the same dichotomies in slightly different forms. Either way I am more sensitive than I wish to admit. My sensitivity and my horniness are at odds.

The next day I found a quiet meadow to journal far from the madding crowd. Ace walked by in that special way that only happens in junior high when the person you are crushing on finds you in some quiet place. We chatted about going swing dancing. I got up for a hug. My chest pressing into her felt instantly familiar, warm, soothing. We held the hug for a long time. Then she left.

A week later Ace and I met at Kezar, a bar and restaurant in my neighborhood with a Latin voodoo theme. Along the walls were Gothic altars with Saraswati and Ganesh statues. Two little skeletons held a banner that said: *Juntos por siempre*. Light filtered through big metal stars punctuated by tiny stars. Ace pulled out a list of torn papers that she'd composed with a friend, each holding a suggestion of what we could do: snuggle on the couch, hold hands, watch a movie, play poker, make out …

I didn't think Ace and I would be lovers. Our interactions had been full of awkward fits and starts. My own attraction wavered from interested to indifferent. Back at my place I put on my pajamas and glasses, changing into something a little too comfortable.

"Hand me your glasses." She cleaned them with the inside of her T-shirt. I liked this detailed act of caring. We sat on my couch and I read her embarrassing passages from my old journals. We got up and danced a little around the room. She hugged me.

"That was a great hug we had at Fabulosa," she said.

"Why are you referencing other hugs when we are hugging now?"

She came in for a kiss very slowly. Her lips were thin, soft, dry. I felt a little jolt of desire. We continued to kiss. I opened my eyes for a minute; hers were widely gazing at me.

"Are you looking at me?"

"Yes."

She moved away and the kissing evaporated. We ended up in my bedroom. I thought this might lead to something. Instead she took leave after an awkward goodbye.

I gave up on Ace again. We exchanged some unsatisfying text messages. She went off with friends to camp in Guerneville for her birthday.

The next time I saw her was at a party at Lydia's. Lydia had a funky, spacious loft apartment. Ace had a little molly so her quirkiness was even more apparent.

"So are you going to take me home?" she asked.

Why would I take Ace home? She was interested in me but there was something so aloof about her. I knew it would never last. But I was so lonely. All my friends at the party were coupled. This was the very loft Quince had moved to shortly after our breakup. I needed the night to have a happy ending.

Back at my apartment I showed Ace to my room and then went to the bathroom. When I came back she was in bed with the covers pulled up. This passive pose concerned me.

She looked around my room. "You have so many talents, like art and coaching and tarot. But you don't seem to use them."

"That's a pretty harsh thing to say. And really bad timing."

"I just mean you should do more."

"Making it worse."

I thought about just closing the door and leaving her in there. But it was my bedroom. I turned around to leave.

"Hey, hey wait," she said, getting up. She had a tank top and cotton shorts on.

"I just meant I'm impressed by you. Don't be mad. I know you do all these things. It's all over your room and you have like a million journals." At this time everyone seemed to be reading *Getting the Love You Want,* which talks about how we seek childhood patterns in adult relationships. I wondered if I was drawn to Ace because she was critical like my dad. This wasn't the first time she had said something that made me feel defensive.

She kissed me and I kissed her back. We got on the bed. We cuddled under the covers. I didn't feel like starting sex that way.

"I need you to sit up on your knees," I said. She sat up so we were facing each other. We began to kiss. Nothing came very naturally between us. Each wanted more from the other: more initiation, more touch, more topping. Though Ace claimed to be a top, I straddled her, pulsing my hips into hers.

"Have you ever used a double dildo?" she asked

"Don't talk about the double dildo," I said.

"Why, you don't like it?"

"I have never used one. But many lovers have alluded to it as if it's Bigfoot or the Great Pumpkin. If you have one let's do it, otherwise it's all hearsay and myth."

The double dildo was always one trip to Good Vibrations away, but all my relationships had ended before the purchase was made. I had been without dildos or any sex toys for about four years. I lost some in the breakup with Quince, I threw others away, I hadn't been motivated to go buy more.

Ace saw the hickies on my neck and the bruises on my breasts. I could see her almost ask, and then sigh and think better of it. Yusuf was marking his territory. When I accused him of it later he said: "like a dog."

Ace moved so she was above me and explored me with her hand. My pussy tingled under her mysterious touch. She seemed to be everywhere at once. I couldn't tell if she was inside or around the small shapes of me. But then she just stopped. Moved away. Laid back on the bed where she had started.

I didn't want to be in a position of demanding she finish. I never like someone getting me stirred up, wet, wanting, and then moving away, leaving my body full of questions, the question of every abrupt ending: *Why did you stop? Why did it end?*

"I need to put my mouth guard on," she said, hands behind her head, arms in two triangles.

"I feel like we are an old married couple."

I was too naked all of a sudden. I put on my panties and my Team Awkward tank top. I wanted to ask her why she stopped. But instead I just snuggled into her. We were both quiet for a while.

Ace took out her mouth guard and started kissing me, touching my breasts, breathing into my ear.

"You're ramping up again?" I asked.

"Yes, are you tired now?"

"I could revive."

Ace's hand was on me and then in me. Earlier she said she liked simultaneous sex. I had experienced this before. Often tops with a foot in the stone butch world like things simultaneous, they don't want all the focus on themselves, they experience the thrill of another's pleasure as if it were their own. They will go to any length to reach at me while I am reaching at them.

I moved my panties off again, took off my shirt. I felt her over her underwear, letting my fingers learn like I was touching a piano for the first time. Her moans indicated I was playing some chords. Then her breath pace quickened, her little moans were on top of each other. She came quickly, which made me so wet. She needed no recovery time.

"Do you like outside or inside?" she asked. Everyone has a different language for the body. These terms were a bit tame for me. I prefer "Do you want me to touch your clit or fuck you?" But okay.

"I like both."

"So two hands?" Her words got lost in my neck.

"Sure, or back and forth."

"Tell me a secret," said Ace.

"I have shared many secrets just being naked here with you."

I was getting close to climaxing, so I started ramping up my fantasies, mostly images of breasts. Just simple round units of measurement: moons, earths, suns. I played other little scenarios quickly in my mind. A hitchhiker giving a man a blowjob in the back seat of a car, a woman pressed up against glass taken from behind. So many quick scenes.

A friend once told me: "I came the other night thinking of you being taken from behind by a gorgeous black man. You never know what will work." These are the conversations I want to be having about sex. Naked truth.

"I like that you are traveling to other places with me right here," Ace said. This statement was such a gift. In both my relationships with Harper and Quince they felt either disgusted or mildly tolerant of my fantasies, both of them claiming to not fantasize.

"What is one of your fantasies?" I asked.

"Sticking trees inside you, and cars." She bore into me with her steady eyes. "Too soon?"

"No."

"Also jamming a lamppost into you."

"So it hurts?"

"Yes."

"Do you want to fist me?"

"I don't know, it seems kind of tight in there."

"I've never been fisted. How would you do it?"

"One finger at a time."

I came with a Ginsbergian howl, grasping for pillows. Then we slept.

The next morning she asked me to climb on top of her.

"Can I take these off?" I said tugging on her gray boy shorts.

"No. Can I take these off?"

"Yes. You can do whatever you want to me, you don't have to ask." I slipped off my panties.

I leaned over her, feeding her my breasts. "I can take deep pressure on my nipples and breasts," I said. "Harder."

"Can I watch you masturbate?" she asked.

"Already?"

The whole point of sex was to have a break from my one-woman show. But I complied. And she touched me all along my breasts, stomach, legs. Goosebumps lined my thighs, like she was my fluffer.

"I'm going to take over now," said Ace, climbing on top of me. Her fingers inside. Once again I felt that naughty joy of a woman just slipping in without permission. It's so different than when a man does this. Between two queer people it so different. We share a story. I responded to her ministrations with what she would later refer to as my "cum scream." After orgasm when I am buzzing with delight, my whole body awake on the cellular level but overall spent, I feel innocent, a virgin again, like my fantasies were worth it. It is said Aphrodite became a virgin again in the ocean after her numerous sexual encounters. I had gone back into the ocean, emerging salt-kissed and fresh.

In another session she asked if I wanted to go down on her. I declined. In truth I wasn't ready for her to be that much of a woman for me. I was even disappointed when she told me to stick my fingers inside. In clothes she was ambiguous but more male. Sometimes she kept her clothes on during sex, and I liked this. Even in just her men's cotton underwear she looked manly but in the way only a woman can. Based on how she touched me and what she said, she became man or woman. If I licked her she was a woman, though nothing was finite. For some, their stuff is always their dick, whether they have a dildo on or not. For Ace it varied.

Duality of pleasures. I took pleasure in the body of a man and the body of a woman. I leave the moment for my fantasies. I am here, there, nowhere at once. I find riches in the way a woman is dressed as a man, undresses to reveal a goddess-shaped body, then fucks me in a "masculine" way. Then holds me close as only a woman can—myself as a woman in a woman's arms.

I enjoy being the only woman in the bed. And yet I worship the feminine too. I love to anoint myself at the altar of a woman's body, to caress and squeeze breasts, to touch her until the wetness is on my hands, to make her sigh, to bring her over, to thrust inside her, to kiss everywhere, to find the pleasure in our womanly shapes pressed into each other. What is it about a woman that looks like a man? *Why does it make me helpless?*

After she left I felt satiated. But didn't know where it would lead. Yusuf wasn't responding to my texts. He seemed to have marked his territory, then abandoned it. To distract myself I purged my home à la Marie Kondo. I found the most bisexual document I own. It was one of those lists of the qualities you want in a partner. The title was: "Man 2004." In 2006 I crossed out "Man" and wrote "Woman" and left everything else the same.

Ace didn't send satisfactory post-sex texts.

I wrote her a half hour after she left: "Thank you for sharing yourself with me."

She wrote: "Thank you and you are welcome." Then silence.

She texted again at 10pm: "Thinking of you." Which was too little too late. I remembered that when we had already started to have sex she abruptly stopped and wanted to put in her mouth guard. I was sure I should give up on Ace. And I wondered where Yusuf went.

The next day I journaled in block letters variations on the sentiment: "Zero Fucks Given. I am done with Ace and Yusuf and dating people." They both started texting but I didn't respond for one whole day — a text eternity.

I had a phone call with Ace explaining to her that I didn't feel good about the lack of affirming post-sex texts.

"You keep rejecting me. This isn't my usual course. Being rejected again and again. And then me pursuing you again and again," she said.

"I don't want to see you again." We got off the phone.

The anger I felt quickly passed. A couple days later I went to a queer party called Mango at El Rio bar. I found my friend Talia and we joined our single friends on the dance floor, our eyes aggressively searching for mates. The dancing was just a pretense for our animal hunt. Maybe tonight would be the night we found a girlfriend. The person we would run errands with, adopt a dog with, wear coordinating outfits with, and have sex with until we stopped having sex. And then it would be time for couple's therapy. Either way, all roads lead to therapy.

Talia and I left to eat dinner at a Thai restaurant across the street. I asked if we could go say hi to Ace next store door in Virgil's. I was behaving like a teenager.

We walked over and she was standing outside with a big smile wearing a Canadian tuxedo with a plaid shirt. Hair pulled back in a ponytail. I thought I glimpsed a quick flicker in her eyes that said: *Oh you are that special person I think about these days when I think about relationships/sex/lust.* I hugged her. She said she was leaving and asked if I wanted to come back home with her.

"I do want to, but I shouldn't," I said. In my mind this meant *because you don't make me feel good about myself.*

She looked at me, then slipped away between two cars. A few minutes later she texted: "Rejection number 5."

But then I got lonely again a couple days later. I was in Oakland finishing up a life coaching training weekend. I texted her: "Wanna watch a movie?"

"So you want me to pick you up?" she asked. I did.

We planned to watch a movie on her sofa. What a luxury to have a sofa in your bedroom. I sat with my back to her.

"Can you scratch my back a little?" I asked.

She scratched. Then she petted me. Her hands reached greedily around to my breasts. Her lips and hot breath were on my shoulder and the edge of my neck. I was pressing against her. She had so much to explore, so much for her hands to do on the front and side of me, on my thighs, all with my back to her. My breath deepened.

"Come to bed," she said.

She was on top of me. The missionary position is such a boring name for an enticing, delectable pressure of body to body. This is the only thing missionaries got right.

Her legs were long. Mine were bent around her. The universal image of reception and aggression like there was something she just had to put into me. Something I needed. After a while of humping, kissing, neck nibbling she said: "Shall I put something on?"

"Music? Yes, what do you have?"

"Not music."

"Oh. Yes. Put something on."

I was naked. She had her t-shirt and boxers on. She put on some jeans and a beige-colored cock.

"That looks big."

"Too big?"

"No. Let's try it."

I was guiding it into the elusive entrance I searched for with my tampon as a jeune fille. The tip finally flipped past a narrow opening for a bigger one. She thrust in me from above. My whole body opened and warmed around her. Before long she was making those delicious quick moans, endearingly feminine.

They increased. She was in in in me. Then she came and came to stillness. Like a premature ejaculating teenage boy. But she wasn't just a boy. And her quick pleasure pleased me to no end. I loved that she could come like this without my hands. If she was a cis boy it would be a cliché for her to come before me. I don't know if she ever felt like a woman but she had lived in the world and been treated like one and because of that it was different than just being with a man.

I have had to use my hands for so many things in life—for massaging people, for writing, for sex. And I like it, I do. But this I also liked. Having this woman, teenager, man, boy lover grunting into me. And then being still. She took care of me with her fingers. Her face close to mine. When I came she put her hand over my mouth to spare her roommates but also because she knew I would like it.

One of the sweetest things Ace said to me was this: "There's no point in my coming after you come. You coming is me coming."

Late the next night I texted Yusuf: "One hour until your birthday. Wish we were having birthday sex."

I wore a red bathrobe two sizes too big. My nose was congested so some of my breaths were really snorts. The night before I pumped yeast medicine up my pussy and later that day blood starting flowing out of it. The entrance to my vagina itched. There was a heating pad over my stomach. I was too cold to bother washing my hair so it acquired a greasy sheen. But Yusuf didn't need to know any of that. I sent him an older pic of me in my scandalous black nighty with the mesh skirt and black sequined thong. We scheduled a date for a couple of days later.

When that day came he texted. "Can we postpone until the weekend, I am swamped at work."

To which I replied: "What's work's name? Is she blond?"

I already knew Yusuf had another "girl" as he put it. I asked if we should have a threesome. He said, "She would be so jealous, she doesn't look like you." I flushed at the unexpected compliment, even though it was at someone else's expense.

A couple days later I was house sitting with Hilary. We watched the sex scenes from *Blue Is the Warmest Color.*

"They just did a close up of her *pussy,*" said Hilary, drawing out the word in pleased awe. Only in a French fantasy would a near virgin have that kind of sex—so many positions, so much scissoring the first go round—but what a joy to behold.

I texted both Ace and Yusuf: "What are you wearing?"

No response.

I scrolled around Tinder and found the best profile ever: "I'm single and pregnant. I do and live comedy. Come at me."

Second best. A feminine lady named David who wrote only: "My name is not David."

In the morning I got two photos. Yusuf's was all chest, one hand taking the selfie the other covering his cock where it might have photo bombed the picture. Ace was wearing a shirt with the chest open. They both looked good. And they both wanted photos of me. I sent them a pic in a white see-through t-shirt, my nipple propped over the edge.

While I had sex with Ace or Yusuf, my roommates were usually in the living room watching a "Friends" re-run marathon laughing hysterically, their hilarity punctuating our sex like a sitcom laugh track.

Ace and Yusuf both liked to pick me up with my legs wrapped around them and fling me down on the bed so they were on top of me. They also liked to put an arm under my leg to shove me open so their cocks could go deeper.

A documentary's theme is discovered in the edit. A collage is so much chaos until you step away. Things always have an inherent pattern but time and distance are required for us to see it. There have been several times in my life when I have dated two people at once. It never lasts more than a couple of months. It never feels fitting to my nature yet it excites me. I found a sort of hodgepodge wholeness in having Yusuf and Ace in my life at once.

Yusuf opened the car door with a hand-fluttering royal flourish, called me princess, paid for every meal, told me how hot I was, deferred to me in everything, and had a generally sunny disposition. Ace was deadpan, with a flat affect, sometimes brooding, and said little cutting things wrapped as jokes that made me feel terrible about myself.

So these duo relationships left me in clip, rotating back and forth between the good cop and the bad cop, the one who lifts me up and the one who brings me down. My multiplicity, threaded through my bisexual nature, found expression in their contrasts. Allegra likes to point out that bisexuality isn't about masculine and feminine, it's about wanting sameness and difference.

Bi-phobia doesn't begin to describe it. It's actually a phobia of ambiguity—of things that are neither here nor there. And was I trying to weave together two threads of my being by dating two lovers at once, not clearly drawn always on sex, but on their treatment of me. In other words, I couldn't have survived Ace without Yusuf. When one burned me the other was there to provide salve. I explored dating and casual sex with more confidence when I had Quince as my girlfriend, my anchor to return to. Without her I was just flung out on my own.

In my restless 20s I couldn't fully appreciate the domestic love of Harper. In my exploratory thirties I still wanted lots of sex with men. In my later thirties I was finally ready to "settle" down. And that began the hardest period. Just because I wanted it doesn't mean I wasn't afraid of putting everything into one person, afraid of loss. Nor did it mean I would find that person.

The brief times of dating two at once kept me safe from anyone being able to leave me fully alone. When I told Ace I was dating someone new she said: "Don't use me to keep yourself safe from being vulnerable to her." But that is exactly what I was doing. Because it was a long time since someone had my back. So I maintained my own back and cultivated detachment through safety in numbers.

On Tinder I searched for a handsome butch or androgynous woman. One with breasts I could grab and kiss and a soft body I could snuggle into. On Tinder I found tons of men but few women. The men were quick to respond, forward with making plans to meet. I will never fully understand the motivations of men. Though when I try to assign deeper meaning the simplest explanations apply: They want to stick their dick in me.

I was beholden to no one. Under no butch rules to not date cis men. No man could entertain paranoia that I really wanted to be with a woman. No one could accuse me of cheating. I made no agreements, no promises. People could have me, my body, but only during the time that they had me. I was free.

I went on a date at Samovar Tea House with a woman from Tinder. We were flirting in full-color flourishes. When she said she didn't want kids I said I wanted to propose. We both had to go, she to a meeting and me to give a massage. She walked me to my bus on 18th Street. She stopped suddenly, turned to hold me in her gaze and said, "You don't date cisgendered men, do you?"

Her tone was serious and hostile. Everything seemed to hinge on my answer. And I should have said: "I date whoever I want. I just met you 30 minutes ago." But I didn't. I said I hadn't dated a cis man in a while and probably wouldn't again. Which was a lie. Her words had pushed me up against a wall. I had looked into her severe eyes and told her what she wanted to hear. I cringe myself to sleep recollecting these moments of self-betrayal.

I loved to be pressed belly down into the bed; smothered into softness by a woman or man. With a man I liked to disappear as they disappear inside of me. My pleasure came from believing in the moment that I existed purely for their pleasure. The more I gave myself over to pleasing them the more they protected the revelation of my own pleasure. It was never a simple game of sadist and masochist. The more I submitted the more feminist they became. There was a tenderness awakened in men when I insisted on being on my knees or tied to the bed. Sometimes this tenderness happened in the bedroom. Sometimes it showed up more subtly in our day-to-day interactions. Sometimes, I am sure, they confused it with love. There was a great freedom in tossing myself aside, of looking after their pleasure first and finding that my lover became my pleasure's boldest defender.

The more decency I surrender, the more their sexual generosity is sparked. Everyone's needs are met.

Ever since Quince, I settled for halfway loves. I thought I had found something lasting with the celebrity…but I had not. I was in partnerships that I knew were temporary with Finn, Ace, Yusuf. There's a freedom to this. I could be my true self without fear of abandonment. I didn't have to change them because they weren't mine. There was even a thrill to never knowing how long it would last. When we had sex I gave everything, I even loved them in the moments we united. It was adult- and sex-positive. We mingled among our married friends, knowing they weren't enjoying all the edges we inhabited.

And it was also the saddest thing ever because I was still so wired for deep commitment. I didn't plan to be a slut. I hadn't met my wife yet, so in the meantime another me was born. I used to be cherished. I used to be someone's everything and they were mine. Troy was mine, Harper, Quince. There is a lizard part of my female brain that hopelessly equates sex with love. That wonders how two people can do such a thing and not fall madly in love. That wonders how I can do such a thing outside the canopy of a love with nothing to hold on to.

The problem with being a woman is sometimes after sex I feel this small golden rope come out of my pussy; it links to the person I slept with. The further the distance they are from me emotionally, physically, the more I feel this terrible tug. I am opened up and at their mercy. They have walked away somehow with my energy and only having them inside me again brings relief.

But that's only sometimes. If it were every time it would destroy me.

Ace had her clothes on and I was naked on top of her.

"Do you want me to be mean to you?" she asked.

"What's our safe word?" I countered.

"It's ow, ow, ow, that hurts."

I was feeling vulnerable lately, wanting her to be tender and loving towards me. Wanting her to cherish me. But that seemed boring. I wasn't seeing Ace for tenderness. I was seeing her for excitement. So I asked her to be mean to me.

I know reader, I know. I am exhausting! You would be too if you shared all your inner world.

"Go get the cock and wash it and bring it back here." I snuck through the hallway, past my roommate's doors, holding a concealed cock. I made it back undetected and set it on the bedside table.

"Climb on top of me backwards."

She knew I was freezing so she cocooned me in my fluffy feather duvet. My ass faced her.

"Take off your panties." I slid the lacy black panties off.

I lay forward so my chest was on her thighs. I held the back of her knees with my hands. She spanked me. Then rubbed her hands gently over my cheeks. Then spanked me, not hard enough to make me scream or beg for mercy. I loved that the front part of my body was so warm, so nestled to her, and that my ass was exposed to the elements and her whims. Then she spanked me really hard, the sharp sting sailing up my legs and I screamed out and clutched her tighter even though she was the source of the pain. I moved my hands down to her ankles and held on there.

Ace said she always seemed to date women at their kinkiest. I think about that. Yeah, this was my kinkiest.

She put her jeans on and had the cock that matches her skin color peering out. She made me mount her reverse cowgirl style. It singes, sears into me, hitting the back of some internal flesh that wants to be left alone.

I couldn't do that position for long so I had her climb on top of me, my thighs opened up to take her. She came so quickly like this. We were both intensely satisfied by the orgasm of the other. At first her sounds were too womanly. Then I couldn't get enough. I listened with every part of my ear, listening as someone listens for a sound that could save them. That she could come inside me like a man but still be a woman fed me deeply.

"Hold on to my shoulder I'm going to move you." I clung monkey-like to Ace and she placed me on my back sideways on the bed so my neck was tilting over the edge. Then she explored me with her fingers. She made me come with her hands.

Yusuf and I got back to our weekly dates. He was still seeing the other girl. He picked me up in his tiny car. I asked him continuation questions on the few threads of his life I knew of: his mom, his sister, his boxing. We shared plates at Magnolia's on Haight Street: dates wrapped in bacon, devils on horseback.

In my bedroom Yusuf found a new way to tie me up. He wrapped silky rope around my arms and torso. I climbed on top of him and our hips fused. From time to time he tightened the rope. Her never had the look of the sadist in his eyes. His gaze was steady with the warmth of the trustworthy. All these theatrics were exhilarating but we couldn't come that way. He placed me below him and locked me in a tight box with his arms and torso as he thrust into me, his chest toppling into me, his heartbeat so fast, his body so hot, his breath the quickness of a runner. For once he didn't take care of me. That's when I realized he was stoned. I prompted him to get between my legs, give those quick licks of the tongue that did the trick. We spooned each other all night, but something was fading away.

18: DOUBLE FANTASY

My fantasies were eluding me, so I watched porn to create something new.

A young woman with huge breasts is on a bed sitting on white sheets. You never see the man who speaks to her, seems to be filming her, and then fucks her. He is all around her, his hand grabbing, his voice disembodied. He is the all-seeing eye of the camera. She becomes every young woman wanting to explore the archetype of the slut. Her breasts bounce under her white t-shirt. He reaches out to grab them. She wears blue eye shadow, her face painted and at odds with her casual clothes. He asks for a peek at her pussy, which looks like a symmetrical oyster. Then she covers it back up. Her shirt comes off. He is everyman, hungry for something she has in bounty: soft, fresh, insatiable youth and beauty. His face and torso are never revealed. He has gray legs and his paltry body hair is wispy and hideous. Every porn is *Beauty and the Beast* stripped of any pretense of romance. It's a chance for the actress to meet the Bogeyman and just let him do what he must instead of wondering anymore. His cock rubs up and down her big breasts. Her eyes look up for instruction, outlined in kohl, always asking *what's next*.

Finally she is on the bed, the camera over her. Their sexes slap against each other with as much ceremony as someone slapping a rug against a fence to whip out the dust. Slap, slap, slap, slap. She looks nauseous. In close-up the cock and the pussy, hair-free, look silly, make-believe, rubbery. It ends with him coming in her. When he comes in her mouth she looks visibly ill, unable to sustain the illusion. This one will not make it into the fantasy file.

What might have been the vast cosmos of my fantasies if I

wasn't raised on images of hot rape written by men, on scenes where the woman gets thrown down on the ground and the man comes and rescues her? There must be so much more than these tales of rescue and bludgeoning. The women of earth's first twilights, of caves, the women of jungles, the woman of farms, the women of prairies, must have had their own luscious musings. But of what?

Thanksgiving night I rode BART to Ace's place in Oakland. I texted her before departure to confirm the time. She wrote: "I got my period. I just want to lie around and argue."

She picked me up in her truck at MacArthur Station in Oakland. I'd now been crossing the bridge for sex for a couple of years, for Finn and others. They picked me up at MacArthur Station or Lake Merritt. In the beginning they came out and greeted me. Later they just sat in the front seat as I hopped in.

Once in her room she had me lie belly down on the sofa, using her fingers to drive inside me. She struck some primal place of helplessness and surrender. I knew I couldn't come that way but I could be panting in this position for a sexual eternity. The rest of my body became peripheral. I lived in a small space in and around my sex. She was beating at a secret door inside me. I looked for the rest of me but it wasn't there. I needed to release this building pressure, this helpless new heartbeat. Breathy moans came from me. I felt self-conscious belly down, ass up, all naked on the sofa and her with naked legs and a 1980s hoodie framing her boyish face.

"You want to turn over?"

I turned over because it was all too much. I needed it to go somewhere or I would just be a hungry animal with one pulse in one location, only that.

When I came I needed to anchor myself. I squeezed her torso with one hand, the sofa with the other, and screamed to let loose all the electricity she had built up in me.

You never know which time will be the last time. The last time Ace and I had sex I was wearing a Say Anything t-shirt, sleeves cut off, John Cusack holding the stereo up over his head. Ace wore a faded t-shirt with Vanity Smurf admiring himself in a mirror.

"John Cusack and Vanity Smurf are having sex right now. Combined with us that's double gay sex," I said.

Ace didn't put on the big double-dipped cock I'd grown to like. She put on a smaller purple cock.

"Because I want to fuck you really hard," she explained.

She straddled me and poured lube on it. Then she held me in her marble stare.

"Are you ready for some cold cock?" I was.

Once inside she held my ass in her warm hands and slapped me across my right cheek, the left hand still cradling me. She had gotten really good at all manner of slapping. Our warm-up had become me lying on top of her, legs bent around her while she slapped me on the ass. Then she would search for evidence with her fingers.

"This makes you so wet," she said. "You're always so ready. Such a sex kitten. You should reject me sometimes."

I felt exposed. I was just a common open mouth of a woman ceaselessly begging for cock to go in. She wanted me to play a game of withholding. I had no game. I did want sex most of the time. I probably needed someone who wanted it as much as I did. Ace had a teasing style of talking that was getting more and more hard to bear. She was a scientist, I her experiment. She would say something nice and look at my face for a reaction. Then say something mean and look for a reaction. She seemed to not differentiate between the two. But I did.

I told Ace it was over on the phone. Her flat affect was in full passive force, though I did hear more sighing than usual.

"It seems like there is no place to talk about this. Like you have already made up your mind."

"We can talk about this. And I have already made up my mind."

Maybe her flat affect was rubbing off on me. When I got off the phone I wasn't sad. We had achieved a pretty successful friends-with-benefits thing.

When a relationship dwindled I always visited my ex's Facebook page, sometimes scrolling all the way down to when they still wore dresses. I avoided the dashing pictures. I found some old one where their fashion was faulty, their skin scratchy, their face frozen in an off-kilter expression. I said to myself *See they're not that hot, just let them go.*

I couldn't visit Yusuf on Facebook as we were never friends there. Things were winding down with him too. He texted that he was going to Paris for most of the winter. We made plans to see each other when he got back knowing we wouldn't. There was an ease and grace to this. Yusuf and I never did anything in the day together, he only existed at night, driving me in his little car, taking me to dinner, ravishing me in my bed. He was the perfect man for me in that he didn't want to be my boyfriend or have a future or to break my vagina having his children. He only wanted what I wanted, which was to enjoy each other's company, date, have sex, snuggle. Neither of us showed signs of a growing affection. We were effusive in our compliments about each other's bodies, the currency we shared. We treated each other with kindness and respect.

Ace took up more mental space than Yusuf, which speaks to the secondary place of men in my life at that time. Or maybe it was just that Ace and I processed and Yusuf and I just ate and had sex.

It was my mom I went to therapy with, even though it was my dad whom I didn't speak to for seven years. I'm more vulnerable to women. I am a Mama's Girl.

19: WHIP ME, LEATHER DADDY

I found myself unattached again, so it was time to explore the outer edges of sex, its tantric circles, its kinky parties, its devious overtures in the night. Athena was getting kinkier by the day. It was like witnessing someone join a fitness craze except hearing about someone's workout is desperately boring while hearing about someone getting tied up and whipped is infinitely fascinating. Athena and Hilary were both blossoming sexually post-divorce.

The party was called Crave. The invite read: "An inclusive women's party—we warmly welcome queer, transgender, gender nonconforming and cross-dressing kinksters at this event. Please note that cisgender men will be politely asked to leave. … come relax and kick back in your comfiest pajama pants, onesies, boxers, nighties or slippers!"

It was located at the Citadel, San Francisco's "premier dungeon space." Though their logo showed a castle on the hill it was in fact a building tucked away on a nondescript street in the Tenderloin District. You had to look for red double doors behind a metal gate.

Though I'm no Pollyanna, this party was already pushing my comfort zone. I went with Athena and Talia. On the ride over to meet Athena, Talia and I discussed what we were comfortable with.

"We've been friends for years but never done kinky stuff together," I said.

"I'm going to keep my clothes on but I'm open to whatever."

We walked to the entrance and were greeted by a young man

who didn't ask for IDs. We ascended the stairs and were met by three women in lingerie. One of them appeared to be a trans woman. They exuded joviality in their bright smiles. I realized I was finally at the slumber party I never knew I wanted to attend.

The first room had a bar with hors d'oeuvres of ranch dressing and celery and carrot sticks, open faced BLTs on thick French bread, brownies (with a gluten-free option of course) and a hot chocolate making station. The place smelled of the aftermath of the Industrial Revolution: metal, wires, cement things whose only odor is a kind of iron bitterness. San Franciscans like to make their playgrounds out of warehouses. A leather-clad lady was selling ropes, whips, and sex toys. Above a curved white leather sofa was a "fish tank," a small glass rectangle where compact BDSM scenes would later ensue.

More erotic virginity lost! On the table was a place to write your name on a sticker and add your New Year's resolution. There was also a sign-up sheet with only one slot left for the fuck machine. I pictured it as an electric bull with an erection on its back that you straddled. I wanted to put my name on the list, but I wasn't ready to commit.

Most people were wearing lingerie but there were also pajama bottoms and t-shirt combos, long silk robes over lingerie. Across from the sofas was the dungeon, two doorless openings chained off with a sign instructing that only people doing scenes could enter. Black and red metal beams ran along the roof and down in pillars. We found a seat where we had a full view of two scenes.

In the first, a naked person was tied to a wooded structure shaped as two X's facing each other. They wore a collar and sported an erect penis. A woman in a white teddy was whipping them with a long black whip. In another area, a femme in tight black slacks, shirt, and kitten heels was bending a woman over a black leather beam and spanking her with her bare hands. We caught sight of Athena and returned with her to the locker area. She took off her pants to reveal thigh-high socks, black panties, a black cotton bra and high heels. She layered a Japanese style robe over it. She was all smiles and beauty, clearly in her element.

"Can I take my shirt off here?" I knew strip clubs required nipples to be covered when alcohol was served.

"You can be completely naked here," she said.

I took off my clothes and put on my nightie with the bra top and the see-through mesh skirt. Under that I put a short red mini skirt that just covered my lacy maroon panties. I put on lace-trimmed black socks that ended just under my knees. Talia wore her pajama bottoms and a t-shirt. Now that we were properly undressed for the fete, we made our way back into the beverage socializing room. I made myself a mocha with marshmallows. Talia tried to convince me to sign up for the fuck machine, a whole new dimension of peer pressure. I wanted to see the 10:30pm demo first.

Talia introduced me to a woman with short black hair and kind blue eyes dressed head to toe in leather. I couldn't help noticing that behind Leather Daddy was a woman in a red leather teddy. Her hands were tied behind her back as another woman pulled her arms further behind her. Everywhere I looked there was something extraordinary happening in the periphery.

"Have you ever done a scene?" Leather Daddy asked, snapping my focus back.

"Do you like pain?" asked Daddy. Athena and Talia were clearly curious about my answer.

"I don't like a ton of pain. I like that line of pleasure and pain. I want to experiment and find my edge."

"Okay, I'm going to get set up. We can try a few things and see how it feels."

"That sounds great. I'll meet you in there."

The floor of the dungeon was cast in colored light squares like a 1970s disco. There were bowing bars, human-sized cages, a round table to be pinned to, a mattress on the floor covered by a sheet with metal chain link creating a permeable barrier. Leather Daddy had her gear set in front of one of the St Andrew's Crosses.

"What are you wanting to experience?" Here was the question. Instead of sexual acts just happening as in every film or novel or porn ever made, I was being *asked to communicate what I really wanted.*

"I like ass spanking and whipping. We can experiment with pain levels. Would you like pulling my hair?"

"Yes I like hair pulling," she said.

"Do I need a safe word?"

"Sure, do you have one you like?"

I didn't have a new one and didn't want to recycle the one I used with Channing ("Thai Noodle") or any lover since. "We can use 'celery' I guess."

"Yeah, you may just get out 'cel' and I'll back off. How do you feel about having rope around your breasts?" As we talked a voluptuous Latina woman in a teddy was being bent over a black bar. Her dom began spanking her and whispering in her ear. Another woman screamed out in yelps that matched the sound of her being struck.

"Yes, rope around the breasts sound good," I said. "Standing in the Way of Control" was playing.

All the music was great. Lots of pop diva ballads, none of the dark industrial I had feared.

"Do you feel comfortable taking off this nightie?" Off the nightie went along with the little red skirt. Athena and Talia were on the sofas watching through a big doorway. When I looked over, their eyes sparkled, they looked on the verge of a giggle, they gave a thumbs up. Leather Daddy wound the rope below and around my breasts so they were framed. It was not smooth silky rope, but course and scratchy. She put leather handcuffs on me.

"Turn around and put your hands up." She pointed at the wooden X of the Cross. There was a metal hook for the cuffs to link into. "If that's too high I can bring a rope down to meet it."

"Yeah it's a bit of a stretch."

She looped rope through so I could bring my arms down a little.

"You can also do thumbs up or down for pain levels. Are you ready?"

"Yes."

She began whipping my ass so hard it stung, all too much too fast.

"That was like a level 10, I was looking for more of a level 4. Let's work up to that."

"Sorry, I get so excited."

She got a good rhythm going and quickly achieved a fine balance between pleasure and pain. Fiona Apple was singing "Criminal" in the background. I told her I couldn't handle any whipping on the side of my body so she stayed focused on my back, butt, and legs. I thought I would want to scream out but I wasn't moved to make any sounds. Fiona screamed for me about angles and devils.

I looked through the X at the Latina woman who was now being fisted. Her eyes were closed and she was moaning. I watched her as my body pulsed back and forth from the whip.

Leather Daddy pulled my hair and my neck back so far I could almost see Athena and Talia behind me. I loved the animal roughness of it. The way my neck was almost stretched too far. I am very protective of my neck yet I love for it to be held and to stretch as my hair gets pulled. Letting someone control my neck is my way of letting go of control and entering risk and trust.

"Can you do some after care in between?" I asked.

"Sure." She whipped and then soothed me with caresses bringing me into more full engagement with the experience. It was hard to fathom that my friends were nearby watching me. I had come a long way since being Harper's girlfriend, having shy masturbatory sex and not knowing what I wanted or how to ask for it.

Then she put her thigh out as a sort of ledge and bent me over it. She spanked me. This position, the body contact, brought my skin to life. A retro Madonna song, "Don't Tell Me," came on. This electronic folk song has a plaintive way of saying: do what you want and don't let people stop you from it.

She started spanking harder than I would usually allow. I let myself see how much pain I could take. I let sounds come out, whimpers and moans.

"How was that?" she asked, caressing my butt.

"That was good. I took some more pain for you."

"I appreciate that."

She unhooked my wrists, took off the cuffs, unwound me. She looked me in the eyes.

"It was really nice to connect with you," she said.

"You too." I felt alive with electricity.

"Do you want to get tied up and suspended sometime?"

"Sure, I've never done it but I'd like to try."

"Let's exchange contacts. There's a place on Tuesday nights that I go to." (Don't get excited about me being suspended. I never got to play with Leather Daddy again).

We hugged. My whole body was shaking. The shaking got smaller but never subsided through the night.

I joined Athena and Talia for the fucking machine demonstration. It was not, as I had imagined, a mechanical bull with a dildo. The receiver was in a swing lying back with feet in stirrups as if giving birth. The fuck machine looked like a small movie projector with a large dildo on the end. A tall femme with spikey pink hair was operating the machine. She got on her knees, put a dental damn over the woman's pussy and licked her. And then penetrated her with the machine. It was all a bit much for me.

Athena and I sat on the sofa for a while chatting. I ate a BLT and celery sticks with ranch dressing. What a comfortingly predictable party snack is celery with ranch dressing. No wonder I picked it as my safe word. I walked back into the dungeon. Just above us in the "aquarium," a naked woman was being spanked.

Talia came up behind me and rested her hands just below my shoulders on my arms. It felt sweet. Like she was framing me. She massaged my shoulders with a wonderfully firm touch. In front of us a tall woman in kitten heels, classy black pants, and a tight black blouse, and full makeup was fucking a bent over woman with a dildo. She was doing it with an attitude that said *That's right bitch that's what needs to be done.*

"Do you guys want to do a scene?" asked Athena.

"Yes, let's do!" I said. "Let's go over to that bed."

We spread clean white sheets over the floor level plastic mattress. I draped myself over Talia in spank position so that my lower half was over her, butt up, and my upper body was draped over Athena, who stroked my hair. Talia spanked me with her hands and various paddles. I felt so loved.

Next it was Athena's turn. "How do you want me?"

"On all fours," I said.

Who was I? Athena was my friend, sister wife, priestess, witch woman. We had never had sexy time unless you counted eight years ago when we kissed under the mistletoe in front of Hilary just for laughs. Though I found her beautiful, I had never wanted to be her lover or vice versa. Then how was it she was in a bra and panties on all fours in front of me? Talia began spanking away.

"Can I pull your hair?" I whispered into her ear.

"You can do whatever you want, I'm your little bitch," she said.

She giggled as Talia spanked her. She was letting us witness her submissive self. I felt honored that she trusted us with this. I pulled her ponytail back as Talia spanked alternate cheeks. I looked at Athena's svelte body, the mild wave in her spine that I fretted about because I knew she had chronic back pain. But she seemed alright now. I spanked her.

"Can I pinch your nipples?" I asked.

"Yes," she said.

I pinched her nipples hard. I was caught up in a moment. More than anything else I did that night, that was the strangest line to cross. When you get to your edge, there's another edge, just out of reach, just a nipple away.

"That was amazing!" said Athena.

Then we draped Talia over us and alternatively massaged her and spanked her ass. Leather Daddy was nearby at yet another X whipping another woman with wavy black hair and big tits. Beyoncé was singing "Partition," telling her Daddy how she wanted it with her lyrics, and I had to reposition myself to watch Leather Daddy as I spanked Talia.

I wondered if I should be totally focused on Talia and not have a wandering eye. But I figured the whole point of this kind of public sex was an immersive feeling. Leather Daddy walked over to her sub, took hold of her big soft breast and squeezed. It was incredibly hot. I am sucker for that particular act. When she stepped back the woman looked so wistful, stoned, satisfied, like my massage clients looked after an hour-long massage. There are so many roads to therapy, release, pleasure.

The three of us changed our clothes. "Girls we vini vidi viched that sex party," I said. Athena got in a Lyft. I got in Talia's car and she drove me home. We were pretty quiet. I felt so comfortable with myself. I could have just been a voyeur but I stepped into the action.

Horny Reader, guess what? You could choose your own adventure and end the book right here. Listen to this editor make a compelling case for that:

I think there's something about ending this memoir at the sex party that could make for a much more compelling conclusion… For me, this is a denouement in more ways than I think you give it credit for. How remarkable to both show up and leave without a lover, per se, and to be okay with that because you discover more of yourself while you're there. How remarkable that your friends, for a brief moment, become lover-like. How remarkable that all of your experiences with your lovers until now have allowed you the assuredness and curiosity to arrive here, to strip down (there's that 'shedding' again), to have your friends behind your back, and so on. I think you could dive deeper into these sex-party scenes as a culmination of what you've told us so far in the book.

So there you go! All done. Close the book.

Or you can ride this tawdry-ass wave until it crashes into the cold, dead sand.

20: BILLIE AND THE RADICAL FAERIES OF MENDOCINO

Coco came over in her glittery skirt and sat on my bed as I primped at my vanity. When I first met her she was super wasted and sat on Quince's lap and I wasn't jealous because she was that fabulous drunk girl. By day she was a corporate badass and by night so fun to party with. You know that scene in the movie where the dressed-to-kill femme takes over a boardroom and gives an epic presentation and wins the client? I'm sure that's not what Coco did (or what anyone with a corporate job does) but it's how I pictured her.

"Let's look at our Tinder matches," she said. We had matched with a couple of the same Masculine of Center women. "Here, you can take Billie, who is a stunning black woman with two sexy face shots and no words about herself."

She showed me another girl with serious eyes and short black hair.

"You might like her."

"No," I said, "too skinny. You go for it."

"Naw. Now that I am doing Olympic lifting I don't like the skinny ones either." Don't you just love Coco? Party girl, businesswoman, Olympic lifting!

"Oh, I almost forgot, I matched with this cute girl just to make sure you wouldn't miss her. Look. Her name's Bo," I said.

"Hold on, oh, she already matched with me. She's cute." (Coco and Bo will fall in love and I will take FULL credit for it and tell this story to anyone who will listen.)

"Should I ask Billie to meet us out tonight?"

"Sure, "she said.

There is some rule of dating regarding not asking someone out as soon as you match. And another cautions against crowded events lacking the initial intimacy required of a meet cute.

I texted her anyway. She responded that she would like to meet up but she was already going to a queer party in Oakland called Ships in the Night. Of course she was. Being single and queer is like improv, you have to say *yes* to everything social.

I pulled a dress out of the closet that had a black skirt and a polka dot top with a sliver of a belt in between.

"Yeah I love you in that one," said Coco.

"You've seen it before?"

"A bunch of times. But I've known you for years. It will be new to everyone else."

I put it on but made a mental note to buy new dresses or get new friends. I put on heels I bought for sex, the kind that are only comfortable when horizontal and no weight bearing is involved. I asked Coco if we would be Lyft chauffeured or if I would need sensible shoes.

"We will be Lyfted, wear those, they look hot."

We went to Guerrilla Dyke bar at Blind Cat. This was the neighborhood I lived in when I first moved to San Francisco, when I first met Kunal and Quince. It had become much more gentrified with hipster coffee shops and vegan donuts.

It was a parade of faces that I had and hadn't matched with on Tinder or OkCupid. I resisted the urge to swipe my hand as I walked past them. I immediately regretted wearing my sex heels for walking.

The organizer announced that they weren't letting enough of us in from the big queue forming outside so she directed us to Pop's Bar further down 24th Street. I tottered along in pain realizing that Sarah Jessica Parker must have had a procedure to put metal splints into her ankles and I was suddenly angry at her for hiding this from All Women.

Talia took pity on me and gave me a piggyback ride. Once in the bar I removed my heels and we all danced about distractedly. I shoveled Coco and Talia into the photo booth and we posed away. When we walked back to the booth a few minutes later, no photos had come out. I hailed a barman.

"This may be a high-maintenance request, but my photo never came out of the booth."

"A reasonable request." He shoved his hand down the slot and came up with four sets of photos. The first three weren't ours but I recognized them as some of the Cool Kids in the queer scene, too cool to ask for help. I would have gone about distributing the photos but it was time to go to our next engagement at the Lookout bar for an Ugly Sweater lesbian party.

I was approached by a lady bro who was clearly bridge and tunnel. She looked relaxed enough that she must have had a parking space in front of her house. Her mullet was not ironic and her striped shirt and outdated jeans implied a suburban casualness.

"Are you *gay*?" she asked, full of accusation. It came out like, "Are you *even* gay?"

"Yes, I'm queer."

"You *are*?"

"Yes, why else would I be here?"

"You could just be a straight ally. So what do you do?"

I did so many things (see Mandala of Me, front of book, for a full list) that I never knew how to answer this question.

"I'm a life coach."

"Oh I need that, I'm a mess."

I quickly escaped her.

I was left with that old disappointment. Everyone thinks I'm the straight ally, never the flaming bisexual queer lesbian I am. The party's demographic was mostly power lesbians in ambiguous suits, who usually stick to their own kind. I asked Talia to leave the bar with her arm around me so I could feel like I had a date for a moment. After we parted it was like many of my departures from queer events, I left without ceremony all alone into the sifting mists and muted tones of the San Francisco night.

I followed up the next day with a text to Billie.

"How was Ships in The Night, do I have a lot of competition now?"

"You have nothing to worry about," she texted.

We made a plan for her to meet me in the city. I suggested we go watch the ice skaters at Union Square. This is such a joyous sight, it's like the opening credits of *Love Actually*. Everyone is so happy when ice skating. And I am happy watching. It's safer for everyone if I am just watching.

On the day of our date I went shopping at Target with Allegra.

I had recently purchased some cozy gold and black lounge pants that were all the rage among the lazy. Allegra grabbed a pair and I bought ones for Celeste so we could be matching.

Just then a text from Billie came. "The weather's pretty bad. Should we have a plan B for tonight?"

"Yes, any ideas?"

She sent me links to three fun options: bowling, Urban Putt mini golf, and standup comedy.

"Which should I choose? Maybe standup?" I asked Allegra.

"Hmmm maybe that's not the best idea for a first date."

"You're saying that because you think she will hear my loud, crazy laugh and she will be turned off."

"No … well yes, exactly."

"But shouldn't she like me, just as I am?"

"Sure, but not on the first date."

I texted Billie back. "How about Urban Putt?"

"That's what I was thinking!"

I didn't even know our fair city had an indoor pee wee golf hipster bar. A woman behind a tall desk greeted me. I let her know I was meeting someone.

I moved to a high table at the front bar. Then I saw Billie: handsome face, long legs, nicely dressed, sensual lips, warm smile. I was startled by how attractive she was. I took in her brown eyes, her short Afro, her overall disarming presence. I responded like a lovestruck fool in a cartoon. My eyes popped out like slinkies, smoke blew out of my ears, my tongue unfolded like a rug and my heart bounded down it and fell at her feet. Luckily she didn't notice.

"You're really tall," I said. We hugged. She smelled freshly showered with a hint of jasmine.

"It just got really busy in here," she said. "How about we have a drink?" I tried to adjust to how tall, dark, and handsome she was.

"Sure, I'm going to get something to eat too."

I munched on sashimi with avocado and taro chips as we discussed our love of memoirs. She was reading Kim Gordon's *Girl in a Band*. I made a note to get it out of the library.

She is tall, gorgeous, smart, well read. I was wondering what the catch was. In the bar young technorati were lined up and putting along. Finally the line died down. We approached the long lacquered wooden floor interrupted by ultragreen golf grass. Each hole was a distinct SF scene in miniature: The Painted Ladies, Ocean Beach Windmill, Lotta's Fountain, Transamerica Pyramid.

My game started out pretty well. We entered a spooky, heavily decorated underwater area. When we emerged to the other side I was swiping big nothings trying to get the ball up a little, ruthless green hill.

"Would you like a lesson?" asked Billie.

"Yes please."

She came behind me, pressing her hips into my behind, explaining things I wasn't listening to, caught up in the heat of her jeans against me, her chest on my back. She moved away.

I swung and missed.

"Did that help? Or do you need another lesson?" She was all smiles.

"I need another lesson."

She mounted me again. This time she put her hands over my hands and swung for me. I could have done that all night.

We finished up the game. She wanted to check out a drag show at Aunt Charlie's in the Tenderloin. After all, what's a first date without drag queens? We arrived too late, the ladies were just mingling and drinking cocktails. We approached the bar, usually a moment of date suicide for me as I rarely drink alcohol. Billie reviewed the merits of various beers with the elderly bartender and settled on a Stella.

"Can I have a hot toddy with no alcohol in it please?"

"So just hot water then, basically?" said the bartender.

The bartender and Billie cracked up together. I resisted the temptation to say that hot toddies also have honey and cloves stuck into an orange slice thank you very much. But I guess not at a dive bar in the Tenderloin.

We sat against high cushioned benches across from the bar. Billie mentioned her celebrity crush on Jennifer Connelly, but complained she had gotten too skinny.

"I resemble her," I said.

"You do actually."

"I'm in a weird place with my femme celebrity crush on Drew Barrymore. I don't usually have actress crushes because they are such *ladies*. But Drew was my exception. My friend Wells recently made me watch her videos, interviews, her famous boob flashing Lettermen show. She was different from what I imagined."

"Why did Wells have to ruin the fantasy for you?"

"Exactly. Rude, right?"

Our conversation wound down.

"I'm going to walk to BART," she said. "Do you want to order your Lyft?" If I ordered it now there would be no time for a goodbye kiss. But I didn't know what else to do, so I put in my request. We went outside.

The Tenderloin was all somber gray and moody blues and dark awnings. People with hard histories limped by. The big SUV Lyft arrived too soon. She gave me a quick kiss on the lips. I jumped into the back seat. There was a woman driver and a man in the front. Next to me was a young woman.

"We were all watching to see if there was going to be a kiss goodnight," said the driver.

"Why was it so brief?" asked the woman next to me.

"I didn't want to keep you waiting," I said, liking the attention.

"We were enjoying the show," said the guy. "Was that a first date?"

"Yes it was."

"It looked promising," said the driver.

"If we get married you can all come to the wedding."

Right when I was settled in bed I got a text from Billie: "That goodnight kiss was too brief. I won't let that happen again."

"I agree. Let's meet up this week."

"Yes I will find another excuse to get behind you," she said. Swoon.

I texted Hilary a picture of Billie. She sent me a video of the scene in *Animal House* where a horny boy is calmly sitting on his bed looking at a girlie magazine when a beautiful woman in a red negligée flies through his window to the tune of epic horns and flops on his bed as he exclaims: "Thank you God!" I was the horny boy in this scenario.

The next week, Wells and my other roommate helped me prep for my date. I put a black lace tank top over my mesh nighty. I squeezed myself into a red pencil skirt. I met her at a little upstairs sushi restaurant in Soma. She looked stunning in tight blue jeans and a blue and black flannel that did not conceal her big breasts. She told me about her parents. Her dad was a major league sports player. She said she had grown up comfortably, leading some of the politicized activist girls she dated to accuse her of being a "Cosby Kid." Theo Cosby in fact. And when she visited her Kansas relatives they called her "Hollywood."

We ordered luscious thin slices of hamachi on a bed of curling white radish and a couple of fancy rolls. I told her about my life coaching career. Just as the bill came I could feel my stomach was not full. Elusive sushi, always either too much or not enough. Allegra says just order tempura or you'll never be full.

Outside we planned on a Lyft.

"Where do you want to go?" asked Billie.

"We could go to my place. Or a wine bar in my neighborhood."

"Let's go to the wine bar."

At tiny Ino Vino on Carl Street they poured goblet sized wine glasses and all the servers had intact Italian accents as if they just flew in from Venice. I proceeded to order an entire pizza and eat most of it as we talked. And because I have no game, I heard myself saying, "Your parents must have been really good looking."

She gave me a full open smile.

"They were actually." She showed me a picture of her family when she was younger. They were posed on a sports field. Two handsome brothers in polyester, her pretty mom who shared Billie's' Egyptian eyes, and her tall dad sporting a moustache. Like all photos taken in the early eighties it was lit with a groovy orange glow.

We were flung out into the Cole Valley night. By day it's all baby carriages, joggers, coffee shop writers. At night the young come in for romance.

"Do you want to head home or come up for a bit? I have about an hour and half, then I am off to Sonoma County. In the morning I'm doing tarot readings at a Winter Solstice Crafts Fair."

"Sure, I'll come up."

We sat on my couch. I put my leg over her. We talked about her new job at Peets Coffee doing accounting. We talked about our love of memoirs. I told her I started reading *Girl in a Band* and was loving it. Forty-five minutes passed. I wanted to be brave and just lean in for a kiss but I couldn't find the courage.

"I have to leave soon to get on the road. Are we going to make out?" I said in Aries bluntness.

"Yes, yes."

We kissed. Her lips like silky pillows, her smell subtle and sweet, her body emanating heat.

"Let's go into your bedroom," she said. "Your outfit is amazing by the way. I've been trying to not stare at your tits all night."

"My roommates helped me pick it out."

"Oh, so I didn't have a chance."

She unraveled me down to my nightie. We got her down to her t-shirt and underwear. I noticed a woman's purple bra underneath instead of the sports bra I expected. She climbed on top of me.

"Can you please take your shirt off?," I asked. "I haven't seen breasts in a long time."

She obliged, pulling her shirt off the "boy way" with both hands grasping behind her neck.

She had her hips between my thighs.

"I can't believe I have to leave soon," I said. "I should just cancel."

"Yes you should. If I had a car I would stay with you tonight and drive you up tomorrow."

"It's okay. We'll just save some delight for our next date."

On our third date I invited Billie to my place for dinner so it was perfectly clear how the date would culminate. We kissed as soon as we closed my bedroom door. She lifted me up, thighs around her torso, and threw me on the bed. It was only weeks ago that Ace and Yusuf were doing this. After a while she was between my thighs with her mouth.

"I'm gonna crack the code," she said.

We entered a blissful stretch of dating where we couldn't get enough of each other. "Don't look at me with those sorcery eyes," she'd say with awe and affection. She called me the *master of touch*.

Billie was housesitting for a friend in Oakland so we had the place to ourselves. She lost her apartment in SF when she broke up with her girlfriend. She had been staying with her friends, her Grammy, and house sitting.

A little light brown dog greeted me at the door with snarling growls. Billie had baked us a tofu pot pie. After dinner she played jazz records with lyrics, the only jazz I enjoy, the opposite of the noodling stuff Kunal loved. She held the dog's two paws and danced a little cha cha, shimmying her shoulders back and fourth. That killed me.

The kitchen was a big, open-air one with doors and a stairway leading to the bedrooms. She pushed my willing body against a closet door and kids jackets fell on my face. Not happy with this, she threw me against another wall and a kid's Christmas felt artwork started coming off in my hair. She lifted me to straddle her and stormed up the stairs, perfectly carrying my weight. Until the last stair, where she lost her footing and fell forward on me, deftly cradling my neck so it was a painless fall. Then she tied my wrists to the banister. She stood above me with an erection supplied by a recent trip to Good Vibrations. She looked so grand standing over me, stroking liquid onto her dildo cock. Then she came down to my level. And pulsed into me as I clutched her back. Afterwards we panted, catching our breath, all tangled up in each other.

"It scares me how much I like you," she said. "You are too good for me. When I have a good thing I always sabotage it."

This is what I now call a thesis statement. When a lover states a thesis statement like "I'm afraid of commitment" or "I'm not looking for anything serious" or "I don't want kids, ever," it's true. THE THESIS STATEMENT IS ALWAYS TRUE. Always believe it and act accordingly.

The next morning on BART I peeled a little felt Christmas wreath off my hair. I couldn't believe how this relationship, born of Tinder, was progressing so beautifully. I tucked the thesis statement away, too deliciously satisfied to let it take root.

"Fade Into You" by Mazzy Star became our song, even though it was released in the early nineties. Its timeless hum, its reverberating sweetness, that smoldering voice peering in and out of the mists like a moon posing while the clouds danced before it. The poetical lyrics never land, they only float up and out. One of the times it played on the "Sex Playlist" Billie made for us, I saw a dream image of us dancing in a warm night under a star-sprinkled sky — our wedding. Emotion caught in my throat. How could this image peek out of my subconscious so soon? We had only just met.

Billie was always saying, "We've known each other before, in another lifetime, maybe many lifetimes."

I texted: "I just played our song three times."

She responded: "I just watched the video. We're so fucked."

I like the moves of sex. My lover is on top of me clicking my knees open by shoving them to the side with their knees, driving an arm under my leg to open me up so they can get at me, quickly pulling my whole body down away from the headboard where all sex eventually crashes into. I like one hand holding both my wrists or both their hands circling my wrists so I am pinned with them above me while they kiss and bite my neck, stomach, the sensitive flesh around my hip bones. I luxuriate in the secret choreography of it.

I had been thinking about masculine and feminine, butch and femme, myself as a sexual being. How the sex of a woman just drops off at a certain point after our stomach, how a discreet curtain parts, how under the veil so much of us tucks inward and into itself. What remains in shrouded view—the clit, the labia, the opening—varies so much from woman to woman. How I have a little tongue that sticks out between my lips. I feel the round warmth of Billie and want to push myself inside, want to rock her to my rhythm. I can teeter totter in sex, unafraid of falling.

Billie and I decided to spend a mellow New Year's Eve at my place. It was a long time since I had done that with someone. Then my friend B invited us to a Guerneville AirBNB and we accepted. We were put in the "Love Shack," a detached square cozy box of a room containing a bed and not much else. Billie helped me put on the new sateen bed sheets she suggested I purchase the week before. They were kind of slippery.

"I wish I would have brought my jersey sheets," I said.

We had to go to the hardware store and buy a heater for the Love Shack. But it lived up to its name. After an early evening romp in the sateen sheets I would have liked to just go to a café or snuggle in bed but Billie wanted to start the Eve at the emblematic gay Rainbow Cattle Club.

A skinny older gay man in a cowboy shirt greeted us at the

door with "Well now, there is an attractive couple!" Billie had three rum and cokes in quick succession. I wished she hadn't. As a child I was always sipping my mom's coke and then making a sour face when I realized it had rum in it.

Finally, evening hit and we all made a big feast back at the house. B brought her girlfriend and there was one other couple. Everyone brought dogs, in true lesbian fashion, so they were constantly circling around our ankles. After dinner we all got in the hot tub and everyone but me was showing their alcohol intake by changes in speech.

In the hot tub Billie's words were slurred, in the living room too. My eyelids drooped, I wanted to go hide out in the Love Shack. I wanted to climb into my Grace Jones memoir. I French exited from the main house into our room. After a while she followed.

"I'm sorry I got so drunk. I messed everything up." She kept repeating the sentence: "With you I don't need to drink, we just have fun, sex, talk about books."

I was stone sober and she was blithering in her own world. She went on and on in the rants of the inebriated, tunneling further into darkness. I couldn't stay on track with her. She was upset again and again, claiming she saw disappointment, anger, sadness, condescension on my face. I kept trying to bring us back and she kept spiraling, escalating, saying it was all ruined, saying that the good ones always leave, that she knew it was our last night and that this would break her heart.

After a good half hour of her mania rubbing me raw, my fears came pouring in and I spoke them. "Maybe I am just not good at making love stay. I am good at so many things. But maybe not this."

In the middle of the night Billie's drunk snoring woke me. She starfished her body across the bed and would not be moved. I bluffed that I was going to the sofa in the big house.

"No no I'll go. I'm the one who messed up." Then she went. I stared at the ceiling, brooding. This was all a huge red flag.

She came back to bed in the morning, I helped her into the covers, she spooned me, then she kissed me, then we were into it, my hands on her wetness, our bodies arching into each other, pressing, fusing,.

She licked me with her finger inside but it didn't feel right. My pussy, like most, shifts throughout the month so different things feel good at different times. And I don't always know how to tell people exactly what I want so I said, "Slow down, listen to my pussy's rhythm, she'll tell you what to do." Eventually she found just the right motion with her finger, just the right pressure with her tongue. She cracked the code.

In the late afternoon, in bed, we finally talked. The thesis statement began to reveal itself. The sabotage of us had begun. And I would continue to naively think that I would be an exception, that I could skirt around the thesis statement, fates be damned.

She pulled the sheets up and over both of us. She explained that her alcoholism had only recently become problematic. Things had got progressively worse since her mom died suddenly four years ago. She wanted to quit but wasn't sure if she could. On our first date I knew there had to be a catch. And here it was. I was tempted to protect myself. To grieve the loss of our potential and move on. But there was something about Billie that I trusted. I wanted to know her more. There was a gentleness in the way she played with the dog, there was a kindness in her eyes. I felt tenderness for her story of losing both her parents, one to death, the other to abandonment. And how that had not hardened her against love.

I discussed her alcoholism with Allegra in her kitchen with the yellow table and the black and white checkered floor. She still lived kitty corner to me off Cole Street. I assumed she would be alarmed and suggest I move on. Billie had begun the process of AA and telling her loved ones she was quitting for good.

"You know April, many people struggle with this in our queer community. She wants to quit. Why not see how it goes?"

Billie promised not to drink. Everyone in AA told her that she shouldn't date anyone while starting recovery. But I ignored the prognosis just as I had ignored the thesis statement.

We had great dates and even greater sex. Only a week later she failed to meet me when she said she would. I waited for her in Dolores Park. We were going to see *Purple Rain* to honor the passing of Prince. I kept texting and calling. Finally I went home. As the early evening hours gave way to the darker shades of night I watched the play of car lights across my bedroom ceiling. I finally called around midnight. Her words were slurred.

"Have you been drinking?" I asked.

"No, I haven't, I just went to dinner."

This went on for a while, her voice rising and falling, her sentences incoherent. She tried to change the subject and ask how my night had been but I was focused.

"On your mother's grave, have you been drinking?"

"Yes I was drinking."

"And you lied to me about it."

"No I didn't lie."

"I asked you three times."

"Baby why are you being so serious, accusing me? You don't understand. You don't understand what it is to lose a mom."

She texted me several times and called me six times. I let it ring, I let it all simmer for the night. I didn't know which I feared more, her being an alcoholic or her lying to me. I knew they were intimately related.

We had some sobering talks about our relationship over the phone. I said we should take some space.

"That's a terrible idea," she said.

She wrote me email letters:

What can I do to make this better? I want to fight for you, April. What do you need from me to make this work? I'm willing to do anything to fight for us. Everything leads up to this moment right now. There is a reason why we met. We should see where it takes us. I'm scared to death of losing you. Tell me what you need from me. I know I fucked up, but please let me make this right.

I wrote back to her right away.

Dear Billie,

You know that once the clouds and fog of alcohol are cleared you will be a force of nature, an outstanding powerful woman who can do anything.

Though of course I must put it on pause. I will miss you. I feel sorry for myself that you flashed possibility and then snatched it away.

Love, April

We agreed to not see each other for four months and then meet for a date on Valentine's Day. But I only made it four days. That Friday night hit and I was so lonely. The Cure did this to me with their "Friday I'm in Love" shit.

Then Saturday night hit and I was confused. I texted: "I feel like I am supposed to be the strong one here that gives you boundaries. But all I want to do is be with you."

"Should I come over?"

If only someone would have yanked me out of this madness. How come lifeguards are there when you swim but not when you are doing truly dangerous things like dating beautiful, emotionally unavailable boozy women? .

We had more weeks of bliss, snuggling against her silky body, laughing while watching old episodes of *Parks and Rec.* I really wanted Billie to be my person, my love, my wife someday. I wanted it so bad that I overlooked all the warning signs. I returned again and again to the innocence of new love. I'd say, "Did we really meet on Tinder?" She'd say, "Everything leads up to a moment."

I thought maybe I wouldn't have to sit this one out. When the music stopped maybe I could get a chair.

"How did I end up with this little white woman on top me?" she'd joke. Just think of all her ancestors, their songs and stories, their struggles, their bliss, all to make Billie, only for her to end up with a little white woman on top of her. She then accused me of trying to crawl inside her, which is exactly what I wanted to do.

When I saw Billie I would say *babe, babe, babe, babe, babe*. I would say it into her back as a whisper as she slept. When we break up she will say she can still hear my voice like an echo.

Billie had me totally pussymatized. When you find a truly perfect pussy it's hard to focus on anything else. Her pussy and I had our own parallel relationship that was full of passion, mutual trust, unconditional love. Her pussy had asked me to be girlfriends right away and then promptly asked me to marry her. I said "Yes!" and we tied the knot in a quiet civic ceremony totally sanctioned by all existing and future marriage laws.

I told Billie that sometimes her pussy and I felt her theatrics interfered with the purity of our relationship. I lobbied for her to stop sabotaging us and short of that if we could have our own relationship that she wouldn't interfere with. But she stubbornly maintained that I had to deal with her if I wanted any kind of a relationship with her pussy.

"But we're married!" I pleaded.

I steered us into a basketball role play. She would start out in long silky basketball shorts and a "wifey lovie" tank top. She'd strap on the brown member we got at Good Vibes. She would say I was just her San Francisco piece, she had a girl in every city, as she entered me.

She was often very attentive. I could see that she was loyal and wanted to spend most of her free time with me. I loved this kind of attention. I needed lots of attention, which is why I prefer not to have dogs or babies or demanding careers to compete with.

But her focus was erratic. When I wanted to relax with her by a pool, hang out with her at party, go to a spa with her, she would disappear, breaking our intimacy. So instead of lounging by a hotel pool with her I would go on a frantic search, wondering why she had been gone for two hours.

Billie offered to drive me to my writing group and then pick me up. I sat in the lovely upstairs apartment with women discussing our memoirs. Yes, this very memoir! I sent my required twenty pages in early to our facilitator, Karen Bjorneby, every two weeks. She told us to have *the arrogance of male writers* and it was worth it just to hear her say that.

During the group, Billie called several times, splitting my focus. I wondered why she didn't text. I went into the kitchen where coffee, tea and wine were set out for our enjoyment, and texted her. She said she was lost. I texted her the address again. I sat back down with my ladies. Then we all heard a door open, which caused everyone alarm. I got up and explained it was probably my girlfriend. She appeared at the doorway with a distant look in her eyes. I gathered my stuff and we left together.

She was frazzled and lost. In a mood. She was driving poorly, mixing up her words.

"Do you want me to drive?" I asked.

"No, no I'm fine."

"Are you on drugs or something?"

"No baby, I'm just upset. I talked to my brothers today. My younger brother is getting married and he isn't inviting me to the wedding."

She continued her erratic driving. The city became a foreign territory she couldn't navigate. On 18th Street she bumped into the car in front of us. Everything came to a thudding halt. The driver got out and Billie and I met him between our cars. He slowly studied the back of his bumper as if at an archeological dig. It was the type of tap you give another car when you are parking. People began to honk from behind.

"Let's drive over there and pull over." I motioned for the driver to turn onto Collingswood.

"There was nothing wrong with his car," I said as we got back in.

"I know," said Billie.

We dutifully turned.

"We should just go," I said. The driver was pulled over waiting for us.

"If you say so, I will," she replied.

"Go! Drive! Fast!" I was strangely enjoying the feeling that we were reckless teenagers. We are adults for so long and invincible youths for such a short time.

You could say it was a hit and run but really it was a time-saving device for everyone. Then we were racing up Collingswood to Market. Billie turned and I shrieked as she was about to turn into a dead-end. We zoomed onto Market on fire until we hit a red light. A driver pulled up and we froze. But it was only a big, soon-to-be-obsolete taxicab. The light changed and we sped ahead.

It felt like we were both driving, as Billie was swervy and confused, letting me guide her. Rain pelted down onto the car, instantly fogging the windows. We struggled to turn on different switches to clear the view. I considered the fact that we might crash or just never find a parking space. I was no longer enjoying the ride. Finally I got in the driver's seat and looked for parking at my mom's house. Then we planned to take a Lyft home. There was no parking anywhere and the rain made the night closed in and scary. I called my mom and she cheerfully volunteered to drive us home. I sat in the front seat with her hoping Billie didn't say anything weird. I was thankful to my mom for being so willing to come out at ten o'clock at night to drive us home only to return and have to find parking again.

I wondered if this was what it felt like for my mom to be managing her alcoholic cokehead boyfriend Jeff. You feel like you have your stuff together in comparison to them. You are always averting your gaze from yourself and keeping an eye on what crazy thing they might do next, often when you least expect it.

When we got to my bedroom I finally admitted to myself that Billie was drunk.

"The problem with you only lying when you are drunk is you lie about being drunk."

She put her head in her hands and became silent, no eye contact, which drove me mad.

"I should go," she said.

"Don't go."

I hate it when people abandon me to my bedroom. I hate watching their figure slip through my door while I wonder if I will ever see them again.

"You don't deserve this." She packed her things into her navy Hershel backpack. I clung to her.

"You don't understand," she said. "The only person who really accepted me and loved me was my mom, and she is gone."

When Billie was drunk she felt the loss of her mom most acutely. Talking about her mom somehow helped Billie escape the possibilities of me.

She untangled herself from me and put on her jacket. She was overcome by spirits I couldn't access. She was slow, sad, remote, already half departed. I lost my patience. Tears forming in my eyes, I lay face down in the bed.

"Baby, what are you doing? Look at me," she pleaded, her tall frame suddenly over me on the bed.

"It's okay. I'm ready for you to go now." She kept asking me to look at her and I kept maneuvering myself away like the child who thinks she can't be seen because her eyes are covered.

"Look at me," she said. It was only minutes ago that she had her head in her hands, keeping her eyes from me. I guess this drives women mad, when you won't look at them.

After a while she pried my hands apart. I looked at her. We took off her clothes and got in bed, holding each other. In the morning her evil twin was gone and my sweet Billie was back.

She started attending AA meetings almost daily. In my journal I wrote: "I need to make a chart of our relationship, one that lists the good days and the bad days." We made it about a week with no incidents or fights.

We went to a lesbian therapist who just let Billie talk the whole time. It seemed Billie was in her own therapy session that I was just witnessing instead of us working on our relationship.

I devised an argument-resolution style with Billie that she agreed to. I would speak as her and she would speak as me. It was a profound experience of each of us stepping into the other's shoes.

I said, "Okay April, as Billie, I want you to know that I love you and I am sorry I have been lying to you."

Billie said, "As April, I'm telling you that if you drink again I'm going to break up with you." And she did and I didn't.

I took a nine-day trip to Italy with Coco. I let Billie borrow my car while I was gone—not exercising my best judgment. She agreed to pick Coco and me up from the airport. I texted her as soon as we were waiting for our baggage but she didn't answer. I called. Nothing. Coco was exhausted and hopped in a Lyft. I should have joined her but instead I called Billie again and again. Finally she answered.

"Sorry babe. I fell asleep. Do you want me to come now?"

"I guess so."

She arrived 40 minutes later. I had told myself she was just tired, had fallen asleep. She came and hugged me and put my bag away. She drove us out of the international terminal. She was in that heightened state, driving erratically.

"Please tell me you aren't drunk."

"Do you want to drive?"

"Yes, pull into this gas station."

I drove us home with my shoulders bunched up to my ears. This was the third drunk driving incident. The one through the Castro I had treated like we were both teenagers on the run until it got serious. Now she was driving us on a five-lane highways, risking our lives.

We didn't even have the energy to fight when we got back to my place. We both fell asleep.

Billie was doing accounting at a startup, spending her free time watching movies and "Murder She Wrote," never exercising, just going through the motions. Something changed one night when we were going to the last Tranny Shack drag queen show at Oasis. I bowed out at the last minute due to premenstrual complications.

In the middle of the night I got a text with a photo of her and John Cameron Mitchell, the genius behind the greatest musical of all time, *Hedwig and the Angry Inch.* I was flooded with excitement and regret.

The friendship with John Cameron Mitchell revived Billie like he was Jack's magic beans. He invited us to go to a small screening of his newest film, an adaptation of Neil Gaiman's *How to Talk to Girls at Parties.* John wanted our help in finding a venue to view it. I looked into ATA on Valencia but that proved unnecessary. John had found a perfect place: Armistead Maupin's home in the Castro. I was a longtime fan of *Tales of the City* in book and televised form. As Billie and I looked for Armistead's apartment we pretended it was totally normal that we were about to be kicking it with Maupin and Mitchell.

The door opened and Maupin's husband Christopher Turner, looking like a Ken Doll supermodel, greeted us.

He ushered us through a railroad hallway to the backyard. And there was Armistead standing in the backyard talking to a perky young woman that could have been a young Laura Linney. Armistead wore jeans and suspenders over a long-sleeved blue shirt. His face was cheerfully pink.

John arrived with his cherubic smile and his signature faded t-shirt and baggy sweats that one usually associates with the depressed, though perhaps in John's case he was still decompressing from all those years in sequin dresses and platform heels. Armistead introduced a young woman as his neighbor, saying his place was like Barbary Lane with different generations all around. Then he introduced her to John, noting that John wrote *Hedwig and the Angry Inch.*

"Did you say itch?" asked John. "That's what it becomes I guess." We all laughed.

We made our way to the living room where I desperately wished I could photograph their bookshelf. I recognized Starhawk's *The Fifth Sacred Thing.* John sat to the side of the flatscreen TV. Billie was next to him and Armistead was next to me.

Christopher breezed in and out. We were offered wine, which Billie declined. Armistead handed us his philo vape. And I thought: *No big deal I'm just having my first vape with a literary genius and a Tony Award winning playwright.* John didn't partake too much, he wanted to stay lucid for the screening, where he was particularly focused on sound quality.

John and Billie brought up the film *The King's Speech* agreeing they didn't care for it.

"I liked it," I said in unison with Armistead, in high-pitched schoolgirl voices. He was practically spooning me!

The movie was an elaborate space-age punk fantasy starring Elle Fanning and Nicole Kidman, set in 1970s London. Sci-Fi isn't my genre but I enjoyed the colorful spectacle of the film. *Hedwig* was one of my all time favorite films so it would be hard for anything to glow next to it.

We moved into the dining room where we were treated to delicious Burmese takeout. The food was creamy and spicy and conversation flowed easily. Christopher set a camera and took a photo of us all. When we said goodbye to John at the door I said: "I am still reviewing your movie, the costumes, the colors, it will continue in my dreams."

And it did. John was featured all throughout my dreams that night. He got a woman pregnant but then no one was sure what was to be done with the creation. When I told him about it later he said, wistfully: "Yes what is to be done with the creation?" As if it was quite natural that I had peered into such an intimate part of his artistic life.

The next day Armistead proudly displayed our group photo on his Facebook page. We all had a sparkle in our eyes and full smiles.

This could be the happy ending where "Fade Into You" plays at our wedding as we dance under the stars on a warm summer night. But no. Not even John Cameron Mitchell and Armistead Maupin could save my dysfunctional relationship.

Strangely, the final straw happened at a Radical Faery Halloween Festival in Booneville. Some of the faeries were radical and some were just faeries as was patiently explained to me several times over the course of the weekend.

We shared a doublewide trailer with John and some other queer men. John and Billie were teaming up for the DJ set. This marked Billie's triumphant return to being a DJ. I was so excited for her. I saw the potential of the artist to transmute pain into creation. She was stifled, running numbers for startups, sitting in an office, when she could be putting her profound knowledge and passion for music to use.

We all got ready for the festivities together. The dance hall was festooned with long flowing fabrics and featured a sex and snuggle room and a teahouse room. Partygoers were dressed in velveteen, sequined gowns, and regalia that would rival that of a '70s fag ball. I asked Billie not to do a bunch of MDMA because we would be out of sync, her tripping with me trying to sleep, or her having post-drug exhaustion tomorrow with me chipper and ready to go.

The dance started at 11 and didn't heat up until midnight, which was way past my bedtime. I forced myself to dance anyway. I delighted in seeing John and Billie laughing and hugging each other behind the DJ booth. He was a fairy goddess mother to her and she was his new muse. I was just about to leave but decided to visit the tearoom.

I slipped under a long satin curtain and entered a lovely space with fabrics, Turkish rugs, low tables, and amber light. A man handed me a decorated porcelain teacup and saucer of Darjeeling, bourbon, and apple cider vinegar. Tea and alcohol was de rigueur for gay gatherings those days. I saw a man in black with black eyeliner giving aggressive, fast-paced tarot readings. I asked how much the readings were.

"Sit down," he said, waving my question away.

I sat across from him and cut the deck as directed. The first card was the Art card, which I think of as a card about soul mates and wholeness, bisexuality, as it depicts a woman and a man in one body—and also about creative expression through art. I looked at the figure and thought about all the creative projects I wanted to complete, from drawings, to movies, to memoirs(!) The gist of the reading was: You are thinking too much about the big picture all the time. You need to finish what you started.

"Now go away," he said.

I said goodnight to Billie, who was sad to see me go.

She woke me up at 3:30am talking in her outside voice and stirring me from a deep sleep. She had taken a big dose of MDMA. Later that morning I got up to volunteer in the kitchen. Billie admitted that was a noble venture but said: "Don't leave me."

"But you are just going to sleep and I have energy," I said.

I helped some men put tables out and adorn them with long tablecloths and sarongs, a sarong being nothing more than a hippie tablecloth. When I came back to our trailer, Billie was gone—and so was my car. Everyone was being couply, packing up, chatting. John was cuddling on the foldout sofa in the living room with a young New Age guy. I told him Billie took off without telling me, with my car, presumably to get herself breakfast.

"She was probably just hungry, I'm sure she'll be back soon," he said.

I packed up all our stuff, noting that we had a cooler full of food Billie could have snacked on until she found me. It would have been one thing if she zoomed back in 30 minutes. But she had now been gone for over an hour.

I went up the hill towards a pond I had visited the day before with a bunch of young guys who bravely skinny-dipped in the bracing muddy water.

The hill was steeper than I remembered. I climbed and climbed. It had been cold and raining but the sun finally peeked out. I was wearing too many layers and had to wipe sweat from my forehead.

I took off my sweater and tied it around my hips. A golden light rose up around the tips of the redwoods. I said to myself: "If I see a rainbow, I will stay with Billie and we will find a good therapist. If I don't I will break up with her."

Three ravens circled around each other and then glided away. When I got to the pond I walked out onto the little dock. I looked into the murky water but could only see a distorted image of myself among the redwood trees. I threw a stone in the water and watched all the circles rippling across each other. I turned my back on the pond and began descending the hill.

I finally admitted that Billie was going to keep abandoning me until there was nothing left to abandon because I would be gone. Her exit with my car was not a discrete incident but part of a pattern of events, hewn from deep inside her subconscious with the intent to unravel us. Her drinking and her lies were all part of a festering self-hatred, the scope of which was beyond my capacity. There was nothing I could feed her hungry ghosts because their nature was to remain hungry.

"Love your fate," said Karen Blixen in *Out of Africa* as her farm dried up, her lover's plane crashed, her body deteriorated. Love your fate.

I thought maybe I spotted a sad little rainbow at the end of the sky hugging some trees, but I had to really look hard to see it. I had to strain to find the violet band. And I realized I didn't want to see it. And that was an even more important sign.

I would miss the nights with Billie when less was required of us. Our love found fulfillment in the night, when I slept on my side pressed into her side, my arm over her torso, my hand between her breasts in an animal gesture of bliss. The same unifying poses my childhood cats preferred when napping in piles against each other in the afternoons.

Billie and I could remain functional for about four days at a time. But then she would drink. And then we would fight. The day requires commitments, truth, follow-through, stability, patience and understanding. After every betrayal I would return to the night in search of reunification. She was eager to please, lost in the intimate places of me. She always held me afterwards while my breath slowed down. Pressed against her I felt wholeness and ease. But then the day came again.

As I walked down the hill I walked back into my own shoes. I recommitted to myself. I said: "I'm going to take care of you April. I am going to get you home, we're going home." I felt relief and freedom. This voice inside me was strong and true and I loved it more than I loved Billie and more than I loved romantic love.

Two hours later, Billie still wasn't back. During those two hours I became a woman unto herself, a woman unattached.

Billie walked into the double wide ready to receive the anger she had elicited. She played her part, the one where she was just innocently going into town for breakfast, no big deal, nothing to do with the thesis statement.

This shouldn't have been the tipping point. The time we had a date to see *Purple Rain* after Prince died and she was drunk and just went AWOL should have been. Or the two times she was supposed to pick me up at the airport and didn't. Or perhaps the times she endangered us by driving drunk. Or the many times she lied to my face. Just when it was the time in the vacation by the pool to hold hands and be intimate, Billie was gone. She was the ocean. I loved and revered her but it was never safe to have my back to her.

I barked at her to pack up the car. Then I barked at her to stop that and go get her DJ stuff. She followed like the punished child she, for historical reasons, wanted to be. I had become someone angry who barked and yelled.

As we drove off the land an enormous rainbow arched just ahead. The fates were mocking me. I wanted to reach up and wipe it out of the sky. In a tarot book I once read that if you get a card that says yes and that makes you feel terrible, and makes you wish it was no, then that's your answer. No. Rainbow or not, I was done with Billie. She yelled as we drove into the rainbow.

"Why are you making such a big deal out of this? I just went to breakfast!"

"You took off with my car for hours without telling me. It's just one thing after another," I screamed back. I had the car, I was driving. I savored this last chance to have some control over the situation. And then I went silent. My body was still in the car but I had evaporated from our relationship.

"This is so unfair!" she yelled. Then she pleaded, and then she apologized in detail for the car and for everything. We drove down 101 to Sonoma County. By the time we got off the highway at the PG and E power cables near North Santa Rosa, she had changed tack.

"Don't end it, baby, you're so kind, so positive and grounding, I love to snuggle you, you are the best snuggler ever."

I pulled over in front of a local market. She did what she always did when I tried to kick her out of my car after her deplorable behavior. She sat down, seat-belted herself in and refused to move. I moved her stuff to the pavement. She got out of the car and I drove away high on my ability to take care of myself. On the fact that, though I couldn't avoid harm and in fact occasionally ran toward it, I could at least remove myself when the time came.

The day I broke up with Billie was the day before Halloween. In the weeks leading up to it we had talked about different couple costumes to wear but never settled on anything.

I couldn't bring myself to go to a party. Instead I sat on my Cole Street stoop enjoying the high spirits of my 3-year-old niece who dressed as a lady bug. I drank from my mom's flask and dressed as a nihilist `a la *The Big Lebowski.*

The next day I was onto the stage of grief called rage. I was commuting to Oakland on BART to see a life coaching client. I put my earphones in and listened to Ani DiFranco's song Untouchable Face. It features many"fuck you's," and I was singing and screaming along with her. I was born in San Francisco. All my life, on public transportation, I've listened to the piercing din of feuding couples, sports fans cheering, drunk and careless teenagers and their amplified music, to the cries of all the lonely, unheard souls. Now it was my turn. People had to hear me scream. It felt so good.

One of my editors thought I should end right there with: *It felt so good*. But I can tell you aren't ready to say goodbye. Also, I could never decide on just one ending so you are about to read four of them. Because FREEDOM!

21: SOULFUL PAGAN ENDING

Mom and I went to Ocean Beach as the sun leaned low in the sky, already planning on leaving us though it was only 4pm. Pagans off all ages sat on blankets around a huge castle of sand with candles and lanterns pushed into its nooks. We set sacred space through songs and chants. The sun was a gentle glow so you could almost look right at it.

The winter solstice tradition is to jump into the ocean naked, cleansing the self of the old and readying for the new. The air was mild and there was no wind. I had brought my purple towel but couldn't imagine shedding my eight layers down to my birthday suit. I looked away from our sandcastle into the ocean. One brave soul after another walked into the chilly waters. They warned us it was dangerous and we should take a buddy. I looked at my mom and said: "You only live once!" Then I bounded towards the ocean.

"Find a buddy," she yelled, ever the mom.

I shed my layers as I ran towards the water. As I passed a blond woman my age and height she asked, "Will you be my buddy?"

"Yes!"

We scampered into the bracing water. Just ahead people were plunging under the tide, a verisimilitude of flesh and sea. I got waist deep and splashed my face three times with water. When I came out, to my surprise, my limbs hadn't come unattached from my torso and my extremities weren't frostbitten. I was so cold I was warm, invigorated, energy spiraling through my body.

After the ritual my mood shifted. I stopped going back and forth about my feelings for Billie. Those feelings would still sneak back in the early hours of the day while I was under the covers.

But my biggest burden was left in the ocean.

I took a Lyft ride home. The passengers were talking about dating. Our older white male driver was single as was the spunky young woman in the front passenger seat. I mentioned I was bisexual. The woman up front said, "I only have one problem with you bisexuals." I braced myself for ridicule.

"Ya'll are greedy!" she said and then laughed.

"I just want boobs, pussy, and cock!" I said. "How is that greedy? Who wouldn't want that?"

"Bisexuals are like Toyota Priuses, people love to hate them," said the driver. We all laughed.

Prince died and with him a whole world of poetry, gender ambiguity, shades of purple. How would we keep the legacy alive? I thought back to all the '80s icons who influenced me: Bowie, Madonna, Cyndi Lauper. Their sexual expressions were coded. You had to be a detective. Thirty years later, you could openly joke with strangers in a cab about wanting the entire spectrum of human experience instead of focusing on only half of it.

My friend said he wanted me to hang out with his 2-year-old daughter. "I want her to be queer. It's contagious right?"

"Highly," I confirmed

22: SELF-REFLECTION ENDING

As I entered what I liked to call my second 30s, I was still not "settled down" in the way we are taught to be. I didn't have a wife or a husband. I often found myself humming a line from "All That Jazz": "No I'm no one's wife but oh I love my life." Remember back in the beginning of the book when I was singing *Sweet Charity* ? And now I've progressed to *Chicago*. That's a nice bookend, no? It may not surprise you to learn that I believe my life is a musical.

I was an amazon on the loose who loves women and men and gender non-conforming dreamboats. My life overflowed with art, with appreciation from my coaching clients, with my great wide-open heart even after all these lovers, all these endings and beginnings. I cherished my concentric and overlapping friendships circles. And my family members were the great loves of my life.

I was still dating various people and enjoying the connections for their own sake. I was comfortable with the certainty of my hard-won love for myself. As I lost erotic virginity I gained self-esteem, an intertwining double helix of growth. The more I loved myself the more I spoke my needs and my truth. I shed veils of shame not only through sexual exploration but through belly dancing, artistic expression, travel, and my work as a life coach.

I wonder what Salome felt as she shed the last veil. As one poet describes it: "The veils fell round her like coiling mists shot through by topaz suns and amethysts." Was her body glistening and oiled? Did she feel an electric buzzing through her meridians? Was she warm? Did she finally feel free?

The closeness of the city, its angry noises and unfriendly faces were wearing me down. But mostly I longed for the quiet country girl I once was. Before I was in sync with my phone and computer I was in sync with milk thistles, Gravenstein apples, lemon balm, miner's lettuce, redwood trees, and pungent bay laurel leaves.

I looked at the pocket doors that were once opened to unite my room with Quince's. They had been closed tight for seven years. I recalled the excitement I felt moving into this place that Allegra found for me on Craigslist. But Allegra had moved out of the apartment kitty corner from me. Celeste had moved out of her place ten blocks away. They both moved into better versions of the places they once lived. When Allegra's old pink apartment got painted gray I saw it as a curtain closing on this chapter of my life.

I told Wells and my roommates that I was moving out. I took a picture of my boudoir bedroom and its curved window. It was once laden with fabrics and art, the four-poster bed the setting for my own private pillowbook. Now it was just a blank room with a beige rug.

Leaving The Velvet Temple felt like pulling up roots from rock. I kept saying to myself *I take nothing from it* but I took it hard. The end of my lease to San Francisco, the end of a daily friendship with Wells, saying goodbye to the place where Quince and I lived. I knew I'd likely never live across the street from my sister again.

Of course I didn't go directly back to Sonoma County. You know me better than that by now. I ease into these big transitions in a circuitous way. I moved in with a female lover in Oakland. And yes I am purposely not giving her a name because I've got to start weaning you off the tit, my loves. We both knew it was temporary. She had just purchased a house surrounded by cement and I wanted to return to the country. I was so delighted to have domestic bliss again, to cook for someone and snuggle at night, that I began to question whether I really wanted to return to Sonoma County. Would it be a new beginning or just a nostalgic rerun?

Then one day I showed up at the home of Hilary and her new wife to take their four-year-old son Doc on an adventure, just the two of us. I packed up a picnic and we were out the door. Doc stood on the stoop as I locked his door behind us.

"Do you have a home Auntie April? A real home?" He said this out of the blue like a fucking miniature sorcerer! I turned around and looked into his big eyes as mine began to tear up.

A week later, I packed up my car, I was single again, and drove back across the Golden Gate Bridge to the place I once shared with my mom and Allegra. The same one I returned to after Spain. The one where I was part of Levi's sexual debut- and learned to finally talk dirty. The Blue Witch House, where I could collect myself.

23: BIG GAY ENDING!

I jumped out of Celeste's car, a vision of gold and white. Every Pride my sisters, mom, and over 20 of our queer friends wear matching outfits with our Pride theme screen-printed on them. All the queers, lesbians, dykes, trans men and women, gay men, and allies were dripping across the plains and valleys of Dolores Park. The park where I met Quince and said goodbye to her and had countless picnics and bisexual barbeques, countless days like this, the Dyke March leading to the crescendo of a week of San Francisco pride celebrations.

Our crew set up day camp on a flat area underneath one of the park's iconic giant palm trees. A kitty pool was filled with water and beer. Two hours later I was drunk on champagne and whiskey, my one day of indulgence. Our friends were dunking each other, wrestler style, into the kitty pool, beer cans, and all. One friend had me get on my knees and open my mouth so she could pour frothy Champaign directly in it.

I felt flirty and free and the whole city had wings. I made a solo lap all along the hills and valleys to tent set ups, young femme girls entangled, lusty butches on the make, pods of dykes with spikey hair, sporty folks holding hands with ladies in tutus; a horizontal parade of triumphant queer love. It was a brisk June day, big clouds gliding across the sun bringing intermittent shade.

I stopped by Finn's tent. She and her friends had raw oysters, whiskey, and burritos to share. I took a swig of Finn's whiskey, appreciating her sly smile as I threw it back. A man in his 20s passed by—sparkling green eyes, a tan face, muscular arms, and cute crocodile patterned shorts. One of my Pride goals was kiss a hot gay man.

"Can I kiss you?" I asked, full of liquid courage. Without hesitation he offered up his lips. The kiss felt like an effortless testament to freedom.

On some witchy gay instinct I rushed back to my crew just as the song "Raise Your Glass" by P!NK was playing on our portable speaker. I was in a flash of intoxication that ran beyond alcohol, fueled by a love still getting named, a love that ran through the veins of this city and every city and every country.

We got in makeshift rows to do our Pride flashmob. Queers gathered in tents and sprawled on blankets and stood with drinks to watch this out-of-the-blue show of choreographed moves. My mom took swigs of Courvoisier from the vulva-shaped flask I gave her. I was between my sisters, one of my favorite places to be. We strutted, spun, and flung our hands up to the sky, because the best way to be queer is to dance. And just then the clouds gave the sun back.

24: CIRCLE-BACK ENDING

"Where's Quince," I asked, suddenly frantic.

"The condom broke," Kunal said with less doom than I thought the moment warranted.

Everything sped up. We saw that a robe was missing. We searched around the hallways, down the dizzy, awful carpets.

We found her in a small windowless "spa room." She was as naked as Godiva in the hot tub, drunk and strangely comfortable. A security guard had been alerted right as we arrived and he was circling her. He made no attempt to hide that he relished his role. There was something absurdly grotesque about the contrast between Quince's naked body in the tub and the security guard wearing a bulky uniform and heavy boots.

Naked Quince was the highlight of the evening, perhaps the year, for the security team who had been watching her on their monitors.

We tried to reason with her. How had Kunal and I become the "parents," the "couple" and Quince our petulant child? Quince and I were the couple! Much to the chagrin of the security team, we got her robe back on.

In the room she explained that the condom had been stuck inside her. Every lesbian's worst nightmare. Most lesbians who have sex with a man have a "hysterical pregnancy," irrationally convinced they are knocked up when there is no chance. But she was understandably worried.

Defeated, we all got back into bed. I spooned Quince and Kunal spooned me. This could have been that delicious bisexual moment of having both. But it wasn't. In theory I love the idea of having sex with a woman and a man at once. But a theory explains known facts and a threesome is a leap into the unknown. And this was Quince's idea. I have never wanted any one static thing. In that moment I wanted Quince's small smooth body, not Kunal's hairy, clumsy manliness that spurted its semen into condoms that got stuck inside my girlfriend. He went into the bathroom to shower.

I lay on my back and held Quince's perfect body against me, her head in the nook of my neck, my arm around her so she was a John Lennon to my Yoko Ono. I looked up at the blank ceiling and remembered that the first time Quince really said it was without words. We were in a hostel room, snuggled in bed. She pointed up to the ceiling where someone had written the word: "Love."

EPILOGUE

One editor said: "A memoir is more than just a listing of events. Its poignancy comes from the truths its author discovers along the way. What are your truths, April?" Are you getting how devastating all this editorial feedback is? Anyhow, I'll throw in some truths here though I get that it's a bit late in the game for that.

I wasn't able to fully give birth to Sumaya, though I'm glad I tried. I took my belly button piercing out just weeks after being home from Thailand. I catch glimpses of Sumaya from time to time. She is impulsive and as brave as she is fragile. She had me take a summer trip to Paris and Catalonia. One night she made me march through the streets of the queer beach town of Sitges near Barcelona all dressed up in my belly dance finery. I went into a lesbian bar called La Marocha and did a spontaneous performance for the patrons. This time I didn't come to Spain an emotional wreck from a breakup and the collective trauma of 9/11. Yes, during a few of the more romantic moments I was lonely for a partner, but I was happy with my own good company.

Valentina, the mom of the Spanish family I stayed with, wrote me a postcard years after I left them. *Sumaya you think we have forgotten you. But we will never forget you.*

Isabel Allende said it was the sins she didn't commit that caused her the most regret. Life is long, and there is still so much to do. But I don't imagine I will suffer from regret. Forget about *50 First Dates*. I have been on over a hundred and without the amnesia of Drew Barrymore's character.

These dates always start promising with clean necks, thoughtful sartorial choices, and high hopes. And they end, well, you know.

You are probably wondering what my beautiful sisters are up to. Celeste is rocking her Somatica sex coaching business in addition to being a top-notch cougar. She lives with her platonic wife Sven and her ex Dimitry and his girlfriend Shelby. Remember Sven? Allegra and Shellie are married with two children. My Pops is likely reincarnated as an Indian holy man or a rich housewife with ten kids. I hope my nephew Devin has all the intellectual stimulation and freedom that his life on earth could never quite give him this time around and all the sashimi too. My mom is writing poetry, giving tarot readings, and dancing in the revolution.

At that tantric workshop at Harbin Hot Springs, when asked what the best sex I ever had was I said it was with a man. When a young man at a festival asked, I said it was with a woman. There are many more genders than these, and many more questions that may never be answered.

All the lovers in the book added to some mural continually drawn on my soul that I will only see when I die. I lost track of Yusuf! Would love to have sex with him again. I miss you, Billie. And I'm sorry.

I wonder if I will ever again find a lover who writes texts like: *Let's do take on the world, Beauty.*

I know myself best when I am swimming under water, in the deep quiet, alone and immersed in everything at once.

Acknowledgements

The first person to read this when it was *Dating in the Time of Terror* ™ was Cousin Kate Hirschman. She gave me tons of great edits. Instead of applying them I let them scare me away for five years. Then there was my fellow wizard Stephan DePaoli. I can't remember any of his feedback but we had a nice meal. He probably mentioned the story needed an arc. Ever so thankful to Naomi Rosenblatt, my publisher at Heliotrope Books, who made this all happen.

Next up was Karen Barneby who is mentioned in these pages. I was so lucky to have her eyes and brain on this.

Jake Whitney read most of it and was super encouraging. Athena Barouxis edited the Mexico trip and the sex party. I should write a whole book about her because she is always having the most interesting sexcapades ever. Seth Andrea McCoy reminded me to show, don't tell.

Very thankful to my sisters, Allegra Hirschman and Celeste Hirschman, who are always my writing champions and editors. I got the line: *the clouds gave the sun back* from my nephew.

So much gratitude for my Jackson's—Talia Jackson, who did my hair and make up for my book cover shoot and handles my social media. And Indigo Jackson, my creative assistant.

Lynn Gardner gave me sensitive, helpful feedback. Robin Rinaldi forged a path through the jungle, removing 40,000 words. Bless her. And mentored me along the way and did another full edit. Read her memoir The Wild Oats Project! Kate Evans read the whole darn thing and gave great feedback. Read her books Call it Wonder and Wanderland. The last two women are on my podcast! Heart Centerfold!

Dr. Lauren Shufran is quoted in these pages as the editor who pleaded with me to be sane, to properly edit, and we all know I couldn't do THAT. Rachel Averbuck also hoped I would, you know, edit this properly and she had all kinds of ideas of how I could mine my truth to do so. That was the turning point. When I realized I was addicted to editors and failing at finishing. And that's when I become a home wrecker of the fourth wall so I could talk directly to YOU, gentle reader.

The title for this book was inspired by a line in Whit Hill's excellent memoir, *Not About Modanna* (Heliotrope Books, 2011).

Thank you, writing teachers: Margaret Shepard, Mrs. Osborne, Joyce Griffith, Ken Valentine, Karyn Bjorneby, Richard Speaks, Denis Bostrom, Dina Ciraulo.

I can't believe you read the acknowledgements. That's so fetch.

Photo © 2024 Lydia Daniller

About the Author

April Hirschman is the author of the self-help book *Best Breakup Ever!* She is a sex and relationship coach, a life coach, belly dancer, filmmaker, yoga instructor, tarot card reader, artist, standup comedian, Thai massage instructor, and one of the 10 priestesses you should know in the 21st century! She has a belly dance troupe with her sisters. She is the host of the Heart Centerfold Memoir podcast. Her writing has appeared in Common Ground and Medium.

Aprilhirschman.com

www.ingramcontent.com/pod-product-compliance
Lightning Source LLC
LaVergne TN
LVHW091043080826
845145LV00002B/604

* 9 7 8 1 9 5 6 4 7 4 4 3 5 *